Insecure Times

'This student-friendly text is a welcome addition to current social policy literature. The theme of "insecurity" integrates a wide range of contemporary issues in an original and stimulating manner.'

Nick Ellison, University of Durham

As we enter the new millennium, a concern for insecurity has resurfaced at the core of the social science project. *Insecure Times* brings together a diverse group of editors and contributors to provide a systematic and holistic analysis of insecurity – and security – that is long overdue. Insecurity has unquestionably generated intolerable levels of fear, anxiety, hopelessness and powerlessness in European and North American societies, yet it can sometimes be a force for empowerment and liberation.

The first section of the book develops a political economy of insecurity and looks at how insecurity is generated. The second part examines some of the more specific and immediate causes of insecurity. How is it, for example, that insecurity has been fostered by an important range of institutions: labour markets, the welfare state, housing and in the family? The final section portrays insecurity as a lived experience in a selection of case studies, and the conclusion acknowledges the dialectical quality of insecurity. When uncertainty and complexity are permanent features of a society, a material basis for security remains a necessary component for a better life, yet it must be complemented with an equal concern for autonomy and empowerment.

The editors: **John Vail** is Lecturer and in the Department of Social Policy at the University of Newcastle. He is the author of *Peace, Land and Bread*. **Jane Wheelock** is Reader in the Department of Social Policy at the University of Newcastle. She has jointly edited a number of books, including most recently *Work and Idleness: The Political Economy of Full Employment* (with John Vail), and *Households, Work and Economic Change: A Comparative Institutional Perspective* (with Åge Mariussen). **Michael Hill** is Visiting Professor in the Department of Social Policy and Politics at Goldsmiths' College, University of London. He is the author of a number of books, including *Social Policy: A Comparative Analysis*, *The Policy Process: A Reader*, and *The Policy Process in the Modern State*, now in its third edition.

Insecure Times

Living with insecurity in
contemporary society

**Edited by
John Vail, Jane Wheelock
and Michael Hill**

London and New York

First published 1999
by Routledge
11 New Fetter Lane, London EC4P 4EE

Simultaneously published in the USA and Canada
by Routledge
29 West 35th Street, New York, NY 10001

Routledge is an imprint of the Taylor & Francis Group

Typeset in Baskerville by Routledge
Printed and bound in Great Britain by Clays Ltd, St Ives PLC

British Library Cataloguing in Publication Data
A catalogue record for this book is available from the British Library

Library of Congress Cataloging in Publication Data
Insecure Times: Living with insecurity in contemporary society /
Edited by John Vail, Jane Wheelock and Michael Hill.
    Includes bibliographical references and index.
    1. Social security – Great Britain. 2. Security (psychology) –
Great Britain. 3. Family – Great Britain. 4. Great Britain –
economic conditions – 1997– . 5. Great Britain –
social conditions – 1945– . I. Vail, John, 1955– II. Wheelock, Jane,
1944– . III. Hill, Michael J. (Michael James), 1937– .
HD7165.I57   1999   99-22355
368.4'00941–dc21   CIP

ISBN 0–415–17093–1 (hbk)
ISBN 0–415–17094–X (pbk)

Contents

12 Boys will be boys: social insecurity and crime

BEATRIX CAMPBELL

13 Democratic vistas: imagining a twenty-first-century security

JOHN VAIL

184

199

Contributors

Beatrix Campbell, freelance writer and journalist

Michael Hill, Visiting Professor, Goldsmiths' College, London; Emeritus Professor, Department of Social Policy, University of Newcastle

Alex Howard, Tutor Organiser, Workers' Educational Association, Northern District

Philip Lowe, Duke of Northumberland Professor of Rural Economy; Director, Centre for Rural Economy, University of Newcastle

Robert MacDonald, Reader in Sociology, University of Teesside

Suzanne Moffatt, Department of Epidemiology and Public Health, University of Newcastle

Peter Phillimore, Department of Social Policy, University of Newcastle

Bob Simpson, Department of Anthropology, University of Durham

John Vail, Department of Social Policy, University of Newcastle

Neil Ward, Department of Geography, University of Newcastle

Jane Wheelock, Reader in Social Policy, University of Newcastle

Roberta Woods, Staff Tutor in Social Sciences, The Open University

Preface

The idea for this book started in the Department of Social Policy at Newcastle University. At one of our early departmental research away-days in late 1995, Jane Wheelock suggested that the issue of insecurity could provide a focus for the shared concerns of social policy researchers in a multi-disciplinary department such as ours. Others in the department picked up on the idea with enthusiasm, and the department's research groups in Family Studies, Health Studies and Political Economy all looked at the ways in which a focus on insecurity could inform their research. Michael Hill and John Vail from the Political Economy group joined Jane Wheelock in the task of developing a book proposal. Roberta Woods was also closely involved at this stage, and has happily contributed a chapter despite her move to Ruskin College and then to the Local Government Information Unit. As the book proposal took shape, contributors outside the department were drawn in, but it remains focused on research undertaken by people with a close association with the Department of Social Policy and Newcastle University.

Insecure Times has been a collective effort, and the editors would like to express their gratitude to all those who have taken part. There were such wide-ranging comments and suggestions from the participants at an editorial seminar in 1997 that the editors began to rue the task they had taken on. The Political Economy group provided an invaluable forum in which to hone a political economy of insecurity. In addition, the department's public seminar series of 1997/8 was devoted to the theme of insecurity, providing more helpful feedback.

The editors would also like to thank Routledge, and particularly Mari Shullaw, Senior Editor in Sociology, for consistent and constructive support. Had we known how difficult the task of applying the concept of insecurity to issues in social policy would prove, we might never have started. Authors have not just been unfailingly responsive to editorial suggestions; they have contributed to a joint collaborative effort. There are many other people who have kept us going, and acknowledgements are made in individual chapters. Jane Wheelock would like to express her particular thanks to Åge Mariussen and to Nordlands Research Institute, Bodø. Two visits to northern Norway as a Visiting Research Associate provided a haven in which to develop ideas and gain feedback on early drafts of the chapters on capitalism and insecurity and on labour market insecurity.

It is our conviction that insecurity is a key concept with which to illuminate approaches to social policy into the next millennium. *Insecure Times* are indeed very much the spirit of the era in which we live. Since we started developing our take on the political economy of insecurity, other authors have picked up on insecurity in a variety of different guises. We hope that the reader will find inspiration from the unique synthesis that we present here. We see this book as a starting point, and look forward to further discussion. The first steps are to see how insecurity is generated, how it is institutionalised in policy, and to understand its impact on people's everyday lives. The next steps are to see what changes we can all make.

John Vail
Jane Wheelock
Michael Hill
December 1998

1 Insecure times

Conceptualising insecurity and security

John Vail

Introduction

Popular commentators seeking to define the *zeitgeist*, the spirit of the times, often rely on the familiar Chinese saying, 'may you live in interesting times' (which lamented those who had the misfortune of living in such an era) to describe the perils of the contemporary moment. Those of us living in modern society at the end of the millennium could well be characterised instead as doomed to live in 'insecure times'. Insecurity has seeped in to the fabric of our lives, and has become the template of our daily lived experience and the nightmare vision of our dreams and expectations.

At first glance this hardly qualifies as an insight of earth-shattering proportions, for the spread of insecurity is present for all to see and experience in their everyday lives. Bob Dylan once wryly remarked that 'you don't need a weatherman to know which way the wind blows', in order to lampoon those in the 1960s who failed to recognise the winds of change which were sweeping Western societies. Nor, one might be inclined to argue, is a collection of academics necessary to confirm that our lives at the end of the 1990s are growing increasingly insecure. The aim of this book is not merely to confirm the conventional wisdom, but rather to deepen our knowledge and understanding of insecurity, to provide an explanation of its roots and to offer our thoughts on how a better foundation for security can be constructed in the coming years. By way of a brief introduction, we would like to begin with a collage of stories that dramatise how these winds of insecurity are raging in our insecure times.

Living in insecure times

There is perhaps no more fitting tale for our insecure times than the story that appeared in the 19 February 1998 issue of the *Guardian*, detailing efforts by international agencies such as the World Bank and the British Overseas Development Agency to improve the environment in Bangladesh. These efforts had backfired horribly. The Bengali rural population traditionally drank from shallow hand-dug wells, but pollution of these water sources caused cholera epidemics. The government, with the financial assistance of aid agencies, sank into the banks of the Ganges Delta three million new wells, which now provide nearly 95 per cent of the drinking water in Bangladesh. However, the wells had never been tested for arsenic concentrations until five years ago, when it was discovered that the water contained extremely toxic levels of arsenic that were slowly poisoning Bangladeshi villagers. Nearly 30 million citizens are currently at risk from the poisoning – which could lead to debilitating and fatal diseases such as cancer – but because the concentrations are rising every year, many millions more could be at risk in the future.

This unanticipated disaster is symptomatic of the ecological predicament that has come to characterise these insecure times. Although Western societies have become relatively insulated from the age-old 'natural' insecurities of famine, premature death and illness, human action has created the potential for even greater insecurity (Beck, 1992). Our best efforts at shaping our world to make ourselves more secure have paradoxically led to even greater insecurity (what we call in a later section the 'insecurity dilemma'). Hardly a week goes by in our lives without some new danger, a new environmental, health or consumption scare emerging to unnerve us. Individuals feel increasingly vulnerable and powerless, unable to predict with any certainty where or when the next critical danger may arise, whether they have fully escaped exposure from the previous crisis, or whether they can reasonably expect to find a residence, workplace or lifestyle that is secure.

One of the hallmarks of insecure times is the extension of insecurity across broad sections of the population. The epidemic of middle-class anxiety that currently plagues Western societies is a telling sign of this development: the middle classes are uneasy about their present economic prospects and fearful about their children's future (Pahl, 1995). A characteristic development in this regard is the growing fear in the United States that the 'American Dream', the country's dominant ideology, may be coming to an end. 'I ran for president', said Bill Clinton in 1995, 'because I believed the American Dream was at risk for millions of our fellow citizens' (Hochschild, 1995). The celebration of this unifying vision – the belief that all citizens have a reasonable chance and expectation of success – has been almost second nature for most Americans; indeed, its taken-for-granted quality has encouraged people to discount those aspects of American society which made the fulfilment of the Dream for all its citizens an impossibility.

However, the power of the American Dream to organise social relations or to inspire myth is rapidly eroding under the pressures of profound economic and social change. The premise that opportunity is open to all has become harder to assert against a growing inequality (both economic and racial) that can no longer be excused as a temporary aberration but is increasingly recognised as a deeply intractable feature of American society. The rich are getting richer, the poor (the largest component of whom are people in work) are getting poorer, and the middle classes in the 1990s are being driven to either extreme (Galbraith, 1997). Nor can the reasonable likelihood of success be sustained in economically insecure times. The insecurity of employment, which has always been the fate of working-class lives, has now become the lived experience of the middle classes. A recognition that the issue of insecurity is inescapably linked to the question of power in society as well as a compelling explanation of why the topic of insecurity has suddenly taken centre stage in our social and political life.

Our insecure time is also tainted by its proximity to the third millennium and by the apocalyptic anxieties that typically pervade these turning points. Millennial fears always concern unresolved conflicts of the present as well as anxiety about the unknown future, and are especially articulated in popular culture. One of the prominent themes at the end of the 1990s is our morbid preoccupation with conspiracies. The fixation with alien invasions in popular movies like *Independence Day* or *Men in Black* and television shows such as the *X Files* exemplify the conspiratorial mindset. In the *X Files*, the paranoid imagination has come completely unglued. The world is controlled by chain-smoking men in dark suits who run the media, the military and the government; our political leaders, whose 'official versions' of the truth can no longer be trusted, have entered into Faustian bargains with mysterious outsiders; the cult of secrecy and art of the cover-up, exemplified by the supposed crash of a UFO at a site in Roswell, New Mexico which operates as the central motif in all of the films and shows above, are now the very crux of political engagement. The popular catchphrases of the *X Files* –'The Truth is out there' and 'I want to believe' – are perfect representations of the neuroses of insecure times.

It has been argued that we are living in an era of social reflexivity, a time when people are required to make more and more informed decisions for themselves, yet ironically, the more we know, the less secure we feel (Giddens, 1992). The conspiratorial mentality is not merely a way of simplifying and ordering the chaos of modern insecurity, it is a way of transforming the unknown itself into an arena of stability and certainty. It is also an exercise in political fantasy which allows us to displace real political concerns into the realm of the unreal and unseen enemy. In the paranoid imagination, real power is no longer held by unaccountable governments or rapacious corporations, agencies which at least hold out the possibility of being transformed by purposeful human action, but rather in the hidden interstices of an unreal world that is both unknowable and unreachable. In insecure times, where powerlessness is the norm and scepticism an ingrained habit, the democratisation of misinformation and withdrawal from public life espoused by the *X Files* has come to seem like the sanest strategy of all.

Why we are writing

The editors believe it is essential that insecure times should be realistically documented rather than ignored or obscured, and that the agents of this insecurity need to be challenged directly on their policies and values. We accordingly see this volume as both a process of intellectual debate and as an act of political engagement. The rise in insecurity in contemporary society which this book dramatises has been immensely destructive of human potential and social justice. Insecurity damages individual lives, it destroys self-worth and self-esteem, and it has generated intolerable levels of fear, anxiety, hopelessness and powerlessness in European and North American societies. Each of these has severely weakened the possibilities of individual autonomy, trust, reciprocity and collective engagement and commitment. This book will provide ample evidence in support of this argument.

Insecurity has always been a central focus in social policy debates in Europe and the United States. In the years after the Second World War, the experience of more than two decades of worldwide insecurity cast a long shadow over the national policy-making agenda. The Great Depression of the 1930s had affected industrialised nations throughout the world: high rates of unemployment left families destitute, growth rates plummeted, international trade languished. This economic insecurity was paralleled by political insecurities which led, in 1939, to the outbreak of what rapidly became a worldwide war. Once peace was declared, governments in most of the developed industrialised economies focused their attention on establishing policies to underpin social and economic security, nationally and internationally. Keynesian policies of full employment were backed up by the development of welfare states. The priority given to policies to underpin this 'regime of security' went largely unquestioned under the dominant political paradigm of social democracy in the first world. (Jane Wheelock describes the establishment of a 'regime of security' during the postwar golden era in Chapter 2.) But, following the worldwide economic problems of the 1970s, the dominant political paradigm shifted dramatically. The desirability of pursuing policies to promote security became contested, with the New Right arguing that state intervention in welfare and the economy merely encouraged dependency. The newly dominant political right believed markets provided a context in which individual initiative and enterprise could flourish and economic growth could prosper. The Reagan government in the US and the Thatcher government in Britain led the 1980s policy retreat from state-based security and the switch to the market as evidenced by privatisation of state industries and services. Not all developed economies abandoned social democracy, but many began to colour their policies with a new individualism that drew inspiration from the ideas of the social market.

As we reach the end of the 1990s, the problems that insecurity gives rise to are once again at the top of the political agenda. How should we evaluate the trade-off between the high unemployment/low inequality labour market of Europe versus the low unemployment/high inequality labour market of the United States and Great Britain? How should a welfare state designed to meet the imperatives of a mass production, mass consumption economy and a patriarchal family system reliant on a single male breadwinner be reconfigured to take into account the profound economic and social changes of the past decades? How can the social problems of homelessness, deteriorating inner cities, mass poverty and environmental degradation be addressed by governments whose efficacy and legitimacy have been seemingly weakened by their concessions to the market? There are no straightforward answers to any of these policy dilemmas, and policy makers are struggling to find a new conceptual and ideological framework to enable them to respond consistently and effectively to these insecure times.

The question of insecurity also lies at the heart of social science inquiry. There is hardly an academic area – in social theory, social policy, international relations, economics, political science, geography, environmental sciences – that is left untouched by a concern for our subject. We recognise the important contributions that have already been made to the study of insecurity by researchers across various academic disciplines. However, it is our belief that a single volume, which can bring together many of these various threads into a systematic and holistic analysis of insecurity, is long overdue. The chapters of our book investigate the roots of insecurity in the structures of capitalism (Chapter 2), the state (Chapter 3) and philosophical ideas (Chapter 4); explore the institutional manifestations of insecurity in the labour market, housing, the welfare state and the family (Chapters 5–8); and examine the lived experience of insecurity in terms of young people, rural communities and working-class communities plagued with economic, social and environmental insecurity (Chapters 9–12).

The remainder of this introduction undertakes three tasks. The first is to offer a definition of security and insecurity, beginning with a brief discussion of how insecurity can be distinguished from risk and then exploring how these definitions are used in social arenas. The next task is to analyse the critical conceptual issues of insecurity that underpin the chapters in the collection. This task divides into four parts. The insecurity dilemma examines how insecurity results from the unintentional consequences of human action. Insecurity and social power looks at how insecurity is perpetuated by structures of power in society. The social construction of insecurity uncovers the way in which insecurity is defined as a matter of social concern, while the dialectic of insecurity identifies the way in which insecurity can become a positive force for personal liberation and empowerment. Each of these analytical sections draws upon empirical examples from chapters in the book to illustrate the overall argument. Finally, a brief outline of the chapters themselves and the plan of the book is provided.

Security, insecurity and risk

Every conception of insecurity implicitly embraces a notion of what security is: what it means to be secure, how this security is guaranteed and what it is that people need to be secured against in the first place. The two concepts are so closely linked, both analytically and practically, that it makes little sense to discuss them in isolation from each other. Throughout the social sciences, the term 'insecurity' is used interchangeably with risk, anxiety, uncertainty and other synonyms. Without overemphasising the significance of terminology, it is important to state at the outset why this collection has concentrated on insecurity rather than risk, which appears to be the current vogue (Beck, 1992; Franklin, 1998), and to reassure our readers that it is not simply a cynical marketing ploy aimed at product differentiation.

Risk has come to signify aspects of danger, or threats to people's livelihood, which are in theory accessible to some form of calculation; in other words, they are uncertainties that can be transformed into probabilities (Douglas and Wildavsky, 1982). This may be applied to any number of areas of social life where the hazards people face can be estimated: these include the likelihood of getting cancer, or having an automobile accident, or losing a job. Risk implies a level of objectivity and abstraction that distances us from a direct engagement with what we actually fear. Beck has argued that the sensibility of risk requires us to ignore our own senses. Dangers are perceived through reliance on scientific or professional expertise rather than through our own apprehension. This expertise maintains that it can 'accurately' measure the precise nature and degree of threat (Beck, 1995).[1]

Insecurity, on the other hand, is a form of uncertainty that, by its very nature, is not immediately amenable to this sort of calculation, so that it is not meaningful to speak in the language of probabilities.[2] Insecurity refers instead to processes that are presently taking a painful toll on people's lives, as well as to the psychological state of mind that is a consequence of this daily brutalising experience. It has an immediacy that can not be avoided or displaced into the realm of probability: an individual who is hungry or homeless, or has a bad job, or is seriously ill does not need to calculate the likelihood of disaster striking because they are already living this fate.[3]

The way in which the two terms are used in everyday life also betrays a subtle difference. When we talk about 'taking risks', or partaking in 'risky activities', or of being a 'good risk', we normally refer to activities in which only a minority of the population engage. These phrases immediately conjure up familiar images of heroic mountain climbers ascending Everest, or bold explorers seeking new discoveries, or creative entrepreneurs winning funds for their latest venture. The elitist and gender connotations of the term are inescapable: these are activities that are typically (although not exclusively) undertaken by men with ample financial resources. Working-class women, burdened with caring responsibilities and trying to make ends meet for their families, cannot afford to be enticed by the prospect of risking everything for the simple reason that they have too much to lose.

Insecurity carries no such symbolic baggage: it is something most of us are familiar with and something few of us – with important exceptions that are treated in a later section – are eager to embrace. The metaphor of a merchant ship expresses this distinction nicely. On the bridge, the risk-seeking explorers and adventurers seeking their fortune dine at the captain's table and are free to roam the ship while contemplating their future in the bright sunlight and cool ocean breeze; below decks, however, the insecure workers are trapped in a dismal, unsafe and unhealthy subterranean existence and dream of nothing more grandiose than surviving until the following day.

Of course, there are important points of convergence as well between the two terms. The development of the postwar welfare state is a good illustration of this. As described in Chapter 3, the development of a system of free and equal access to social services such as education, health care and unemployment insurance actually represented a conscious process of sharing and pooling risks (Baldwin, 1990). On the one hand, it enabled people who were labelled as 'bad risks' by private insurers (the elderly, the disabled, those who had suffered major illnesses in the past) to enjoy the benefits of coverage. It also ensured that people who were highly likely to be insecure in the future – as a result of old age, or catastrophic illness, or loss of job – could expect to receive support when they most needed it. To return to the metaphor of the merchant ship to describe this interrelationship, immigrants who travelled in second-class berths typically fled insecurity in their homelands such as lack of employment opportunities, religious persecution or human rights violations. They made it on board only because their friends and relatives joined together in mutual sacrifice to finance their voyage (no bank would ever have financed such a speculative venture). They shared the risks of this hazardous journey and cushioned themselves against the insecurities (low-paying jobs, bad housing, discrimination) that inevitably faced them when they finally reached their destination. They learned to pool whatever income they received in their new jobs to ensure everyone's survival and allocated a portion of their earnings to be repatriated to their homes to enable others to follow in their footsteps. Insecurity and risk are thus intertwined in both our commonplace vocabulary and our political practices.

Following our common-sense understandings, security/insecurity can be defined in essentially three ways. First, if security is a sense or state of well-being or safety, insecurity is a sense or state of precariousness and fear. Insecurity is thus associated with isolation, as when individuals who are not integrated into the wider social relations of their community feel a high level of anxiety; it can also be caused by the presence of an abnormally high level of external threats (war, crime, environmental hazards, natural disasters). Second, security is the self-assurance and confidence of achieving one's goals, of being able to 'secure' some favourable outcome. Insecurity is a feeling of hopelessness, a constrained sense of self and a belief in the futility of advancement. It is also a sense of powerlessness, an inability to realise one's goals or protect one's interests as well as a heightened awareness of vulnerability to events and forces over which an individual has no control. Third, security is a condition of stability or permanency, where an individual has reliable expectations of continuity in their surroundings and relationships; insecurity is a feeling of uncertainty about the future, about other people's activities or intentions, about the unknown.

The interplay of security and insecurity can be traced across the broad spectrum of social and political life. *Personal security/insecurity* concerns the achievement (or lack thereof) of the minimal conditions of a dignified life: good health, sufficient food and accommodation, physical safety in one's home, workplace, community; rewarding intimate relationships, personal happiness and the ability to participate in public life. *Economic security/insecurity* is conceived as an individual's interaction with the market economy which provides sufficient (or insufficient) material resources to provide the foundation for personal security. This may involve financial security (decent wages and livelihood, guaranteed prices for farmers, reasonable rate of return on investment), job security, protection of property rights or land use patterns, or investment in human capital (education, skills). *Social security/insecurity* is generally seen as minimum protection (or lack thereof) offered by the state to individuals whose personal security is threatened by sudden and drastic changes in their life chances and life situations (economic depression, ill health, natural disasters), or to individuals for predictable contingencies, such as old age, where people lack sufficient resources to meet their needs. Yet it also has a wider connotation as the presence (or absence) of a socially cohesive community and society, where mutual obligations and responsibility are widespread and members of the community are linked together in reciprocal ties. *Political security/insecurity* is concerned in the first place with the stability (or instability) of political institutions and the legitimacy of the political system, the first and fundamental requirement of all governments. This usually has two distinct meanings: internal security, where public order is assured and threats to the legitimacy or stability of the polity are prevented; and national security, which revolves around the defence of the nation from external threats and the system of agreements which the nation has with other states in the international arena. Political security also concerns whether individual citizens enjoy fundamental civil liberties and democratic rights, and whether these are ensured (or threatened) by the acts of governments. Lastly, *environmental security/insecurity* indicates the way in which social actors interact with the natural environment so as to establish a political and economic system that is either protective of or harmful to our eco-system.[4]

Any consideration of security is at the same time a description of the insecurity which could possibly endanger it. What is it that we fear most: the exploitation and inequality of the market, the arbitrary authority of the state, the erosion of the nuclear family, neighbourhood crime, the day-to-day violence that occurs in the home? Every society will prioritise one set of insecurity concerns versus another. The hierarchy of insecurity that is erected is the outcome of processes of social construction involving the state, social divisions and the role of social power, which we explore in the section below.

Conceptual issues in insecurity

The insecurity dilemma

The symbiotic relationship between security and insecurity highlighted above has particular resonance in light of the centrality of unintentional consequences to any explanation of human action and social change. This topic has been one of the critical concerns of the social sciences ever since Adam Smith postulated the existence of an 'invisible hand' which was said to ensure that private decisions made on the basis of self-interest 'promotes an end which was no part of his original intention', namely the collective interest of all. Over time, the unintended consequences of human action have taken on a decidedly negative connotation and this has been the focus of our attention as well. What we are calling the 'insecurity dilemma' is the well-recognised phenomenon that the most well-intentioned efforts to ensure security may sometimes increase insecurity instead.[5] In the elegant phrase of Smith's contemporary, Adam Ferguson, 'history is the result of human action, not of human design'. Human action may precipitate a series of potentially countervailing actions (often referred to as side effects), a fact that is extensively documented in the literature on risk analysis and 'risk trade-offs' (Graham and Wiener, 1995).

It is easy to put these familiar terms into the language of security/insecurity. Unanticipated consequences are optimising behaviour (to create security) by social actors which unintentionally leads to sub-optimal outcomes (insecurity) (Elster, 1989). There may be a number of combinations that can result from this dynamic, as the following examples help demonstrate. First, a proposal to create security may backfire and generate even more insecurity for the actor concerned. The egalitarian wage policies (such as the reduction of wage differentials or the elimination of job classification hierarchies) promoted by trade unions in the 1970s to enhance solidarity across divisions in the working class, unintentionally forged an even larger cleavage between blue-collar and white-collar workers, who felt their particular interests were not being adequately considered. The fragmentation of interest that resulted made co-operation between the two groups less likely and created a troublesome representation dilemma for the unions (Hyman, 1992). Second, attempts to create security for one social actor may unintentionally create greater insecurity for a different actor: new technology may be introduced into the workplace by management in order to generate higher levels of productivity, but this may worsen existing divisions among workers, weaken worker solidarity and make future strike mobilisation less likely.

Third, a policy for security may lead to greater insecurity for all actors concerned: a firm's attempt to increase productivity by means of an increase in the intensity of work will not only exacerbate the sheer wear and tear on workers' bodies and spirit, but it may also violate received workplace norms of fairness that can precipitate higher than normal levels of shop-floor militancy. This could have a substantially negative impact on production schedules and deliveries, thereby reducing productivity and making future co-operation between workers and management much less feasible. Fourth, optimising behaviour by one group may unintentionally produce greater *security* for a different group: successful collective action by workers against individual employers can create an incentive for capitalists to devote greater resources to their own collective organisation, which may allow them to reduce self-destructive competition among firms (Bowman, 1989). Lastly, attempts to make one group secure may indeed make everyone more secure. Higher job security for workers (through tighter legislation prohibiting unfair dismissals or layoffs) may unintentionally provide firms with distinct advantages by lowering turnover rates and training costs and thereby increasing productivity as a whole.

The insecurity dilemma may be observed across all areas of society – the economy, civil society and political life – and has been highlighted in many of the chapters in this collection. Robert MacDonald in Chapter 11 describes how training programmes which were supposed to integrate unemployed youth into the world of work ended up increasing their dependency on state benefits and 'fiddly jobs'. Neil Ward and Phillip Lowe demonstrate in Chapter 10 how middle-class migrants to the countryside, who move in search of greater security and stability, actually create new pressures, anxieties and insecurity for rural dwellers. The Child Support Act was introduced by the British government in 1996 to help preserve conventional family life after divorce by building closer ties between absent fathers and their families, but it actually did more, argues Bob Simpson in Chapter 8, to undermine the security and stability of the family than any government policy for decades.

The ubiquity of the insecurity dilemma has been explained in many different ways: as an inescapable feature of the human existence, or capitalism, or political life, or modernity itself (as Alex Howard discusses further in Chapter 4). The recognition of the inescapable perversity of all human affairs was a central theme of the tragic drama of the ancient Greeks. Here, tragedy was envisioned as a reflection of the hubris of humankind, the mistaken belief that mastery of the world was possible. The reality, the Greek tragedists argued, was that our free choices simply foreclosed our most fervent desires; that human history was actually the unfolding not of mastery, but of fatal errors of judgement and miscalculation that would resound across familial relations, entire communities and even future generations. In the classic case of Sophocles's *Antigone*, Creon, who is described as living 'on the razor's edge of luck', values the security of the state more than he does family ties. He refuses to commute Antigone's death sentence, and in so doing sets in motion a series of disastrous events that end in the death of his son and wife and leave Creon himself desolate and broken in spirit.

Unintentional consequences may actually be endemic to the capitalist system itself, as discussed by Jane Wheelock in Chapter 2. Finally, social theorists have seen the insecurity dilemma as a paradigm for the modern condition. This has a long lineage stretching back as far as the beginnings of nineteenth-century sociological theory. These writers witnessed what could be appropriately called the first 'age of insecurity': the massive upheavals of the century in every dimension of economic, social and political life led to an atmosphere of constant change and transformation where the potential for limitless possibility was matched only by the equal chance of unending misery (Berman, 1982). Modernity was conceptualised as both perpetual disintegration and renewal, and as continual struggle and contradiction.

This theme has resonated in the writings of contemporary social theorists as well. Ulrich Beck sees unintentional consequences as a hallmark of what he calls 'risk society': every institution in society which seeks to legitimate itself through a guarantee of security merely produces even greater possibilities of insecurity. What is particularly frightening in the current context is that unintentional consequences may be global in their impact on insecurity, especially where local disasters, such as the nuclear accident at Chernobyl, have the potential to unleash horrifying consequences on an international scale, a process Beck calls the 'globalisation of side effects' (Beck, 1992). What the insecurity dilemma may reflect, in other words, is the growing interdependence of social action in the modern world, the fact that in our increasingly complex societies, we are more vulnerable to the behaviour of others than ever before. Because the outcomes of human intervention travel along chains of social interdependence, the more extensive these networks are, the greater is the likelihood of unintentional consequences (Giddens, 1990).

Insecurity and social power

The question of who is insecure or how they become insecure is intimately related to the nature of power in society. Which social actors have the power to withstand the hazards of security? Who has the power to escape from circumstances that may constrain security, or the power to ignore the detrimental consequences of insecurity of others; or the power to shift the burden of insecurity onto others? The burden of insecurity typically falls on those who are least equipped to face it: those without economic resources, those who are marginalised because of gender or racial discrimination, those who are ill or infirm, those who are the least organised or the least mobile. Individuals without power resources are less able to shield themselves from the debilitating effects of insecurity and have a much harder time finding substantive alternatives that allow them to minimise or escape from their predicament.

Insecurity is not just about the prior distribution of power but is also the byproduct of intentional and purposeful action by social and political actors to enlarge the scope of their own freedom of choice. Wealthy individuals in the United States, who have prospered enormously from the upheavals of economic restructuring and globalisation, are a telling example of this elitist security, which John Galbraith so aptly characterised as a 'culture of contentment' (Galbraith, 1992). These elites have barricaded themselves into residential bastions of privatised security and abdicated any collective responsibility to the wider community, as evidenced by their refusal to pay a fair share of public services. As described in Chapter 3, the growth of this 'security apartheid' has gone hand in hand with the progressive deterioration of urban America and the criminalisation of the poorest members of society by an increasingly repressive public and private security apparatus.

The ability of the powerful to ignore or even condone the consequences (either intentional or unintentional) of insecurity which their actions have generated for others is another important prerogative. As Beatrix Campbell describes in Chapter 12, many men, whose primary economic activity revolves around criminal behaviour, take immense pride in their lawless masculinity and give little regard to the damage they have wreaked in many of Britain's most deprived inner city communities. Corporation directors may find it convenient, if not relatively painless, to countenance the job insecurity that results from their introduction of new technology or the ecological insecurity that occurs when their production processes indiscriminately poison the air or waters of local or even distant communities. Likewise, political leaders may be more than willing to ignore high levels of insecurity in certain arenas of social life, as exemplified by the wilful denial of the rising inequality that has engulfed both the United States and Great Britain amidst a general prosperity.

It is a hallmark of insecure times that those who have the greatest resources and power will attempt to shift the burden of insecurity onto the weakest members of society. Individuals shift insecurity to other individuals or try and insulate themselves from collective responsibility for insecurity; collective organisations shift insecurity sideways to other groups or privatise it downwards to individuals; states shift insecurity downwards to individuals or groups or laterally to other states. The chapters in this volume provide vivid evidence of this relentless process. Certain individuals may attempt to alleviate their economic insecurity (unemployment), or their insecurity of identity (masculinity), by engaging in criminal activity that severely jeopardises the personal security of others. As Roberta Woods details in Chapter 7, housing associations facing a more uncertain financial environment in the 1990s were forced to conform more closely to the practices of the private rental sector, which necessitated a reduction in the security of tenure of their association tenants.

Corporations respond to the uncertainties of a rapidly changing economy by shifting the costs of restructuring onto workers, who are less equipped to manage such change. The transformation of the labour market, discussed by Jane Wheelock in Chapter 5, is the direct result of these calculations: short-term contracts and reductions of core staff to the bare minimum, subcontracting production or services to smaller firms that bear the brunt of demand fluctuations, flexible hours, more uncertain tenure and higher unemployment are all manifestations of the way the insecurity of economic change is being borne almost entirely by employees. Government leaders may find it convenient to locate toxic waste or garbage incinerators in working-class communities which are already facing unacceptable levels of pollution and other forms of economic insecurity (as discussed by Peter Phillimore and Suzanne Moffatt in Chapter 9).

We find this callous shifting and redistribution of insecurity to be morally, socially and politically unacceptable in a democratic society. It is unacceptable on the grounds of *fairness*: those who are most vulnerable to the burdens of change are the ones required to shoulder the most insecurity. It is unacceptable on the grounds of *equality*: the winners and losers in the insecurity distribution game do not correspond to how much insecurity each actor faces. It is unacceptable on the grounds of *solidarity*: the more individuals are able to insulate themselves from insecurity and off-load their collective responsibilities to others, the harder it is to achieve a spirit of community and mutuality and the more insecure everyone becomes. It is unacceptable on the grounds of *democracy*: because those who are marginalised in the decision-making process that decides on how insecurity should be allocated are all too often those who bear the brunt of it; and because participation in a democratic society is next to impossible if the autonomy of citizens is permanently constrained by the threat of insecurity.

The social construction of insecurity

Insecurity is intimately related not merely to the way in which people become insecure, but to what 'insecurity' itself comes to mean in everyday experience and understanding, as Alex Howard shows in Chapter 4. In the first instance, the construction of insecurity follows what Raymond Williams called the 'paths of social connection' (Williams, 1989: 109). Perceptions of which insecurities are in most urgent need of redress are heavily influenced by factors such as social class, gender, age and sexual preference. These in turn play an important part in determining the extent to which one group of social actors is willing to recognise the legitimacy of another group's claims to be insecure. For instance, perceptions about personal safety are profoundly influenced by gender and race. The everyday precautions which women are forced to undertake to shield themselves from sexual violence or which ethnic groups use to minimise the likelihood of racial attacks may lead these groups to emphasise specific policies (domestic violence shelters or anti-racist training for the police, for example) which may not have a similar priority among the wider population.

The AIDS epidemic in the United States is another excellent illustration of how social divisions matter, in this case highlighting the importance of sexuality. When the disease was in its infancy and largely confined to the gay community, public awareness and government attention was virtually non-existent due to the pervasive bigotry and homophobia of American society and political culture. As Randy Shilts describes in his remarkable book *And the Band Played On*, the news media decided that coverage of the escalating deaths of homosexuals was not warranted or newsworthy; the Reagan government spurned pleas for higher funding for AIDS research because many of its more conservative and religious advisors believed the disease was a 'curse from God'; and public health authorities refused to take stern measures to stop the spread of the epidemic because they were more concerned with their electoral prospects than with the public health. It was not until the death from AIDS of the famous actor and self-proclaimed heterosexual Rock Hudson in 1985, that the spectre of the disease spreading to the wider heterosexual community became overwhelming and AIDS was recognised as a national health crisis. But by then the death toll had escalated to the tens of thousands and hundreds of thousands of gay men were infected with the virus (Shilts, 1987).

Economic power also exerts immense influence on this process. A bank may unilaterally decide to withhold mortgage financing or small business development loans to individuals who live in an area which they deem to be 'insecure' and a 'bad risk' (this is the practice known in the United States as redlining). As a consequence, other lenders, firms and government agencies may decide to disinvest as well, which assures that the anticipated decay will actually take place as the neighbourhood is starved of funds. Corporations that have engaged in a frenzy of 'downsizing' are in essence redefining the very nature of what job security should constitute. Indeed, the neutral language of the word itself is a way of deflecting attention from the brutal insecurity that occurs when people lose their jobs. Another important prerogative of economic power in defining insecurity is exercised through corporate control over the media (both newspapers and television). The mass media plays a key role in deciding how our society is portrayed and what are the critical social problems that exist; corporate domination of the media ensures that the ideas that are advanced in this regard typically conform to the (political and economic) interests of elites (Chomsky, 1989; Philo, 1995).

Political institutions have the power to systematically influence popular conceptions of what constitutes insecurity or what the established hierarchy of insecurities should be. Phillimore and Moffatt (in Chapter 9) describe a whole series of strategies enacted by the Teesside authorities – what they call a policy of 'convenient misrepresentation' – that generated a false consensus about the local hierarchy of insecurity where concern for jobs rather than pollution was dominant. This not only legitimated policy makers' efforts at downplaying the impact of environmental concerns, it served their interests as well.

In this context, Howard Becker's concept of the 'hierarchy of credibility', the common-sense assumptions of what 'everyone knows' and the corresponding opportunity for people to be heard in the exercise of this knowledge, is relevant (Becker, 1967). The power to shape, redefine and manage insecurity is also the power to decide who should be listened to, whose views can be discounted or accepted, whose claim of insecurity can be ignored or denied. European governments have discounted the genuine plight of asylum seekers fleeing political instability, economic hardship and genocide, and instead have created an illusory 'security' crisis and moral panic where the very presence of immigrants in their countries is deemed to constitute an imminent public danger. Police departments (or local communities for that matter) where institutionalised racism may be systemic have every incentive to discount racially motivated crimes as biased exaggerations or 'even-handed' fights, which can lead them to ignore evidence or dismiss witness statements which would demonstrate the racial basis of these acts. In each case, the dominant hierarchy of credibility is essential for protecting entrenched power and privileges against the claims of subordinate groups.

However, this protective cocoon of ignorance and denial may be becoming less and less feasible in these insecure times. Beck has argued that the scale and intensity of modern dangers has escalated to the point where all individuals, regardless of power resources, are equally vulnerable. Smog and nuclear contamination, as he is famous for saying, are 'democratic': they treat the company director, worker, university lecturer, house husband, and movie star exactly the same (Beck, 1992: 36). Beck believes that the fundamental conflict of industrial society between capital and labour has been replaced by this predicament of 'collective self-injury', that what is really at stake is conflict not over the spoils of growth but over the disadvantages of insecurity. An individual's privileges will essentially consist of a reduced disadvantage, reduced by the amount of damages they can manage to shift onto others more marginalised than themselves.[6]

The dialectic of insecurity

Our emphasis to this point has been on how we learn to control or adjust to insecurity, and that insecurity as a social relation of power and subordination needs to be avoided, constrained and reduced. Yet this perspective overlooks the ways in which insecurity may be positively embraced by people in their everyday lives for its liberating and empowering effects. The attractions of risk and uncertainty for people can hardly be underestimated: indeed, one cannot imagine the rich panorama and drama of human life without the interplay of uncertainty and ambiguity. Individuals accept dramatic risks in their personal lives – daredevil sports such as free climbing or hang gliding; drug taking; high-risk sexual activity – because they value the attendant pleasure and excitement more than they acknowledge the potential costs. Uncertainty is a central feature of artistic creation; it can be a burden (the lack of predictability in artists' lives or their alienation from normal work life) yet it may also serve as a stimulus for astonishing creativity.

This dialectic of insecurity can be observed in many arenas of social and political life. Risk taking and uncertainty are essential attributes of a capitalist system, as Jane Wheelock argues in Chapter 5. A firm that decides to make a substantial investment in research and development must estimate the potential profitability over time of the investment (whether it is likely to generate innovations that will increase profit) as well as estimating the likelihood of their competitors making similar levels of investment and their probability of success. None of these calculations can be made with any certainty; no company can ever be sure that they will hit the jackpot, and as a consequence, decisions are largely determined by what Keynes called the 'animal spirits' of investors. In financial markets, a successful entrepreneur may be precisely the person who is willing to embrace the most insecurity, for the greater the risk, the greater the potential return on investment (Mandel, 1996).

The importance of uncertainty is also at the core of philosophical work on social justice and the founding of the welfare state. John Rawls's work is an ingenious attempt to marry self-interest to social justice, by making individual insecurity and vulnerability to the uncertainties of fate into a rationale for collective support for those who may be more vulnerable. In his groundbreaking work, *A Theory of Justice*, Rawls argued that to decide the best principles of justice, one should start behind a 'veil of ignorance'. People should make their choices about the appropriate principles to regulate society without firm knowledge of the position they would occupy or the skills or talents they would be allocated. Under conditions of absolute uncertainty, the most rational choice for an individual is to take account of the worst position which they could conceivably end up occupying. They then minimise the risk of receiving an unacceptable outcome by making the worst possible outcome as acceptable as possible (Rawls, 1971). Some writers have argued that the creation of the postwar welfare state in advanced industrial societies represented just this sort of fusion of self-interest and social justice (Baldwin, 1990).

The area of social life where the dialectic of insecurity is perhaps the most celebrated and the most controversial is the family, as Bob Simpson argues in Chapter 8. A fierce debate has been raging in social policy for the past decade about the consequences of family insecurity, in particular about what is the most appropriate stance to take regarding the steady rise in the number of divorces in modern societies. Clearly, there may be circumstances where divorce serves as a substitute for real commitment, or where one or both parents walk away from their obligations to their children out of convenience or pursuit of personal aggrandisement. Yet divorce also continues to be a powerful resource for those women (and their children) who are trapped in abusive or oppressive relationships. It may also be a way to escape the injustices and difficulties of an unequal and unhappy relationship.

It is indeed in the family where the combative relationship between freedom and security stands in starkest profile. Many commentators argue that divorce is essentially a conflict between parents who seek freedom at the expense of the interests of their children, who in turn require stability and security to flourish. Judith Stacy, on the other hand, argues that the principles of egalitarianism and security collide, and that in most traditional marriages the former has been sacrificed to the latter (Stacy, 1996). The contradiction of marriage – and hence the reason why the liberating aspects of divorce are most in dispute – is that family security has often been predicated on a veiled inequality, where household and caring work were largely the responsibility of the female partner. It is hardly a democratic or egalitarian philosophy to insist that the foundations of security for children should be based on women's inequality; indeed, our conclusion argues that domestic democracy must be at the core of any reconstruction of security in the future.

It is this trade-off between freedom (insecurity) and security that lies at the heart of the dialectical nature of insecurity (see also what Alex Howard has to say in Chapter 4). Freedom has typically been envisaged in two ways: as the absence of external constraints on individual action, and as the ability to perform the actions we desire (Berlin, 1969). Both conceptions relate directly to the issue of security. In the first case, it is well accepted – indeed, this insight is the overwhelming rationale for the welfare state's 'interference' with the market – that narrowing the scope of freedom of individuals or groups is permissible when the constraints are outweighed by a societal interest in greater fairness and security for the entire population. If an individual's ability to work long hours is restricted (by banning overtime or through statutory limits on working hours), this may limit individual freedom of choice, but it provides greater security through a wider distribution of work opportunities or by the potential for a reordering of household work that leads to a renewed family security. Similarly, freedom cannot truly be feasible without accepting the premise that individuals exercise their choices within a framework of responsibilities and obligations to others. The security of living within an environment of mutuality and reciprocity may occasionally require limits on the exercise of freedom.

The second meaning of freedom as purposeful autonomy is the reverse situation. Individuals are willing to surrender a measure of security for the greater exercise of freedom. The trade-off is premised on the expectation that higher levels of uncertainty and unpredictability can nevertheless lead to greater pleasure, creativity and the possibility of fulfilment and reward. The pursuit of freedom at the expense of security may also involve the exercise of power: individuals exercise their free choice to achieve a certain outcome, the accomplishment of which will often result in the restriction of free choice – and hence greater insecurity – for other social actors. In other words, the pursuit of freedom may result in greater insecurity, not just for yourself but for others as well.

Our emphasis on the dialectical quality of insecurity is predicated on the belief that neither of these positions on their own is sufficient. Security would have little meaning if there were no freedom. Likewise, without a modicum of security (personal safety, dignity, material and physical well-being), the pursuit of freedom would be pointless. The recognition of this interdependence is essential to creating a new principle of security where these trade-offs can be negotiated in an egalitarian and fair manner. Free choices should be exercised so long as they do not jeopardise other people's security. We must prevent the illegitimate use of power in the pursuit of freedom. Similarly, the pursuit of security must not promote a stability that is premised on inequality, exclusion or dependency. We must ensure that people are not disempowered by less freedom. Who makes these determinations, the extent to which they are the outcome of a broad social and political debate, the conceptions of fairness, autonomy, equality and security on which they are made: all of these will determine whether the foundation of security is based on democratic or exclusionary principles. We will return to these debates in the conclusion of the book.

Readers' guide

We have divided this book into three main sections. The first develops a political economy of insecurity, and looks at how insecurity is generated. The second part examines some of the more specific and immediate causes of insecurity. How is it that insecurity has been fostered by an important range of institutions: labour markets, the welfare state, housing, the family? The final section portrays insecurity as lived experience in a selection of case studies. The conclusion acknowledges the dialectical quality of insecurity. While uncertainty and complexity are permanent features of society, a material basis for security remains a necessary component for a better life; yet it must be complemented with an equal concern for autonomy and empowerment.

'Generating Insecurity' opens with an examination of the forces within capitalism which promote insecurity. Chapter 2 shows that the current period of post-industrialism may be particularly prone to insecurity. Most social scientists and economists would probably agree that capitalist societies generate insecurity by their very nature, but there are profound disagreements about the significance of this. The bulk of economists argue that capitalism thrives on a degree of uncertainty and see insecurity in terms of opportunity. Other social scientists are more interested in asking at what expense, and at whose expense, the insecurity promoted by capitalist markets operates. 'Who Dreams of Failure?' argues that the economic downside of uncertainty and insecurity has been insufficiently investigated.

The politics of insecurity – in particular the way in which insecurity has been generated as a consequence of state policies – are the focus of Chapter 3. This chapter investigates the diverse methods by which the state provides security in three areas of social life: the economy, civil society and polity. It then goes on to explore the wide range of state activities that can lead to insecurity, including decision-making failures inside the state, the collapse of previous security arrangements, a change in the nature or boundaries of security provision, and a withdrawal from security provision altogether. These concepts are then explored through the use of two case studies drawn from the contemporary period.

'Generating Insecurity' closes with a chapter that acknowledges that insecurity has always been with us, and considers the philosophical and psychological perspectives that have informed debates about insecurity over the ages. A single volume such as this cannot possibly cover all aspects of a social science of insecurity. 'Insecurity: Philosophy and Psychology' (Chapter 4) is intended to set the reader thinking about insecurity in as wide a context as possible. It outlines the philosophical strategies which have been used over the centuries for coping with insecurity, ranging from those which celebrate insecurity to those which deal with its most negative aspects. Its aim is to provide the reader with a set of intellectual perspectives for approaching the moral dilemmas that emerge from a study of insecure times.

Part II, 'Institutionalising Insecurity', deals with four important institutions which have been a battleground between promoting security and insecurity. All four chapters in this section document ways in which public policy has promoted social and economic insecurity through specific policies, whether in the labour market, social security, housing or the family. Chapter 5 shows the ways in which insecurity has been redistributed as the structure of power relations, the gender order, discrimination and state regulation of the labour market have changed over the last quarter century. Chapter 6 demonstrates that employment and social security issues are inextricably, and probably perversely, entangled. Instead of being prepared to enhance their social security roles, states are tending to fall back to merely regulatory responsibilities. More individuals are either forced or encouraged to look – often inappropriately – to the market for security. Against a background that the idea of home has a special place in our conception of security, Chapter 7 analyses the way in which British housing policy under successive Conservative governments exacerbated feelings of insecurity and profoundly damaged the fabric and cohesion of local communities. The final chapter in this section looks at insecurity in everyday family life: unparalleled changes in family life have created new dependencies and inequalities, which have been exacerbated by the state's attempt to use the family as a vehicle for social order.

Four stories of 'Insecurity as Lived Experience' are told in the final part of the book. Two of these focus on Teesside, in northeast England. Chapter 9 shows workers facing joint problems of unemployment arising from restructuring and environmental degradation caused by the very industry that provides many of the jobs. The dominant institutional voices in Teesside, in government and industry, have evaded these contradictions by disconnecting issues of poverty and economic insecurity from matters to do with the urban environment and pollution. Yet though these two sources of insecurity may manifest themselves as distinct and separate, in many respects they compound one another. Chapter 11 looks at the processes, problems and policies encountered by working-class young people as they carve out insecure transitions from school to adulthood. Chapter 10, in contrast, examines the fact that while the perceived tranquillity, change-lessness and security offered by rural areas continues to attract in-migrants from towns and cities, new insecurities for some social groups are generated as a result. Chapter 12 returns to the city, showing that for young men trapped in a relentless ordeal of unemployment and poverty, individual survival rather than collective resistance has been the dominant strategy for dealing with insecurity, with collectivity often articulated in rites of lawlessness rather than constructive engagement.

Acknowledgements

I would like to thank Michael Hill, Robin Humphrey, Ruth Lewis, Peter Phillimore and especially Jane Wheelock for their helpful comments and contributions to this chapter. Kate Thompson is owed a special debt of gratitude for her support during the arduous journey of this book.

Notes

1   Beck's work is extremely sceptical, if not damning, about the feasibility of scientific risk assessment models in today's world. Systems of risk control and insurance, he argues, have been made obsolete by the spectre of large-scale hazards (such as Chernobyl) which are no longer amenable to predictions and whose ecological devastation may be so extensive that insurance becomes meaningless. 'Residual risk society', he writes, 'is a society without assurance, whose insurance cover paradoxi-cally diminishes in proportion to the scale of the hazard' (Beck, 1995: 85).
2   There may of course be crucial barriers that render rational calculation impossible, as risk theorists such as Ulrich Beck and Mary Douglas assert.
3   This is not to say that individuals who feel insecure are necessarily those who are most at risk of experiencing insecurity. This is a familiar paradox in terms of crime, where people's subjective levels of fear sometimes may not match their objective risk of victimisation, as in the case of the elderly, who are objectively the least victimised by crime but who clearly fear it the most. What this indicates is that differential perceptions of insecurity are socially constructed and politically conditioned.
4   Insecurity, like other social disadvantages, may also be cumulative: the effect of one form of insecurity may be reinforced and magnified by the impact of another insecurity arena. People who are most insecure at work are also the ones with the least stable housing accommodations, or suffer the highest levels of food insecurity, or are at risk from the most lethal environmental hazards. In other circumstances, the

diversity of insecurity may produce cross-cutting relationships, where one form of insecurity is counterposed to another: job insecurity has always been seen as a trade-off with environmental security or family insecurity with the pursuit of individual security and freedom.

5   Robert Jarvis, as highlighted by John Vail in Chapter 3, coined the phrase the 'security dilemma' as a way of capturing the familiar problem in international relations when a nation-state's efforts at ensuring national security backfire and generate even higher levels of uncertainty and insecurity (Jarvis, 1978). Brian Job's recent edited book, *The Insecurity Dilemma*, focused on the way in which Third World states are often themselves the largest single source of insecurity for their own populations (Job, 1992). Both of these works are largely confined to the discipline of international relations, whereas our use of the term is intended to broaden the scope of consideration to all aspects of human action.

6   This is an important insight, yet it overlooks the way in which firms, individuals and even states can reap material profits from the production of insecurity. The relentless devastation of the natural environment, as an example, may have distinct economic payoffs even if it jeopardises the wellbeing of others. Wealthy landowners in Indonesia burned millions of acres of forest in the summer of 1997 because it was the most inexpensive way to clear land for cattle farming, even if at the same time it created disastrous air pollution and an epidemic of respiratory diseases across Southeast Asia.

Part I

Generating insecurity

The first chapter in this section, by Jane Wheelock, looks at the economic determinants of insecurity. She reminds us of the extent to which the market is a social construct, not a natural phenomenon, and therefore of the extent to which (contrary to one of the main themes in classical economics) attention needs to be devoted to control over the working of the market. Such control may not only be in the interests of general social welfare but also the effective working of economic institutions themselves. In examining, therefore, the functioning of modern capitalism, Wheelock argues that it is important to recognise a tradition of writing which stresses the way in which market systems go into crisis. Contemporary times can be seen then as a period in which a new crisis, generating insecurity, has emerged after a long postwar 'golden age' in which ways to manage the market seemed to have been achieved.

The theme of the state as a potential manager of markets, and of other sources of insecurity, is then taken up again by John Vail in Chapter 3, from the perspective of political science. Vail explores the ways in which the modern state seems to have abdicated from such a role, and the particular implications of insecurity for groups lacking in political or economic power. He challenges the way this abdication is justified by arguments about the need to let 'natural' economic forces run free, looking particularly at the way arguments about globalism are misused.

Jane Wheelock and John Vail's chapters develop the main thesis of this book, as set out in the introductory chapter, that there are social, economic and political changes occurring in modern societies which are in various respects increasing insecurity. But in Chapter 4, Alex Howard reminds us of the extent to which insecurity must be regarded as a contestable concept, with both objective and subjective aspects. He goes on to show how universal has been the human preoccupation with insecurity and how varied has been the quest for ways of dealing with it.

2 Who dreams of failure?

Insecurity in modern capitalism[1]

Jane Wheelock

...I am alone, exposed
In my own fields with no place to run
From your sharp eyes. I, who a moment back
Paddled in the bright grass, the old farm
Warm as a sack about me, feel the cold
Winds of the world blowing. The patched gate
You left open will never be shut again.
R.S. Thomas, *Invasion on the Farm*,
with permission © Macmillan Publishers Ltd

Does insecurity matter?

The insecurity of the livelihoods made from Welsh hill farming seared through the poetry of R.S. Thomas even in the apparently prosperous mid-1950s. More than a century earlier, Marx and Engels had warned in *The Communist Manifesto* that 'Constant revolutionising of production, uninterrupted disturbance of all social conditions, everlasting uncertainty and agitation' mean that 'all that is solid melts into air' (Marx and Engels, 1848: 53–4). Do capitalist societies generate insecurity by their very nature? Probably most social scientists and economists would agree that they do, but there are profound disagreements about its significance. The bulk of economists argue that capitalism thrives on a degree of uncertainty, seeing insecurity in terms of opportunity, for it is uncertainty that opens up possibilities for profitable investment by business entrepreneurs. Capitalist accumulation and economic growth are the outcome. True, the operation of markets can result in considerable insecurity for sectors of the population – even whole countries – for periods of time; but market forces will ensure a spontaneous movement to a new social order within reasonable time, as economic equilibrium is re-established. Insecurity of livelihoods is an unwanted but necessary byproduct of a market system. Others (including many of those economists who might prefer to call themselves political economists) argue that the insecurity generated by capitalism has important economic, social and individual effects that need to be addressed. They want to ensure that economic activity serves social as well as economic purposes. But insecurity at what expense, and at whose expense? This chapter argues that the economic downside of uncertainty and insecurity has been insufficiently investigated.

The next section draws out the differences between those who see insecurity as a necessary element for the success of capitalist markets, and those who dwell on its problems. The former start from the classical argument that Adam Smith is most famous for: the pursuit of individual self-interest leads to the greater good of society as a whole. It is the invisible hand of the market that makes individual selfishness – and particularly the self-seeking of the capitalist – into the foundation stone for economic growth and the prosperity of all. Insecurity provides the opportunity for the economically fittest to survive. There are two camps in this group. One places most emphasis on the key role that the capitalist entrepreneur plays in ensuring innovation in markets; Joseph Schumpeter and the Austrian school of economists embrace the insecurity this creates with open arms. The other camp acknowledges the inevitable instability in processes of market adjustment as individual capitalists, landowners and employees pursue their own gain, but argue that this is justified by the efficiency with which the factors of production – capital, land and labour – are then applied to the process of economic growth.

For mainstream economists – and for Marx – it is the incentive for capitalists to make profits in a competitive environment that encourages investment in technological change, and thus growth; and in the process, generates insecurity. Marxists acknowledge that capitalism has made huge material advances possible, but they also identify capitalism as the prime suspect in causing quite unacceptable levels of insecurity for the working class and other marginalised groups. Others, for whom Karl Polanyi is the most noted champion, identify the extension of market relations as the source for insecurity. For this group, state regulation is essential to counteract the destructive impact of the spread of markets, and will help to establish much needed security for excluded groups.

Insecurity is a timeless concern that is always with us. However, the existence of business cycles and of long waves of expansion and depression indicate that in economic terms, at least, there is more insecurity at some points in time than others. The third section of the chapter moves on to discuss how the end of the post-Second World War 'golden era' of economic growth, signalled by the 1973 oil crisis, shows the possibility of an intensified structural tendency to insecurity in this *fin de siècle* period. What were the mechanisms that allowed insecurity to be held in check for the quarter century after the Second World War? Why did those mechanisms break down? Was it partly because those groups that had never gained security started to push for their share of the cake, or was it that the inherent tendency of capitalism to generate insecurity was able to reassert itself? Did the decline in economic growth rates trigger this process, as controls over the worst aspects of self-interest and individualism were abrogated by policy makers? In answering these questions, this section will draw out the dimensions through which capitalism generates insecurity, and identify who controls its distribution. The conclusions suggest that the pursuit of gain in capitalist markets lies at the root of all analyses of insecurity, whether positive or negative.

Different views of the significance of insecurity

Celebrating insecurity: insecurity as opportunity

Is insecurity a necessary element for the success of capitalist markets? Economists in the Austrian tradition have been vocal in their support for this proposition, and Joseph Schumpeter still puts the case for capitalist insecurity in as convincing a manner as any. He exemplifies the concerns of economists who have followed in the footsteps of von Hayek to look at markets as institutions which undergo dynamic change under the leadership of enterprising capitalists. Schumpeter started his analysis of capitalism from the psychological predisposition of the entrepreneur. For Schumpeter, capitalism has been singularly effective because it is cast in a purely economic mould, in the sense that 'prizes and penalties are measured in pecuniary terms'. This appeals to, and creates, 'a schema of motives that is unsurpassed in its simplicity and force. The promises of wealth and the threats of destitution that it holds out, it redeems with ruthless promptitude' (Schumpeter, 1954: 73). Such promises attract business people to seek out new markets, look for new methods of production and new forms of organisation, and find new consumer goods. Entrepreneurial success is fascinating enough to draw most of the best brains and generate further success. Indeed, 'The function of the entrepreneur is to reform or revolutionise the pattern of production by exploiting an invention' (1954: 132). Yet Schumpeter acknowledges that the system is neither just nor fair because: 'Spectacular prizes much greater than would have been necessary to call forth the particular effort are thrown to a small minority of winners' (1954: 73). It is capitalism's effectiveness that provides its justification.

How then does capitalism function? Schumpeter sees this as an evolutionary process: 'Industrial mutation…incessantly revolutionises the economic structure *from within*, incessantly destroying the old one, incessantly creating a new one. This Creative Destruction is the essential fact about capitalism' (1954: 83). The perennial gale of creative destruction can cause institutional chaos: in the process, 'many firms have to perish' and it 'so disorganises an industry for the time being as to inflict functionless losses and to create unavoidable unemployment' (1954: 90). Large firms will attempt to control this destructive situation by restrictive practices, insurance and hedging. Competition for Schumpeter is a life and death struggle between giants, who will use any technique to gain the upper hand.[2]

Contemporary economists do not generally use the term insecurity; they discuss risk, and uncertainty. They are interested in how business people respond to these challenges thanks to the possibility of reaping rewards, so that both risk and uncertainty are analysed from the perspective of their impact on capital. Post-Keynesians draw out the distinctions between risk and uncertainty (Skuse, 1994). In the case of risk, probability can be attached to the range of possible outcomes: it is businesses based on speculation that rely on such calculations, in share or currency markets, for example. Short-term decisions about whether to expand or contract output from a given plant may also be based on specific calculations of risk. In the case of uncertainty even the outcomes are unknown, so that G.L.S. Shackle often preferred to call it 'economic unknowledge' instead (Loasby, 1996). Businesses undertaking investment will inevitably do so on the basis of uncertainty, of partial ignorance. Profits are the reward for success in a fight for the survival of the fittest; bankruptcy is the price of failure.[3]

Yet very few economists have concerned themselves with the other side of the coin of the profit incentives seen as essential to induce firms and entrepreneurs to undertake risky or uncertain ventures in a market economy. For what more certain way of ensuring profits than to off load insecurity onto others? Insecurity can be passed on to weaker sections of the community in all sorts of ways. One obvious way of underpinning profits is to pursue strategies which mean that employees bear the brunt of uncertainty, or even risk (the outcome of such strategies is analysed in detail in Chapter 5). Economists have largely ignored the market uncertainty experienced by labour. There is no coherent modern analysis of the impact of insecurity on labour as a factor of production, nor the ways in which it might promote or hinder economic efficiency.

A second important strategy for managing insecurity in the business environment is to limit the impact of competition. Large firms in particular are often in a position to manipulate and control the competitive environment through takeovers or agreements with rival firms, through domination over suppliers or distributors, and a host of other mechanisms.[4] The systematic incentive for firms to control competition allows the insecurity deriving from competition to be passed on to others. The instability of competition encourages strategies which bring forth its opposite: a shift towards a more secure monopolised environment (see, for example, Sawyer, 1982).[5]

Within the neoclassical tradition there is, then, a strong belief that competition, and the insecurity it generates, provides a potent mixture of fear and opportunity which is generally good for business, for efficiency, and therefore for economic growth. At the same time, the disciplinary power of competition is taken as given, so that there is no call to investigate power or distributional relations (see Rothschild, 1971). Indeed, distributional inequality between labour and capital is usually seen as a desirable route to promoting savings, and therefore investment and growth. Competition will limit excessive inequality, and labour will eventually be compensated (at an unspecified time and by an unspecific amount) when economic growth 'trickles down'.

Yet there is also an acknowledgement that too much uncertainty and insecurity are undesirable. Price instability, for example, is particularly to be avoided. When inflation reduces the value of money, the unit of account for measuring costs – and profits – is no longer reliable. Inflation disrupts patterns of bargaining power between employers and employees, or may have unpredictable effects on the prices of other inputs to the production process. Economists and business people are largely in agreement that governments should act to ensure price stability.

Insecurity as destabilising

Karl Marx's political economy provides a fascinating bridge between those who argue that insecurity is on the whole desirable for capitalism and the market system and those who see the levels of insecurity it promotes as unacceptable. Marx acknowledges that capitalism has led to huge increases in material production, and then links this with an analysis which focuses on the exploitation of the working class. Because he takes the view that the basic function of an economic system is to provision all its members, Marx identifies a fundamental problem with capitalism. This is the possibility of a failure of social reproduction, the danger that society may not be able to provision itself in ways that allow it to reproduce itself, materially and socially.[6]

The capitalist class 'during its rule of scarce one hundred years, has created more massive and more colossal productive forces than have all preceding generations together' argued Marx and Engels in the *Communist Manifesto* (Marx and Engels, 1848: 56), yet capitalism is a society which 'has conjured up such gigantic means of production and exchange, [and] is like a sorcerer, who is no longer able to control the powers of the nether world whom he has called up by his spells' (1848: 58). In the three volumes of *Das Kapital* and his other economic writings, Marx develops an analysis of the nature of capital, its relation with the working class, and of inter-capitalist relations to explain the basis for this insecurity and the constant change lying at the heart of capitalist achievements.

Capital achieves what command is possible over this chaotic process through controlling (and exploiting) the labour force, as labour power becomes a commodity, for: 'Labour power is a commodity neither more nor less than sugar. The former is measured by the clock, the latter by the scales' (Marx, 1970: 19). For Marx, a significant dimension to this control is the effort to increase the length of the working day; following the Industrial Revolution, 'Capital celebrated its orgies' of day and night working (Marx, 1912: ch. 10). Capitalist production, Marx argues, involves consuming the natural energies of the worker. Competition between capitalists necessitates innovation. Technological change increases production, but at the same time 'the solid crystal of their organisation based on the old division of labour becomes dissolved and makes way for constant changes' (1912: 464). Capitalist competition 'has the peculiarity that its battles are won less by recruiting than by discharging the army of labour. The generals…compete with one another as to who can discharge most soldiers of industry' (Marx, 1970: 42).

Today, it is Marx's success in exposing the underside of capitalist development that remains morally convincing as he spells out 'the devastation caused by a social anarchy which turns every economical progress into a social calamity' (Marx, 1912: 493). In the postwar golden era of economic growth, one could be sceptical of Marx's dire warnings of capitalist production as 'prodigal with human lives, with living labour, wasting not only blood and flesh, but also nerves and brains' (Marx, 1909: 106). This is less the case as we approach the millennium.

While the class nature of capitalist production provided Marx with his fundamental analytical tool, it is the destruction of institutions that lies at the heart of Karl Polanyi's writings. For Polanyi, this disastrous feature derives from the development of the self-regulating market, whose most prominent characteristic is that it is based on gain. While acknowledging that 'all types of society are limited by economic factors', nineteenth-century civilisation was economic in the unique sense of basing itself on gain; so argues Polanyi in *Origins of Our Time: The Great Transformation*. Vast economic improvement was accompanied by an avalanche of social change, and 'The rate of change is often of no less importance than the direction of change itself' (Polanyi, 1946: 44). For the control of the economic system by the market means nothing less than running society as an adjunct to the market. The market mechanism cannot be allowed to be the sole director of the fate of human beings or they would perish from social exposure, as would landscapes and business enterprises. 'The disintegration of the cultural environment of the victim is then the cause of degradation', becoming a lethal injury to the social institutions in which social existence is embodied (1946: 159). For Polanyi, the good economy is one that provisions the lives of individuals and their societal institutions, for 'a society whose freedoms are purchased at the cost of injustice and insecurity is neither enduring nor good' (Stanfield, 1986: 141).

Polanyi, then, is representative of that group of political economists who find insecurity as an unwanted byproduct of the capitalist self-regulating markets that have contributed so much to the growth of material output. The restlessness of this process is destructive of the lives of people, of institutions, indeed of capital itself. Arthur Okum captures this quality neatly when he says: 'The imperialism of the market's valuation accounts for its contribution, and for its threat to other institutions. It can destroy every other value in sight' (Okum, 1975: 13). The environment becomes part of this destruction. The market-based analysis that preoccupies most of economics has meant that pollution and environmental degradation become classified as 'externalities'. They are 'economic bads' which are not costed within the market mechanism, because by and large environmental and air quality are not owned by anyone in particular but by all of us in general, even on a worldwide scale (Foreman, 1972). Individual firms therefore do not have to pay anyone for their abuse of the environment, unless governments intervene to impose pollution taxes, for example. Nor do individual consumers have to pay for the pollution of the streets they drive through in rush hours, though collectively their children have increasing rates of asthma and other respiratory diseases (see Chapter 9 for a case study of these issues).

Such micro-level market failures are reinforced by macro pressures promoting productivism, whether it be policies to promote economic growth pursued by governments wishing to be re-elected next time, or an advertising industry (which in Britain spends more than the entire education budget) encouraging us all to buy more and more material goods (albeit by dwelling on how much our non-material well-being will be promoted as we find a partner thanks to the deodorant we use, for example). Similarly, as we shall see in Chapter 5 in the case of labour, the collective 'economic good' which derives from a healthy and educated population does not enter into the individual, selfish calculations made by firms or by lifelong learners when seeking training or health, so that society as a whole is shortchanged.

The economic paradigm rejects engagement with the distribution of power in a market economy, and so fails to provide a coherent specification of insecurity. Keynes (1936) was instrumental in exposing the paradoxes that this gives rise to, showing how macro-level market failure can lead to widespread unemployment. Uncertainty provides the opportunity for one set of economic agents – namely firms – to invest. Firms are driven by the prospect of profits to undertake investment, and greater investment leads to capital accumulation and to economic growth. But what Keynes called the 'animal spirits' of business leaders may focus on the dangers of making losses; there may be 'dreams of failure' with business confidence at a sufficiently low ebb for investment decisions to be delayed. Economic growth will not take place in the face of such bad dreams.

However, insecurity provides no opportunity for labour. Firms can frequently see possibilities for maximising profits by reducing costs through labour-saving technologies or organising production in ways which require less labour. In effect, then, insecurity only acts as a *constraint* on labour. Only if households are confident that members can get employment in other firms, industries or locations may they borrow, and so continue to spend, inducing firms to continue to produce. Households will however still have to repay borrowings in the future, so that sooner or later insecurity impacts on labour through a reduction in spending. Even more likely is that insecurity and the threat of unemployment eat away at household savings. Keynes's insight was that the different ways in which employers and employees experience, and respond to, insecurity may in fact lead to cumulative undermining of economic growth if insecurity is perceived as a constraint on both sides.

Keynes was able to identify this resounding case of 'market failure' – the possibility of a cumulative failure to achieve full employment – because neoclassical economists before him had been so concerned to find a way of justifying the rewards that a market system gives to different categories of economic agent. Interest is the reward that financiers who loan money capital get for waiting, for deferring gratification. Profits are the reward for industrialists and service providers who undertake entrepreneurial investment in response to uncertainty and risk, that is, market insecurity. Wages are a reward for the amount of work done, whether in terms of hours or per unit of output; rent is the return for ownership of land. Interestingly, some of the early classical economists thought it essentially unfair that landowners should be able to gain from ownership of a scarce resource, as it put landowners in a position to extort a tax on economic growth (see, for example, Ricardo, 1912 [1817]). However, later economists abandoned any ideas of inequalities of power between owners of any of the 'factors of production'. There was no recognition, for instance, of the fact that workers were highly unlikely to have anything else but their labour to sell.

To sum up, the humanist critique of the capitalist market system sees rewards in excess of what is required for effort being extracted by some, at the expense of insecurity for others (Hobson, 1922, 1928). For all those political economists who are prepared to look at the downside, the need to establish some form of control over the effects of insecurity is morally justified, whether by revolution, state regulation or through much more democratic social control. In the golden age of postwar state-managed capitalism, the unprecedented growth of economic output and the opportunities this provided made it easier to ignore insecurity. Even so, 'one may care less for the efficiency of the capitalist process in producing economic and cultural values than for the kind of human beings it turns out and then leaves to their own devices, free to make a mess of their lives' (Schumpeter, 1954: 129). How far do we now need to turn our attention to the downside again?

The golden age and insecurity

The story of the ending of the postwar economic golden era has been told many times before (for example, Armstrong *et al.* 1984), but here I want to retell it to bring out a rather different storyline, one which looks at its impact on the distribution of the burdens of security and insecurity, and how changes in that distribution have come about. I want to start by asking how the 'security regime' of the quarter-century following the Second World War was made up, before going on to look at the contradictions contained in that security regime, leading to an era which is decisively less secure along a number of significant dimensions, and which might be characterised as a 'regime of insecurity'.[7] The analysis suggests that a key cause of this broad shift from greater to lesser security is the extension of market relations into wider arenas of everyday life. This brings with it greater 'commodification' of human relationships, emphasising individual self-interest at the expense of reciprocal or collective values. At the same time, the extension of markets brings about a change in the institutional forms that competition takes, altering the way in which power is exerted and controlled. For if we look holistically at the 'invisible hand' of the market in a dynamic setting, that hand becomes highly visible through commodification and through institutional change. This highlights elements of the tale of postwar economic periodisation that are sometimes omitted: gender relations, the environment, the role of the welfare state in shaping the economy and institutional fragmentation.

The security regime of the 1950s and 1960s derived from a fit between macro and micro factors which reinforced each other in a virtuous circle. Markets – and individualism – were kept at bay in a number of ways. Cutthroat competition was managed by hierarchically controlled relations within – and in many cases also between – large-scale firms. The establishment of welfare states in developed industrialised nations meant a decommodification of services like health and education. The gender division of labour also helped to keep market relations outside the front door of the household. These factors likewise limited inequalities in the distribution of income, and made for a relatively equitable distribution of insecurity. There was even an element of decommodification at the international level, with the 1946 Bretton Woods agreement providing a framework for managing international trade, currency and capital movements. But as we shall see, this national and international regime of security gave rise to a growth in prosperity which was anchored in an extending market context. This led to a wide variety of contradictions which did much to undermine the conditions for the economic security of growing numbers of institutions and groups. With the ending of this regime of security, and as economic growth declined and income differentials widened, an increase in insecurity became highly likely.

Domestic contradictions

Let us now go back to the start of the story to see how it was that the causal framework for the golden era of economic prosperity also promoted security along a variety of dimensions. The postwar economic order was based on four pillars: an economic regime often labelled as 'Fordist'; a political order based on consensus and a welfare state; a gender order founded in a male breadwinner and female carer division of labour; and an international order reliant on US domination or hegemony. Fordism can be seen as a way of organising production which promoted a virtuous circle of high levels of technological innovation and investment and rising productivity as a basis for economic growth. Mass production was organised in large firms and corporations which were internally controlled by the 'visible hand' of management (Chandler, 1977). Competitive and potentially disruptive market forces were limited by corporate hierarchies deciding to 'make' products internally rather than 'buying' them in the market (Williamson, 1975). High levels of productivity meant high wages for intensive but repetitive work, which in turn enabled the workforce to purchase the new goods produced, with matching mass consumption. The institutional context of the large corporation meant full-time, secure and well-paid Fordist labour contracts negotiated with trade unions, albeit largely for the white, male labour force. Throughout the 1950s and 1960s, unemployment remained low, thanks on the one hand to high levels of economic growth, and on the other to the commitment of postwar states to using Keynesian policies of demand management to maintain employment levels. This reinforced micro-level security of employment at the level of the firm with macro-level security in the labour market as a whole.

It is precisely this workforce security that is credited as one of the important factors undermining the Fordist regime of accumulation (Aglietta, 1979), as labour militancy and higher wages began to reduce profitability for capital (Glyn and Sutcliffe, 1972). The role of women's employment in maintaining Fordism has, however, not been fully recognised, nor have the contradictions for the security regime that this gave rise to. As Bruegel *et al.* (1998) point out, these contradictions have been under-theorised. Women never enjoyed full employment (Campbell, 1976), so that their security has been largely dependent upon marriage to a breadwinner. True, the lure of mass consumption drew women into the labour force as component wage earners (Humphries and Rubery, 1992) but this was usually on a part-time basis, typically on the twilight shift, when husbands were home from full-time breadwinning work and could supervise the children (Stubbs and Wheelock, 1990). Women, in other words, were beginning to take on a double burden of paid as well as unpaid work. In addition, from the labour demand side, firms were happy to employ a 'green' (inexperienced) female labour force at lower wages to undertake repetitive assembly tasks, seen as women's work. Such job segregation, and the discrimination against women that this involved, provided a cushion for employers who were also paying high wages to a secure male labour force.

Women's employment provided a double safety valve for the Fordist regime, as a reserve army of labour, and at low rates of pay.[8] But at a macro level, the double burden of work that women were bearing in a larger and larger proportion of households (Wells, 1998) had a destabilising effect on the conditions for social reproduction (O'Hara, 1995). The social reproduction of the family unit was becoming dependent upon women being prepared to undertake two major roles, not just the domestic caring role on which the postwar gender order was based. Some relief from drudgery was provided by purchase of washing machines and other consumer durables, making households into centres of investment. Household relations became more commodified as labour-saving technology and convenience products were bought. The market was beginning to enter the private world of the household in a big way.

Secure male breadwinner employment had been complemented by a secure (and decommodified) social wage obtained from taxation of growing Fordist incomes. Health, children's education and retirement pensions were provided for by state-led redistribution of income over the life cycle. In addition to providing the conditions for (male) full employment, the welfare state played an important role in shaping the way in which work was organised by ordering the life cycle, structuring hours of work and institutionalising the sexual division of labour (Purdy, 1998). The Beveridge system of social insurance was firmly based on the assumption of a male breadwinner adequately paid to support a non-employed housewife and mother. Her rights to state support were obtained through her husband, and dependent upon his employment status. The security of women – and children – was thus made dependent upon the maintenance of the traditional family, with personal security founded on patriarchal gender relations (Hill, 1997).[9] In other words, their security remained decommodified (for further details, see Chapter 6).

International contradictions

A secure international economic and political base for the historically unprece-dented rates of growth in national incomes and world trade that took place during the golden era was provided by the institutions set up by the Bretton Woods agreement. US economic domination of the First World economy meant that the dollar could become the linchpin of a system of fixed exchange rates, with liberalisation of world trade. As it transpired, the system of nuclear deterrence largely managed to hold the ring in a balance of power between First and Second World during the long Cold War, but growing power imbalances between First and Third World, which facilitated exploitation of natural resources and primary products (Mandel, 1975), eventually precipitated the oil crisis of 1973. That first oil crisis provided a signal for those who cared to see it that the golden era of economic expansion was over, indicating that security in the First World had been purchased, to some extent at least, by off-loading insecurity on to the Third World. Underemployment and unemployment there were higher, product prices were less favourable, and the ensuing debt crisis of the 1980s meant that the Third World exported capital to the First.

Even at the height of postwar economic expansion there had been a number of other indications that insecurity was more likely to be experienced by the less powerful groups in society. There were also ways in which insecurity, particularly of the less powerful, was successfully masked. True, rising incomes largely went along with growing equality in the distribution of income, and full employment ensured that disadvantaged groups such as the young or women, or non-Caucasian immigrants, could often still find jobs. However, the distribution of income was most egalitarian in the Second, communist World, and least so in the Third World (Chenery *et al.*, 1974). Within the advanced capitalist nations, the incomes of the least-well-off households, including those of blacks or immigrants, were regularly raised from poverty levels by female household members seeking employment. Such households therefore had to work more hours to obtain the same standard of living, and had less time to devote to caring. Not only did longer hours of work hide the costs of insecurity; households in some of the richest nations, particularly the US and the UK, were reducing their levels of savings, thereby lowering longer-term security in the interests of maintaining current levels of well-being (Baily *et al.*, 1993). One telltale indicator of growing insecurity even in the golden era that has only recently been brought to light is that health inequalities within the advanced capitalist nations have been widening since the mid-century (Wilkinson, 1996). The failure of economic actors to cost natural resource depletion or degradation of the environment gave a false impression of the levels of growth and security achieved in this period, a failure that national income accounting systems did nothing to put right (Ekins and Max-Neef, 1992; Waring, 1989).

Imbalances between the First and Third Worlds were not the only ones. The collapse of the Bretton Woods system following the first oil crisis signalled radical shifts in the postwar management and regulation of the international economy. US hegemony – with an international policy based on the extension of free trade, a policy likely to protect the already strong – has gradually been replaced by three powerful regional trade blocs: in Western Europe (the EU), in North America (NAFTA) and in Asia (ASEAN), each of which has strengthened the pervasiveness of market mechanisms within their respective regions. Indeed, the much used but often poorly defined concept of 'globalisation' suggests that the

1980s and 1990s have seen a quite new and completely unfettered process of 'marketisation'. The unstoppable extension of market capitalism was confirmed by the collapse of communism in Eastern Europe and the former Soviet Union. Globalisation is also often taken to imply a growing interdependence in the world economy, with nation-states losing the capacity for independent action thanks to an apparent shift to one big self-regulating market.

However, opponents of loose concepts of globalisation have demonstrated that the discipline of 'global' competition is not all that it might seem (Epstein, 1996). In the first place, is the 'global economy' really a new phenomenon? After all, international markets for goods, for example, predate capitalism by a very long way (Sahlins, 1972). Restricting ourselves to the present century, as late as 1991, OECD shares of exports in GDP (at 17.9 per cent) were not so much greater than in 1913 (when they were 16 per cent) (Weiss, 1997). Ruigrok and van Tulder (1995) argue that globalisation should more appropriately be viewed as a strategy pursued by large corporations, rather than as a description of real world changes. Indeed, if a genuinely global economy were developing, global competition should ensure convergence in the price of capital and in rates of savings and investment (Boyer and Drache, 1996; Ruigrok and van Tulder, 1995; Weiss, 1997).

Yet despite the international waves of financial deregulation of the 1980s and 1990s, savings ratios vary substantially between those in the lowest band of countries (US, UK, Australia and Sweden at between 0.5 and 2 per cent), the middle band (Germany and Austria at between 10 and 15 per cent) and the highest band (Japan, Taiwan and Korea at 20 to 25 per cent) (Weiss, 1997). Only bond, currency and futures markets seem genuinely transnational, where global money markets as the 'casino face' of capitalism have rocketed, notably failing to deliver the smooth adjustments that competitive markets are supposed to ensure. It is also worth highlighting that the diffusion of wealth and international economic activity from the North to the South has not taken place either. As Linda Weiss sums up the situation, we have 'not so much a globalised world (where national differences virtually disappear), but rather a more international-ised world (where national and regional differences remain substantial and national institutions remain significant)' (ibid., p. 13).

Boyer and Drache (1996) have pointed to similarities between the *fin de siècle* world economy and that of the interwar period. This throws up questions of how the growing uncertainties and dependencies of what might appropriately be called 'manic depressive economies' are being managed. The old socially constructed rules of the game of competition have changed, so that a control problem arises. Who determines the new rules of the game? Ruigrok and van Tulder (1995) provide a compelling argument that it is core firms in industrial complexes that are able to construct the rules controlling competition, giving them structural control through establishing a powerful institutional embedded-ness inside the value chain – which can stretch from the labour process, supply chains and distribution and consumption, to production technologies – as well as outside the value chain, in terms of finances and relations with government.

There is not space here to go into the variety of strategies used by 'core' firms, which Ruigrok and van Tulder picture as spiders in an industrial web (1995: 65). Suffice it to emphasise that such 'managed competition' is not stable or fixed, for there is a continuing struggle between different competitive trajectories, principally those of Fordism, flexible specialisation and 'Toyotism'. It is nevertheless important to note that what Ruigrok and van Tulder see as core firms' bargaining strategies – but which can also be seen as the ways in which competition is managed through embedding power relations – function as sunk costs so that a core firm is never really as footloose and fancy-free as the globalisation thesis might suggest. Indeed, studying a wide range of literature, Ruigrok and van Tulder come to the conclusion that 'being the first in a given national industry puts a firm in a position to shape dominant institutions, competition rules, and industrial and trade policies' (1995: 217). Despite internationalisation, national embeddedness remains highly significant even to core firms.

A new regime of insecurity?

The institutional foundations of insecurity

Where does this analysis of the changing nature of competition in the international economy since the 1970s take us in terms of the shift to a regime of insecurity? To understand this means looking at how the changing boundaries between market and non-market relations have extended the ways in which insecurity can be offloaded down the institutional power pyramid. Meso-level strategies of flexible specialisation, of embattled Fordism and of Toyotism, as means of maintaining profit rates have each been based on processes which extend markets through institutional fragmentation. The flexible specialisation of networks of small firms operating in the industrial districts of the computing industry in Silicon Valley, California, or of fashion firms around Bologna in northern Italy, as first analysed by Piore and Sabel (1984), are said to be far better adapted to supplying new and rapidly changing markets than the old dinosaur mass producers of Fordism. Leaving aside whether such industrial districts are as widespread as the advocates of flexible specialisation would have us believe, it is clear that even when operating in networks, relations between such small firms will tend to be more reliant upon market relations. Changes in market demand in such an institutional setting can lead rapidly to bankruptcy and the insecurity this entails for the unsuccessful. On the other hand, flexible specialisation is based on partial rather than fully market wage relations, for small firms are frequently reliant upon family and other informal labour.[10]

The large-scale Fordist institutions of industry and government have also sought to respectively maintain profitability and reduce costs with more 'flexible' forms of organisation. The management and production hierarchy of the large corporation was 'hollowed out' (Jessop, 1994) in a variety of organisational changes from the start of the 1980s such as the use of autonomous cost centres, subcontracting, the use of outside consultants and so on. The secure hierarchy of the visible hand of management has been increasingly replaced by the extension of market relations in a system of post-Fordist institutional fragmentation. In other words, imbalanced power relations between large and small firms are further emphasised as large and powerful market institutions seek ways of off-loading market-based risk and the insecurity this entails onto the less powerful.

Although some commentators have seen Toyotism, with its emphasis on lifetime security of employment in core firms, as less insecure than either embattled Fordism or flexible specialisation, Toyotism is in fact a hierarchical combination of the latter two systems. The core firms of Toyotism rely upon a pyramid of supplying firms, where the contractual relationships of just-in-time production and delivery off-load the insecurity of market demand onto firms lower down the hierarchy; labour contracts are correspondingly less and less secure, and again, insecure microbusiness self-employment with only partial wage relations forms the base of the pyramid.

In all these three forms of market-regulated competition, then, we see that the labour force is expected to be more flexible in terms of pressure on the security of the employment contract (also known as numerical flexibility; see Atkinson, 1984). It is however argued that these more flexible ways of organising the production process also allow – or require, depending on your ideological stance – employees or the self-employed to be more flexible in terms of the tasks undertaken (functional flexibility). Michael Mandel (1996) has suggested that the commodification of production knowledge has devalued the dignity of shopfloor workers and middle management as incorporated in their experience, so that employers are in any case less interested in offering long-term employment. In this respect, the undoubted growth of small businesses and self-employment in the developed industrial economies since the end of the 1970s has seen some tendency towards decommodification as the family is used as a safety net (Smith and Wallerstein, 1992). As Chapter 5 will further develop, such decommodification of labour markets becomes a form of protection in times of increasing insecurity of livelihoods, but it is a safety net of distinctly low quality.

Insecurity and inequality

A fundamental source for a growing experience of insecurity has been the sharp rise in inequality in the distribution of income since the end of the 1970s, which has been particularly marked in Britain and the USA, countries which pursued vigorous New Right market-led, deregulationist policies. In Britain, for example, the average real income of the richest fifth of the population rose by 60 per cent between 1979 and 1993, while that of the poorest fifth rose by only 6 per cent (Wells, 1998). Conventional wisdom has it that this rise in inequality in the advanced capitalist economies is due to rising unemployment and to the failure of relatively inflexible European labour market institutions in particular to respond to technological and international competitive changes which particularly affected the less skilled workforce. However, despite an apparently better record of job creation in the much more flexible US labour market environment, wage and income inequality has grown there too (Bernstein *et al.*, 1998). Reliance on incentives gives rise to a win–lose situation, as neo-liberals themselves would accept. Yet widening income differentials over such a protracted period shows that the trickle-down solution to this problem is not functioning. This argument will be followed through in Chapter 5; what is important here is to indicate the ways in which growing inequality affects security.

There is considerable evidence that even middle-earning people had become more conscious of job and income insecurity by the start of the 1990s. Decreased levels of saving (encouraged by financial deregulation and competition to provide loans) and increases in the hours worked by women had masked relatively stagnant wages for many households until that point, while others had found themselves on the rapidly rising tide of incomes for the better off. In Britain, middle-income, house-owning consumers in particular had borrowed extensively on the strength of apparent rises in wealth based on the property-led boom of the second half of the 1980s. The collapse of that boom not only wiped out their rises in wealth, but also meant that debts could no longer be serviced as unemployment threatened (for further details, see Chapter 7). While those affected by policies of labour market flexibility at the lower end of the income range (Will Hutton's bottom 60 per cent of the population (Hutton, 1995)) had experienced rising insecurity throughout the 1970s and 1980s, by the 1990s, the middle-class culture of contentment (Galbraith, 1992) was considerably sharpened by the prospect of being hurled into an abyss of homeless unemployment.

The neo-liberal programme sees strong families as the institutional basis for preventing social disintegration in a flexible and deregulated economy and providing a cushion against market-based insecurity (Mariussen and Wheelock, 1997). Yet at the very time when welfare states have become noticeably less prepared to underwrite security for those faced with unemployment, sickness or old age, social and labour market conditions have also made it more difficult for people to provide for these themselves within their families, as Chapter 6 will demonstrate. Substantial changes in men's and women's relations to the household economy began to become apparent from the 1970s onwards. With rising levels of unemployment, men were no longer the guaranteed breadwinners that they had been, undermining the material basis for the patriarchal ideology which had found expression in the postwar gender order. Yet with wives increasingly employed in the labour market, men have only marginally increased their participation in unpaid work at home. The 'lagged response' of the domestic division of labour to labour market change seems likely to exacerbate social trends towards higher divorce and separation rates, as women find themselves increasingly bearing the costs of providing material and emotional security for themselves and their children regardless of whether they are living with a partner or not (see Folbre, 1994, and the further discussion in Chapter 8).

Yet family break-up leads to support costs for the welfare state and to greater costs in training a future labour force. O'Hara (1995) argues that micro-level contradictions (and instability), particularly in gender roles within the family, have interacted with the changing macro conditions for social reproduction, undermining the basis for postwar prosperity. Policy makers have unfortunately generally failed even to undertake any analysis of the way state policies might promote insecurity in gender roles and family life, let alone turning their attention to supporting appropriate role changes.

Who dreams of failure?

Three leader articles from a random copy of *The Economist* (4–10 April 1998) exemplify the widespread view of insecurity as a desirable feature of the economic system. The first comments: 'For incumbent firms [in the telecommunication industry] the lesson is "change more quickly and more completely than in your worst nightmares".' In crisis-torn Asia, protectionists may argue that 'with unemployment rising and family incomes falling sharply, is no time to be putting people out of work and firms out of business', but the leader view is 'There may be no better time.' Finally, on free trade for South Africa, the view is: 'What works is competition, with its potent mixture of fear and opportunity.'

True, *The Economist* has held to the view that 'everything should get out of the way of free markets' for a hundred and fifty years, as editor-in-chief Rupert Pennant-Rae declared on the occasion of his departure and that paper's anniversary (Ruigrok and van Tulder, 1995: 210), so we should expect any who 'dream of failure' to be severely rounded upon. Yet it is the under-theorisation of insecurity that leads to the kind of optimism that *The Economist* evinces for the opportunities that arise from insecurity.

For we avoid dreams of failure at our peril. Insecurity does not merely open the gate of opportunity. Market insecurity makes it possible to off-load risk onto those least able to protect themselves, while allowing those best able to defend their power to profit from risk. This has potentially dire implications for social reproduction in both its broadest and its narrowest sense. It ignores the impact of market-induced institutional insecurity on long-term economic goals whether for production, for the environment or for the socially based skills of people. A system powered by the market relies on an imagination bounded by narrow self-interest and discounts imaginative construction (Loasby, 1996). A much more knowable fabric for those at the top of the hierarchy, where capital can pay for insurance against risks, can hedge against market uncertainties and can pay for research to narrow its own ignorance, becomes a distinctly insecure environment for those without such power.

It is only those without power who do not get rewarded for facing insecurity. Those who make their living from the calculable risks of financial market speculation, for example, have enjoyed soaring rewards.[11] Neither does the ideology of economic maximisation look to the well-being of the provisioning unit of society, the household. As O'Hara (1995) argues, contradictory relations within the family and between the family and other spheres contributes to instability and uncertainty in social reproduction. Market-based economics takes no account of the institution of gender, and so is blind to one of the central contradictions of postwar capitalism: the double burden of paid and unpaid work undertaken by women. O'Hara draws attention to the way in which macroeconomic uncertainty and family instability reinforce each other, with prospectively disastrous effects on the social structure underlying accumulation.

Issues of labour market, family and institutional insecurity are pursued further in later chapters. It is in the conclusion that we take up the issue of how a belief in the future can be grounded in a humanised incentive system and a collective quest for knowledge, which can be used to reduce the insecurity experienced by those with less power. It is worth trying to shut the gate that R.S. Thomas's Welsh farmer found open.

Notes

1 This phrase is taken from R.S. Thomas's poem, 'On Hearing a Welshman Speak'. I should like to thank Dick Bailey, Alex Howard and John Vail for their thought-provoking comments on earlier drafts, and John Vail in particular for his suggestions for keeping this chapter brief enough.
2 Schumpeter is scathing about the orthodox concept of perfect competition, for the competition which counts is that which strikes at the foundations of existing firms, at 'their very lives' (Schumpeter, 1954: 84). He argues not merely that there are no major examples of long-run rigidity of prices, but that flexible prices are actually likely to destabilise still further: 'Perfect and instantaneous flexibility may even produce functionless catastrophes' (1954: 105).
3 It is ironic that businesses based on speculation where the risk element can in principle be calculated should tend to command higher rates of return than investment in uncertain industrial ventures.
4 Ruigrok and van Tulder (1995) provide a comprehensive review of such bargaining power relations.
5 This is a tradition which often draws on a Marxist corpus of work on 'monopoly capitalism', following on from Rudolf Hilferding's *Finance Capital* (1985) and popularised by Lenin (1970) (see Wheelock, 1983, 1984).
6 Of course Marx also identified a potential failure of economic reproduction with his argument that there is a tendency of the profit rate to fall. That is a complex and controversial tendency, and it is not required for the argument of this chapter.
7 I am grateful to John Vail for suggesting this term, to cover the economic, political and social macro and micro characterisation of the golden era.
8 At a micro level, it also provided women with the economic security of money they called their own, for it seems that only men had a right to personal pocket money out of the (male) household wage (Pahl, 1989).
9 The postwar welfare state has always been largely based on female labour. This derives from the 'mixed economy' of welfare, in the sense that welfare was also delivered through the market (private health and education, prescription charges and so on), and through unpaid caring by voluntary bodies and inside the family. Thus, although the welfare state relieved (predominantly) women of some of their caring responsibilities, it has also tended to be women who have provided any services not available through the state. The expansion of state-provided welfare services that took place in the 1970s was based on the employment of women (Sainsbury, 1994). So, despite the changing institutional structure for its delivery and

the commodification of welfare, it can still be said that women remain the primary providers of care, with men alongside the elderly and children as the major recipients of the security which that care provides.

10 Proponents of flexible specialisation have not in fact done any empirical work on this posited reliance on family labour, but the author has undertaken collaborative work which shows the importance of household labour to the flexibility of micro businesses in Britain, although without evidence for the industrial districts of flexible specialisation. See Wheelock (1992b), Baines and Wheelock (1997).

11 The possibilities for these rewards have been criticised by a major recipient, George Soros.

3 States of insecurity

The political foundations of insecurity

John Vail

The dramatic intensification of insecurity in recent decades is incomprehensible without reference to the activities and policies of states. As other chapters in this volume amply illustrate, political choices have been paramount in unleashing insecurity in the labour market, housing, environment, welfare provision and the family.

However, this chapter is not intended as an exhaustive discussion of these insecurity strategies. The political foundations of insecurity are largely the product of particular historical and political conjunctures and the outcomes of political power and struggle; as such, insecurity may not be embraced in the same way by all states, in all periods, or for the same reasons. The state is equally not a unified actor but rather a differentiated set of institutions and agencies, with distinct levels and arenas of activity from the local, regional and national to the transnational. It would be an impossible task in a single chapter to explain the complex interaction of insecurity at every one of these levels. I have decided to concentrate instead on providing an analytical overview of the way in which the state provides security in three areas of social life (the economy, civil society and the polity) and the range of political actions that produce insecurity. This is followed by a discussion of two case studies of contemporary insecurity which explore the analytical concerns in closer detail.

The state and arenas of security

All democratic capitalist states can arguably be said to concentrate the bulk of their activities in three 'security arenas': the economy, civil society, and the polity (domestic and international). Each of these corresponds to a particular logic of security – capitalist, welfarist and democratic – that involves a distinct set of state strategies, institutions and norms.[1] These tasks are not unique to the state – other social institutions and actors (corporations, the family, the media) are also involved in providing forms of security or generating insecurity – yet no social actor or institution can be said to occupy the same critical role in all three arenas. In each arena, the state carries out a series of strategic objectives and goals that become institutionalised over time into what could be called a 'security regime'. A security regime refers to a set of interlocking, mutually reinforcing policies to foster security that are entrenched in a series of economic, social and political institutions. The ubiquity of the state's involvement, however, does not imply that there is necessarily a single outcome that results from these security logics or that state activities in its security arenas automatically contribute to societal maintenance in any straightforward functional manner.

The state and the economy

In every democratic capitalist society, the state plays a crucial role in the successful operation of the market economy that underpins the economic security of its citizens. As Chapter 2 has shown, markets are far from the natural phenomena portrayed in economists' textbooks – indeed, the notion of a free market is a contradiction in terms – but are political creatures, the product of sustained regulation and governance by the state (Polanyi, 1946). One of the first tasks of the state in this regard is to provide the foundation of stability and predictability that is a necessary precondition for a market economy. All states therefore must seek to establish the rule of law, the establishment and mainte-nance of a sound currency and credit system, an extensive infrastructure, an appropriate system of ownership rules and mechanisms for the use and control of property rights.

Governments also take a more proactive stance in reducing the uncertainty which all economic actors face when contemplating investment. Policies which guarantee material benefits (unemployment insurance, pensions, tax breaks) for low-income households not only improve the livelihoods of the individuals in those households but ensure corporate confidence that demand in the consumer market will be sufficiently high to warrant extra investment. Training and education programmes similarly ensure that investment in the workforce will be profitable. The state is also intimately involved in reducing the insecurity that firms face from market competition. Social policies, such as unemployment insurance, minimum wages, working time restrictions and health and safety regulations, safeguard the reproduction of the work force but also represent a guarantee of market security for high-wage, innovative firms because they help them eliminate cutthroat competition from their low-cost rivals (Swenson, 1997). A reliable system of patents, copyrights and trademarks ensures that investment in cutting-edge research and innovative products will be captured by the firms who invest in these practices and not by their poaching competitors. State-mandated product standards and labelling practices are an effective way of reducing shoddy products that are a threat to decent businesses and consumers alike. Finally, the state may act to increase the security of financial investors by promulgating regulations that prevent fraud or speculative ventures or force firms to exercise 'due diligence' in their practices to ensure that people's livelihoods are not recklessly squandered.

States play an integral role in helping firms maintain the pace of industrial innovation in the face of an uncertain competitive environment. It can assist firms to adapt to rapid technological change and to achieve technological breakthroughs by subsidising research, utilising national procurement policies to support strategic industries, promoting joint ventures to share the high start-up costs of research (for example, semiconductors in Japan, digital television in the United States, or air transport in Europe), and investing in infrastructure to create conditions for the rapid diffusion of new technologies (Ruigrok and van Tulder, 1995). The state may provide stable credit to firms, limit speculative mergers and takeovers that damage long-term investment, and use antitrust regulations to prevent predatory attacks on medium-sized firms. The state can also use its macroeconomic policies to help counteract persistent problems of deficient demand, to prevent low-capacity utilisation from undermining firm profitability, and to stimulate the economy out of business downturns and recessions.

Governments are needed to avoid the sub-optimal outcomes that result from pure reliance on market mechanisms. The state must address the problem of market externalities, the fact that the real costs and benefits of a whole range of public goods – in the environment, health care, housing, education, and transport – are not adequately priced by markets. The value to society of clean air, free libraries and other services far exceeds the profits that could reasonably be captured by individual market actors who would only take into account the benefits to themselves rather than the wider society. If left to the myopia of the market, society would underinvest in these services, so the state intervenes in a variety of social arenas to guarantee that the wider returns to society of these services are realised (Kuttner, 1997). Governments must also institute regulatory agencies (in environmental protection, food processing, utilities, and the like) to protect society from the unrestrained selfishness of corporations that routinely discharge hazardous pollutants into the air and water and manufacture dangerous products.

The state and civil society

The 'welfarist' logic that runs through the state's approach to civil society corresponds primarily, although not exclusively, to the activities and policies of the welfare state. The key security concerns in this arena involve the issues of equality, risk protection, solidarity and social integration. In the case of equality, governments have interfered in the market to alleviate the harmful effects (both socially and politically) of income inequality: progressive income taxes, full employment policies, welfare safety nets and unemployment insurance have all been utilised to redistribute income. States may also act to redress an imbalance of resources owing to other aspects of social power (gender and race as an example) or to prevent discriminatory practices that revolve around these and other social divisions. Policies that guarantee equality of opportunity to important assets such as education, training, health care and paid work are also critical to an egalitarian position. Equality can also be said to require individual access on equal terms to what is considered most valuable in life for everyone (Held, 1995). In other words, security depends on the extent to which governments ensure that individuals have the resources to enjoy basic needs such as housing, clothing, food, holidays, leisure activities or buying their children birthday presents. Equality therefore is not simply a matter of fairness, but about fundamental human rights as well.

The collective arrangements of the postwar welfare states reflected not only redistributive aims but also the desire to reapportion the costs of individual misery through some form of collective risk pooling (Baldwin, 1990).[2] An enduring role for the state in ensuring security is to shield citizens from 'unpredictable risks': occasions when individuals face immediate crises that are beyond their own control – unemployment, catastrophic illnesses, accidents – but which can have collective consequences for society if these individual insecurities are not redressed. The impetus of state action in this regard has typically been to ameliorate the impact of the market on individual life chances (Polanyi, 1946). Minimum wages, unemployment insurance, active labour market policies (retraining, relocation subsidies and so on), enhanced social wages may all be part of a state strategy to 'decommodify' social relations, or in other words, to lessen the reliance people have on the market for their livelihood (Esping-Andersen, 1990). Risk protection, however, is not just a question of enlightened self-interest but of morality as well. 'There is no universally valid moral standard', writes Claus Offe, 'according to which individuals affected by the risks of social insecurity, unmet need or poverty, could possibly be expected to accept this condition fatalistically as a burden imposed against them' (Offe, 1992: 62).

All states have an abiding interest in providing the foundations for a cohesive and well-integrated society. The welfare state was conceived not only as an instrument of equality and risk avoidance but as an agent of moral authority as well; an arena that would promote altruistic action and develop strong ties among different groups in the community (Wolfe, 1989). The state is intimately involved in establishing social relations and practices among members of civil society that promote mutual responsibilities, reciprocal obligations and solidarity. As such, the state regularly decides which activities can be designated as 'socially productive', in other words, that allow citizens to discharge their responsibilities; how obligations are distributed between various social groups; and whether decisions in this regard are made according to egalitarian criteria.[3]

The vitality of civil society depends on whether state activities enhance the autonomy of citizens, or lead to their subordination. To become truly integrated in society, an individual needs the security to be able to choose freely and to engage in reciprocal relations of their own making. But this capacity for self-reliance is strongly linked to access to resources and initial power endowments. If the state system of risk protection collapses or is inadequate, or if redistributive policies have little impact on inequality, individuals will suffer from continual anxiety, low self-esteem and a lack of control over their lives, all of which are destructive of a cohesive community and individual autonomy. The differential capacities for autonomy between social groups are particularly critical in the sphere of gender relations. Women's access to resources, their freedom to escape oppressive relationships, their autonomy and self-determination are all critically influenced by the state (Orloff, 1993). Anna Orloff uses the term 'defamiliasation' – which she sees as a complement to Esping-Andersen's concept of 'decommodification' – to describe state activities that enhance women's personal autonomy and their ability to form autonomous households. In other words, to what extent do public policies provide women with sufficient personal security so they are not compelled to resort to networks of family support (Orloff, 1993)? There are a wide range of state policies that play an important role in this regard: provisions for universal child care or after school activities, the nature of parental leave, regulations on divorce or the nature of child support require-ments, assistance in providing access to paid employment, housing or battered women's shelters, the level of state benefits or caring allowances and how they are allocated (that is, to individuals rather than families). Governments may vary considerably in their policy commitment to autonomy.

Indeed, the state may actually set distinct limits on individual or group autonomy when it fears that the consequences of these choices threaten social cohesion or political stability. Industrial relations systems, for instance, regulate and mediate class conflict through collective bargaining, incomes policies and legal restrictions on collective organisation and forms of collective action by workers (and occasionally employers as well). The state may also intervene to control behaviour it believes undermines dominant social norms or power relations. Family policies that restrict the ease of divorce or prevent the marriage of gay couples or their adoption of children are typically premised on a belief that these forms of autonomy will cause irreparable damage to society. States regularly privilege certain life choices as more desirable than others, a stance that inevitably leads to insecurity for those whose self- determination is compromised.

The state and the political realm

The provision of security in the political realm touches on a number of key issues, of which I have chosen to concentrate on the following: civil liberties, civic participation, citizenship as membership, and national security. Perhaps the first and foremost provision of security by the state consists in limiting the arbitrary use of state power itself, which has long been recognised as a potential source of tyranny. The scope and depth of civil liberties is critical to safeguard personal security and freedom. These include the protection of free speech, the right to protest, freedom of religion, rights of association and movement, right to privacy, rights of criminal suspects and the right to redress in case of maltreat-ment by the state. The preservation of these rights depends in large part on the particular institutional structure of the state: whether rights are given special constitutional standing in the law (as in the case of the American Bill of Rights), whether there is adequate provision for judicial review of rights violations, or whether the actions of state bureaucrats are subject to democratic accountability and oversight (Klug *et al.*, 1996).

The question of civic participation lies precisely at the intersection of civil society and the political realm and involves the development of citizenship as a set of state practices that promote group formation and associability. Do individuals have a sense of wider social responsibility and an awareness and involvement in public affairs? Are groups able to organise freely, pursue their interests, mobilise resources and pressure policy makers? The vitality of the civic community, what Robert Putnam has called the presence of 'social capital', is thought to have a direct bearing on social stability, economic efficiency and successful governance (Putnam, 1995; Wilkinson, 1996). Participation is also absolutely central to a healthy and vital democracy. David Held has argued that the 'capacity of human beings to reason self-consciously, to be self-reflexive, and to be self-determining', in other words, the self-confidence to act on one's interests in groups of one's own choosing, is a prerequisite for an effective citizenship and a more humane society (Held, 1995: 151).

Political participation has generally been viewed as a function of the pervasive influence of social divisions such as race, gender and class (Verba *et al.*, 1995). The state's role, although largely overlooked, is also critical to associational development. Social and economic policies, as noted earlier, which promote personal autonomy and development are likely to have a beneficial effect on levels of participation. The institutional environment plays an important role as well. Because small-scale collective action is more efficacious at the local government level, institutional arrangements, such as the number of constituents per local councillor, or the nature of decision-making authority the locality enjoys, or the range of services it directly controls, all have a determinative impact on the formation of associations and civic responsibility (King and Stoker, 1996). Likewise, participation depends on the extent to which the national government recognises the legitimacy of particular groups, or takes concrete steps – granting special standing, funding, or increased access to information – to provide marginalised groups with wider opportunity of participation in policy formation and evaluation (Cohen and Rogers, 1995). The wider political culture plays a critical role as well, including how young people are trained to be citizens in the education system, or how individuals are trained in critical inquiry, problem solving, independent learning, public speaking and other interpersonal skills that are essential to building a healthy polity (Barber, 1992).

The 'membership' aspect of citizenship – defining who is regarded as a member of the political community – is a fundamental component of every security regime. Citizenship as membership can be viewed as a combination of both inclusionary and exclusionary practices (Sassen, 1996). On the one hand, citizenship is an inclusionary vision of who is deemed to have a legitimate claim to the rights and entitlements within the state's orbit of sovereignty, and to whom reciprocal commitments and responsibilities can be extended. At the same time, it implies a process of closure, of establishing discrete limits to the boundaries of the state's umbrella and defining who does not have the right to belong. Citizenship therefore is essentially an act of providing security for some and creating perpetual insecurity for others (see the next section for further discussion of the latter point). There are any number of state policies that are critical in this regard, including how citizenship rights are acquired in the first place (in most cases by either the principle of birth or of ethnic descent), the level of immigration, policies on refugees and asylum seekers, and the range of welfare state benefits (health coverage, education, poverty assistance) that are extended to non-citizens.

If citizenship operates at the intersection of civil society and the state, the concept of national security involves the relationship between the domestic state and the international system of states. The very notion of the state involves a claim of sovereignty over a specific geographical area. This claim is in turn subject to regulation in the international arena by formal agreements and security arrangements with other states (treaties, arms control agreements, security coalitions such as NATO), by international law and norms (on the use of violence, justifiable intervention) and by specific territorial rights. The standard meaning of the term 'national security' has included three interrelated issues: policies utilised to protect citizens against external threats, policies to lessen unpredictability in the external environment, and policies that deal with instability within the domestic environment that makes the achievement of other security goals harder to accomplish (Lustgarten and Leigh, 1994).

Yet this rather anodyne definition obscures much of what is problematic about the concept. The question of whom, or what, we should fear is never straightforward, and indeed changes over time based on the ebb and flow of power relations and the outcomes of ideological campaigns (Chomsky, 1994). Likewise, the pursuit of national security may often pervert the state's provision of security in other arenas. Actions taken on behalf of 'national security' often go hand in hand with the curtailment of civil liberties: censorship, loyalty tests, surveillance by unaccountable 'security services', internment, the malicious depiction of certain individuals or groups as 'security risks', discouragement and repression of dissent. It may also have a debilitating effect on the political culture: 'far too often the cry of security functions in the political world as a sort of intellectual curare, inducing instant paralysis of thought' (Lustgarten and Leigh, 1994: 21). It gives governments a convenient rationale for greater abuses of power and allows them to abandon any pretence of democratic accountability in the field of security. Finally, states may regularly manipulate or even fabricate external threats and thereby constitute an even greater threat to the safety and security of their own citizens than the supposed enemy.

The political foundations of insecurity

While the scope of state activities to maintain these security arenas is extensive, the range of state actions that can lead to *insecurity* is equally vast. Given the limits of this chapter, it is not possible to provide an exhaustive account of how insecurity is generated in each of the security arenas discussed above. What I offer instead is a broad overview of the various 'insecurity logics' which governments are both plagued with and purposively employ.

In the first place, insecurity is the product of the unanticipated consequences of state policies. The research literature on public policy is replete with examples of unintended side effects, policy failures, lost chances and missed opportunities, all of which increase the likelihood of insecurity being generated for certain actors. When things go wrong with state policies, there are typically any number of reasons that can be identified. Government officials may misdiagnose the problem that needs to be solved in the first place. This may occur because knowledge about the problem was not readily available or officials faced a high degree of uncertainty about which policies might work. Governments may provide a policy prescription that has little chance of working because the value of the policy for officials is purely symbolic, a way of demonstrating and validating their concern for a deeply-felt problem.

Insecurity may reflect critical decision-making failures that are predicated on the way decisions are informed and structured inside the state. Government policies that are intended to reduce insecurity may backfire because officials make little effort to consider the range of possible adverse consequences. This may occur because of problems of co-ordination within the government or the fragmentation of authority within the state. In the American government, as an example, agency jurisdictions are drawn around narrowly focused boundaries that limit oversight responsibilities to a discrete range of activities within single security arenas such as employment, health and environment. The potential for neglecting side effects that spill across domains is consequently quite high. Government policy makers, who have every incentive to ignore the possibility of unintentional consequences, may concentrate their energies on trading off one insecurity against another rather than developing a holistic policy that addresses the consequences of all insecurities at once. If groups directly affected by state action are excluded from the initial policy formation stages, the government may have an easier time ignoring the countervailing losses that may be imposed on those groups.

Robert Jarvis used the term 'security dilemma' to describe the familiar phenomenon when actions taken by the state to increase security actually increase the insecurity of others (Jarvis, 1978). As an example, states have typically justified their sales of armaments to other countries as a way of ensuring regional security and political stability. These actions may actually be used to prop up third world dictators who brutally violate the human rights of their own population (Chomsky, 1994). Similarly, international alliances constructed to limit rivalry between states and to consolidate new norms of co-operation can often heighten mutual fear and resentment. The recent proposal to extend membership in NATO to former Eastern bloc nations (Poland, Hungary and the Czech Republic) was conceived as a way of consolidating democracy in these countries and creating the basis for a new security order in Europe. Yet by refusing to incorporate Russia into the agreement, the plan sends the message that Russia is still to be feared and contained, a policy that greatly risks dividing the continent rather than uniting it.

Insecurity may also occur as the result of the unanticipated decay of an earlier security regime. Mutually reinforcing institutional structures may over time become mutually destructive (Marglin, 1990). The security arrangements of an earlier period may be inappropriate to the demands and pressures of the new external environment, and indeed traditional policy responses may actually exacerbate the new problems that have emerged. These contradictions reflect a poor institutional capacity for social learning on the part of the state as well as the inability to enforce change over the opposition of entrenched interests. For example, the postwar 'golden age' security regime of the advanced industrial societies created a virtuous circle of high employment, rising wages and steadily increasing trade union power that significantly enhanced the security of the working class. Yet at the same time, it created a 'full employment profit squeeze' which undermined accumulation and future growth prospects because of a detrimental effect on profits and an inherent propensity for uncontrolled inflation (Marglin, 1990). The failure of governments across the West to find an appropriate policy response to the 'stagflation crisis' precipitated the unravelling of the postwar security regime (these issues were explored further in Chapter 2).

However, states often deliberately rethink their security arrangements in order to increase the burden of insecurity on certain groups of the population. One of the most commonplace methods in this regard is to alter the nature or boundaries of security provision in exclusionary and particularistic ways. In the case of altering the nature of provision, governments may decrease the monetary value of state benefits, limit the duration of benefits, or link benefits to a requirement for labour market participation which severely discriminates against the disabled and women with caring responsibilities. These may be embraced by governments as an appropriate price to pay for lowering the budget deficit or reducing 'dependency' on the state, but they are tantamount to imposing hardships on the most vulnerable in society. A related strategy is to reorient social insurance provision away from universal benefits derived from citizenship towards selective benefits based on means tests (which again may be the consequence of either budgetary or ideological considerations). It has been well documented that selective targeting of social assistance to the 'truly needy' actually reduces the scope of social protection, enhances inequality and creates long-term dependency (McFate *et al.*, 1995; this topic is also explored in Chapter 6).

Altering the boundaries of security provision may have devastating consequences for insecurity as well. The exclusionary aspects of citizenship play a key role here. Governments can restrict the benefit eligibility of non-citizens, expel refugees and asylum seekers from the country, impose immigration quotas and deny citizenship rights for any number of spurious reasons such as gender, race, ethnicity, sexuality or age. This politicisation of difference is extremely damaging to an individual's life chances. Those excluded from citizenship face tougher prospects on the job market, suffer poorer health and nutrition, and are subject to tighter restrictions on their freedom of movement. Political refugees from oppressive regimes may face the threat of torture and imprisonment if they are returned to their homelands. Indeed, in an era of mass migration between the impoverished South and the affluent North, the question of who has a right to citizenship, and the criteria used to make these decisions, has become a matter of life and death for millions of people (Sassen, 1996). An exclusionary policy may likewise generate damaging side effects. When officials complain about being 'swamped' by outsiders, or maintain that immigration is a destabilising feature of destructive proportions, they are automatically heightening the visibility of the 'aliens within' and paving the way for the subsequent demonisation of these groups in everyday life. The more intense the 'moral panic', the greater the likelihood of discriminatory practices and violence being perpetrated against the disadvantaged.

The state also contributes to insecurity by providing indirect assistance to social agents who want to off-load the costs of insecurity to others. Governments provide tax breaks to firms who ruthlessly shed their staff, shield corporations with horrendous health and safety records from suits by injured workers, and offer incentives to landlords who displace their tenants. A prominent feature of this pattern of 'insecurity redistribution' may be the deliberate enhancement of the range of 'exit' options that powerful social actors can employ which imposes heavy costs on the rest of the population (Hirschman, 1970). The exodus of middle-class Americans from urban school systems in Chicago, New York and Washington is a telling example: as 'class flight' accelerated, the quality of education deteriorated for those who remained. Governments may extend the reach of property rights of businesses in order to insulate them from democratic oversight. Governments engage in these actions out of ideological conviction, the belief that the efficiency gains that accrue from enhancing the freedom of choice of key actors is worth the attendant insecurity. They may equally feel that they have little option but to appease social actors whose co-operation is indispensable to economic and social stability, yet cannot be easily enforced.

At the same time that the state enhances the 'exit' options of some actors, it may deliberately weaken the 'voice' strategies available to subordinate groups. This can include limiting the range of freedom of certain actors on the specious grounds that this will increase the security of others. States can weaken the capacity for group formation and collective action within civil society. There is a wide range of social and political policies that undermine the efficacy of civic participation. The 'hollowing out' of governments as a result of privatisation has transformed citizens from active, thinking subjects to passive consumers: an ethic of public service that relies on altruism, moral concern and self-sacrifice has been replaced by an ethos of 'customer sovereignty'. In Great Britain, the relentless replacement of local government functions by unaccountable quangos, which routinely limit the public's right to information or to attend meetings, has created an inherent bias for passivity and inaction in local politics (Weir and Hall 1994). State actors may purposefully encourage apathy and indifference because it enhances their own security by insulating them from public questioning and because it makes public opinion much easier to manipulate. They may also wish to align themselves with the dominant interests in society that have a material interest in ensuring that resistance to their insecurity redistribution is thwarted.

Another important political foundation of insecurity is the state's critical role in defining what constitutes insecurity in the first place, which is always a question of prioritising key social interests and power over others. For example, every government must evaluate what the balance of risks facing their national economy may be: inflation, unemployment, lack of demand, slow growth, financial instability and the like. In practice, this means deciding, as an example, whether economic policy should emphasise high employment levels or a lower rate of inflation. But neither choice is neutral: certain groups (financial institutions, creditors, shareholders) benefit much more than others from low inflation, just as expansionary policies tend to favour workers and manufacturers.

The process of social construction also concerns the state's indifference to insecurity, its willingness to downplay the relevance of insecurity, or to deny that a problem exists in the first place (see also Chapter 9 where similar behaviour by the local state is explored). Activists in the United States protesting against dioxin poisoning from a public waste incinerator were assured by the local government that the risks were no worse than 'eating 2 or 3 tablespoons of peanut butter over a 30 year period' (Krauss, 1998: 136). Governments may intentionally conceal information about policies that substantially worsen the security of its citizens. A story in the 13 October 1998 edition of the *Guardian* newspaper revealed that Ministry of Agriculture officials in the UK deliberately withheld information from the public about the fact that BSE-contaminated offal had passed into the human food chain or that safeguards in slaughterhouses were routinely ignored. They chose instead to issue blithe reassurances for over five years that British beef could be safely eaten. Individuals who seek to pierce this veil of official secrecy and misinformation are dismissed as irrational hysterics, face police surveillance and official intimidation to dissuade them from action, and have their innovative forms of campaigning and protest criminalised under the law (McKay, 1996).

Finally, perhaps the most pernicious way in which the state generates insecurity is when it withdraws from security provision altogether and transfers responsibility to other social forces such as the market or other collective actors such as the family, churches or voluntary organisations. As noted in Chapter 2, reliance on the market can be extraordinarily devastating to civil society. The market creates vast gulfs of wealth and income that can have profound social consequences including worsening health, higher mortality rates, crime and destruction of community resources (Wilkinson, 1996). The more extensive the 'imperialism' of the market, the more market values and ethos permeate social and political life, the harder it is for society to generate a public morality rooted in values such as trust, co-operation and reciprocity. 'When everything is for sale', writes Robert Kuttner, 'the person who volunteers time, who helps a stranger, who agrees to work for a modest wage out of commitment to the public good, who desists from littering even when no one is looking, who foregoes an opportunity to free ride, begins to feel like a sucker' (Kuttner, 1997: 62–3). A shift in responsibility to the family may be equally problematic. Families may be ill-equipped to take on these new roles; their provision of security may be just as debilitating and damaging to self-esteem as dependency on the state, and their expanded roles may strain family relationships beyond the breaking point.

Paradoxes of security and insecurity: contemporary reflections

The politics of globalisation

There is no question that the nature and development of capitalism has undergone a remarkable transformation in recent decades (as was discussed in Chapter 2). Globalisation has been used as a shorthand to describe a set of common economic processes and trends, including the establishment of systems of global production and trade, the unlimited mobility of financial capital, the diffusion of advanced technology, and the development of institutions and agreements of global economic governance (Hirst and Thompson, 1996). Although various explanations have been offered to account for the origin and evolution of these developments – as a response to profound technological change, as a conscious class strategy – there can be no doubt that globalisation as an economic project would have been unfeasible, if not unthinkable, without the direct, ongoing assistance and direction of the state (referring here primarily to the role of the OECD nations).

The state's critical role in unleashing global finance has been well recognised (Banuri and Schor, 1992). The unilateral decision by the American and British governments in the early 1980s to abolish capital controls sparked a competitive dynamic among the other advanced nation-states, none of whom could afford the *status quo* as capital poured into those countries that relaxed their regulations. By the end of the decade, every OECD nation had removed all significant barriers to cross-border movements of financial assets and the unfettered mobility of an international capital market became a reality (Heilleiner, 1994). States have been equally active in the arena of production and trade. They have provided incentives to finance overseas investment, promoted joint ventures with international partners, helped raise money in capital markets and provided tax subsidies for inward investment of foreign firms, and developed regional production and supply networks (Ruigrok and van Tulder, 1995).

The state also has been instrumental in creating the institutional foundations of a new global constitutionalism as embodied by transnational accords such as the North American Free Trade Act (NAFTA), the General Agreement on Tariffs and Trade (GATT), the Single European Act, or the proposed Multilateral Agreement on Investments (MAI) (Gill, 1998). These initiatives have led to a massive asymmetry of power between capital and other social actors. On the one hand, all of these measures have significantly expanded the range of 'exit' options which capital now enjoys. Capital has the freedom to invest wherever its owners please and under agreements such as NAFTA, governments are forbidden from imposing any performance requirements on foreign companies (for example, a demand for labour quotas or an insistence that a percentage of the firms' R&D be committed there) that do not fall on home companies as well (Panitch, 1996). At the same time, these agreements have enhanced the scope of market discipline, which constrains the freedom of action of subordinate groups. Workers face a downward spiral in terms of their real incomes as a result of corporate downsizing, the shifting of production overseas and mass unemployment. Government officials are prevented from tampering with these agreements – most contain binding lock-in clauses that preclude future governments from exiting the agreement before a preestablished period elapses (often twenty years) – and are forbidden from passing legislation that violates the spirit of the agreements. Under NAFTA, an American corporation has sued the Canadian government for its stringent environmental regulations, which the firm argued constituted a 'restraint of trade' under the logic of the accord (Panitch, 1996).

Globalisation has been accompanied by a remarkable ideological campaign, mounted with evangelical fervour by transnational institutions such as the World Bank, the World Trade Organisation and the International Monetary Fund, to create popular support for an open international order. There have been a number of ideological gambits in this regard that are worth highlighting. It is firmly entrenched within today's conventional wisdom that globalisation is irreversible; indeed, politicians across the political spectrum are united in their fealty to the idea that economic success can only be guaranteed by the active encouragement of internationalisation. On the one hand, this perspective is a convenient excuse if popular support for the project dwindles: policy makers can state with absolute impunity that they have little choice but to accept this new logic regardless of whether the people like it or not. But this rhetoric of powerlessness represents more than just an accommodation to the way in which the world works. It is a conscious strategy to obscure the way in which the world is actively being made by powerful social interests (including national govern-ments).[4] The fact that the establishment and evolution of globalisation has been entirely contingent on wilful political choices should lead logically to the conclusion that what has been made can just as easily be unmade. But the particular genius of the irreversibility thesis lies in its seamless transformation of globalisation into a transhistorical process operating above the domain of human action.

The other primary tenet of the conventional wisdom is that the process of globalisation has made the nation-state largely irrelevant. The thesis of state powerlessness – usually couched in code words that envisage global processes as 'undermining', 'outflanking' or 'marginalising' the state's efficacy – maintains that global economic activity has greatly undermined the autonomy and capacity of the interventionist (i.e., Keynesian) state in the economic realm (Weiss, 1998). The scale of international financial transactions has grown so vast that governments have effectively lost control of their standard instruments of monetary policy. Central banks do not possess sufficient reserves to defend a state's exchange rate once the financial markets have made up their mind to sell a currency. The use of interest rates to attract long-term manufacturing invest-ments is similarly untenable so long as other nations, particularly those with massive weight in the world economy (such as the United States, Germany or Japan), keep their own rates high which effectively forces any country pursuing an independent policy to revise its rates upward.

Fiscal policy is thought to be equally problematic. Financial markets equate budget deficits, which have been traditionally used to stimulate expansion in a sluggish economy, with higher tax burdens on the rich and higher rates of inflation (which are injurious to financial interests) and instantly penalise governments that attempt to direct their economy in this fashion (Block, 1996). The higher tax burdens of social democratic welfare states are thought to be unsustainable as well because they erode the competitive positions of national firms that are exposed to highly competitive international sectors and thereby lay the foundations for slower long-term economic growth. The implication is that all governments are converging on a similar set of policy repertoires – low inflation, minimal regulation, lower taxes and government spending, maximum flexibility – that not surprisingly bear a striking resemblance to the minimalist state envisaged by the neo-liberal proponents of the new global order (Crouch and Streeck, 1997).

While there is no question that the global economic environment has changed the opportunities and constraints facing state actors, it is also true, to paraphrase Mark Twain, that the demise of the state has been greatly exaggerated. In the first place, the loss of efficacy of a particular policy tool should not be equated with a lack of state capacity altogether (Weiss, 1998). Governments continue to enjoy considerable scope in fixing tax rates, setting spending levels and interest rates, and regulating economic activity, without encountering any immovable obstacles. Nor has the 'pervasive logic' of globalisation rendered irrelevant distinct national trajectories in economic policy. Indeed, there are still considerable cross-national differences between governments regarding the size of the public sector, deficits, and effective tax rates (Garrett, 1998). Market actors still rely on the continuous action of national governments for the regulation of tariffs, communications, technology and the environment. Corporations still require a competent public sector, predictable environments, open access to markets and the ability to discipline labour.

If anything, the nation-state's importance to capital to sustain profitability and enhance competitiveness is even more pronounced now than in the past. Indeed, as has been well observed by Douglass North and others, a competent and efficacious state has become a source of competitive advantage for nation states in today's international economy world (North, 1990; World Bank, 1997). In short, as Linda Weiss has argued, we are not witnessing the 'end of state history' but rather an evolving history of state adaptation to new internal and international challenges (Weiss, 1998). The world market may have raised the risks and rewards of particular forms of state behaviour, but there is no reason why the power of the market needs to go unchallenged, a point I will return to in Chapter 13.

Social insecurity: American style

The paradoxes of security and insecurity have reached their starkest contrast in the United States at the end of the 1990s. Amidst all the well-publicised signs of a general prosperity – the lowest unemployment and inflation rates in nearly three decades – an eerie silence persists about the consequences of an insecurity regime that has created a world of hardship and desperation for some that is nearly unimaginable. The indices of this new social insecurity are to be found in nearly every aspect of social life. There has been a precipitous rise in poverty in the United States since the late 1960s, with 22.9 per cent of all families (19.1 per cent of white families; 40.7 per cent of black families) living in relative poverty. Of American children, 21.5 per cent live in poverty as compared to 9.9 per cent in Great Britain or other European nations, where the figure is below 5 per cent (Bernstein *et al.*, 1998). The feminisation of poverty has increased exponentially, with the risk of a single parent with children living in poverty in the United States twelve times greater than in Sweden (McFate *et al.*, 1995: 53).

Twelve per cent of the American population (nearly one-third of whom were in households with someone in full-time work) currently suffer from 'food insecurity', which can include anything from missing the last meal to not knowing where to find the next one. Eleven million Americans, including four million children, are categorised as either moderately or severely hungry (Garosohn, 1997). These developments are mirrored by an extraordinary acceleration of inequality in the past twenty-five years. In the so-called 'wonder years' from 1946 to 1973, all Americans improved their material well-being, but this trend has been reversed in the intervening years. From 1973 to 1995, the income of the top 20 per cent of the population grew by 8 per cent but the bottom 60 per cent lost real income; the poorest 20 per cent lost the most income of all, nearly 15 per cent of an already inadequate living (Galbraith, 1997).

This abysmal failure of social protection has many roots – growth in jobs that do not provide a living wage, the progressive marketisation of society that bestows disproportionate rewards to the advantaged, a precipitous decline in union power – but the role of political choice has been paramount. The real value of the minimum wage still lags behind the 1979 figure: in 1997, someone who worked full-time for fifty weeks at the current minimum wage of $5.15 would earn only $10,300 which falls below the national poverty threshold for a family of two (Pollin and Luce, 1998). There have been radical reductions in the level and scope of many federal programmes including school lunches, food stamps, health insurance, pre-natal care, after-school programmes and disability benefits. Immigrants face tougher eligibility requirements for access to school lunches, food stamps, immunisation programmes and early child learning, and have been barred in several states from the right to education, health care (including emergency services) and other social services.

The 1996 welfare reforms, promulgated under the Orwellian title 'Personal Responsibility Act', dismantled federal regulation of many components of benefit provision and allowed individual states to set their own levels and conditions of benefits. Over two-thirds of the states have imposed new limits on the period in which people can claim benefits and have required people on state assistance to take jobs (regardless of the pay or conditions) or risk losing all payments. These new programmes were supposedly designed to reduce dependency and harness self-reliance, but a recent survey by the US Conference on Mayors found that large numbers of inner city residents risked destitution because of a severe shortfall of jobs in their areas. All of these initiatives have significantly impaired the ability of individuals (particularly women) to pursue their autonomous life projects and have led to a precipitous decline in the quality of life of millions of Americans. Indeed, the social safety net in the United States is more and more beginning to resemble the nineteenth century, when security provision was largely the province of the family, church and charities.

There are wider consequences of this new insecurity as well. The profound inequality of American society has produced what John Galbraith referred to as a 'culture of contentment', the growing disengagement of elites from any form of collective responsibility and solidarity (Galbraith, 1992). Evidence of this social apartheid is visible in every walk of American life. The contented classes send their children to private schools, use private health care, opt out of public pension schemes, vote for regressive taxation policies and restrictive benefits, and reject altogether the possibility of a public sphere. Eight million Americans now live in 'gated communities', privately owned residential developments that feature private security guards, barricades to limit the ease of entry, and a whole series of private leisure amenities (Blakely and Snyder, 1997). In these 'bourgeois utopias', 'security has less to do with personal safety than with the degree of personal insulation, in residential, work, consumption, and travel environments, from "unsavoury" gangs and individuals, even crowds in general' (Davis, 1990: 224).

This social polarisation has its counterpart in the draconian measures of social control launched against the 'dangerous classes' in many American cities. Young people, particularly within the Black and Latino populations, face arbitrary arrest during police dragnets that seal off entire neighbourhoods in search of suspected gang members. They are targeted for highly intimidating and intrusive random searches while driving, an offence that is widely referred to by racial minorities as DWB (Driving While Black). They make up the bulk of those arrested, convicted and sentenced to prison for drug offences even though the vast majority (76 per cent) of illegal drug users in the United States are white (Miller, 1996). The political paranoia about crime, as evidenced by the infamous 'three strikes' policy which imposes life imprisonment for anyone convicted of three offences or by the various 'wars' on drugs, has resulted in the construction of an 'American Gulag'.[5] Prison spending in the US has increased tenfold over the past two decades, from $4 billion to $40 billion. California, which once possessed one of the best public education systems in the world – in 1980 it spent seven times as much on universities as it did on prisons – now devotes more of its budget to prisons than it does to education. There are nearly four million Americans currently in prison, on parole or probation, or awaiting trial, including nearly one in four African-Americans between the ages of 21 and 29 (Miller, 1996). The horrific conditions in these infernos and the abandonment of any hope of rehabilitation such as education, training, drug treatment or psychological counselling has been deplored by Amnesty International as a fundamental violation of human rights (Amnesty International, 1998).

It should come as no great surprise, then, that the willingness to engage in collective obligations has all but disappeared from the worldview of American elites. A belief in risk pooling effectively depends on an ability to appeal to an individual's enlightened self-interest; to persuade someone, in other words, that because they too may one day be vulnerable, it is in their interest to share in the protection of the presently disadvantaged. But as Robert Reich notes, wealthy and powerful Americans have vastly different life experiences from the poor, who are economically, culturally and spatially marginalised. 'The wealthy are no longer under a "veil of ignorance about their futures" ', he writes. 'They know that any social compact is likely to be one sided in their favor' (Reich, 1992: 278). The privatisation of security for American elites is tantamount to condemning millions of their fellow citizens to lives of indescribable insecurity.

Notes

1   The idea of state 'logics' was first formulated by Alford and Friedland (1985), who postulated three such logics: class, bureaucratic and pluralist. I have substituted a welfarist logic, corresponding to the state's interaction with civil society, for their bureaucratic concept.

2   Redistribution may actually be completely incidental to the purpose of risk pooling; there is nothing that prevents the levels of social protection established from being highly unequal. Nevertheless, the egalitarian aspects of risk protection are implicit: the ability of groups or individuals to withstand these crises of insecurity is unevenly distributed.

3   The seeming neutrality of the terms 'cohesion' and 'integration' should not obscure the fact that each of these issues will be resolved in terms of power. The structural inequities of class, race or gender may mean that people are socially integrated (in the labour market, community and family) in fundamentally unequal ways (Levitas, 1997). It may also be the case that the boundaries of the community to whom individuals owe responsibilities may be drawn in narrow, exclusionary ways (see below).

4   As Manfred Bienfield has perceptively noted, none of these political actors operate with the slightest misconception about the fate of the global order. It is obvious that political leaders do not believe in their own myth making about inevitability or else they would not have expended so much effort to create mechanisms that bind members into the agreements (Bienefield, 1994).

5   The rapid expansion of prisons has also been a way of addressing the problems of rural insecurity and poverty. Prisons represent a needed influx of jobs and resources to areas that are in slow decline. As Seth Abramsky has argued, they in essence represent a public works programme for the rural unemployed to incarcerate the urban unemployed (Abramsky, 1998).

4 Insecurity
Philosophy and psychology

Alex Howard

This chapter explores questions more than answers, and sets the scene for what follows by considering philosophical and psychological perspectives on insecurity. It will thereby, I hope, serve as a framework for subsequent discussion.

What kinds of insecurity are most important? Whose insecurity is most significant? Who decides? We may feel more, or less, insecure than we really are, but how is the reality of insecurity to be established, and by whom? How insecure is it 'reasonable' for us to expect to be? Who decides and how?

Insecurity may be exhilarating for those who are confident and competent enough to stay on top. But what of those who keep getting swept under? Are casualties inevitable in a competitive global economy? Is a Darwinian struggle unavoidable? Can we afford to consider, or ignore, social justice and social cohesion? Are those on the political right hard-hearted and selfish in their attitudes towards the insecure? Are they courageous, honest and realistic?

In considering such questions it is worth sampling the range of implicit assumptions, and explicit ways of thinking, about insecurity. The topic can thereby be placed within a larger context, and we can cultivate a more critical and creative approach to the subject and avoid becoming locked into a narrow mind-set.

Feelings of insecurity

Some people appear to feel chronically insecure, however safe their circumstances. Others maintain their confidence, however close to real danger. We look around and see people whom we judge to be too scared or too confident for their own good. How closely, then, do fearful feelings relate to frightening realities? Presumably there is some connection between *feeling* safe and actually *being* secure? But how positive is the correlation? Sometimes it seems very strong. A chronically insecure adult may have been traumatised by a chaotic childhood and a continuously punishing present. On other occasions, though, the correlation may be negative. An overly protected and pampered child may develop such high expectations that the smallest adult uncertainty or setback becomes 'intolerable'.

Some go boldly and recklessly forward with little regard for danger. Others stay rigid and frozen because of exaggerated or illusory constructions of surrounding hazards. For the intrepid, the security of firm dry ground may be dull and dreary. They climb dangerous mountains or sail into storms, thereby risking their very lives. For the timorous (and sometimes the contrary emotion is to be found within the same individuals), their fear of crime is out of all proportion to the real risks.

On the political left, the focus of attention tends to be on protecting people from insecurity. On the political right, the agenda has tended more towards encouraging individuals to be more proactive and entrepreneurial; to face up to insecurity, to take risks, to pick yourself up however many times you may become bankrupt or redundant. This attitude, it is argued, is what creates a healthy dynamic economy and society that can more easily support its genuine social casualties. The left focuses on these casualties, or victims, those who lost in the race to security. It seeks measures to support and protect them. The right pays more attention to winners, those who seized opportunities and won despite the odds. It seeks to encourage the rest of us to be similarly brave. One agenda does not have to exclude the other, but within a polarised political system it does so: too often.

Facts about insecurity

Other chapters in this book analyse material insecurity. There are important statistics about such forms of insecurity that are independent of expectations, value judgements or individual feelings. For example, the probabilities of being sick, unemployed or poor correlate strongly with each other and with social class background. We do not know if a particular individual will get sick or lose his or her job, but we can say that those from the lowest social classes may be four or five times more likely than average to suffer a major illness before age seventy (Black, 1980). Likewise, we may know that in certain categories of employment you may be twice as likely to be made redundant than the average for the country as a whole. All these statistics assume that the existing patterns of incidence will continue into the future, but such assumptions are often not unreasonable.

Even with agreement about the statistics concerning insecurity, there may be disagreement about how to explain them and the consequent moral stance that should be taken. Mortality rates are uneven between social classes. How far is this because of unhealthy behaviour? How far is it due to an unhealthy environment, limited opportunities and unjust circumstances? Are the individuals concerned *ir*responsible or *not* responsible? Are they feckless or victims of an unfair society? Insecurity of employment is very unevenly distributed. Is this because society does not offer enough for some workers? Is it because some workers do not have enough skills and/or motivation to offer society? Who is to blame? Or perhaps nobody should be blamed but nothing much can be done about it anyway?

As many other chapters in this volume argue, *to him that hath shall more be given*. The secure and comfortably situated are best placed to increase their security and comfort still further. Conversely, the poor and vulnerable are most exposed to still further setback. The rich can afford the best environments, services and comforts; the poor may be left with the most depressing, dangerous and polluting places to live and work. Loans to the poor, who need them more, will be unaffordable. The largest and cheapest advances go to the already wealthy. Interest accrues mostly to those who are already well-cosseted by accumulated interest. Private insurance is usually unaffordable to those facing high risks and low incomes. In these and many other ways, inequalities tend to widen unless strenuous collective efforts are made to combat this strong tendency. Social insurance brings protection to the poor but only if the more comfortably situated are prepared to subsidise the less wealthy, fortunate, successful or competent.

Some moral questions are resolvable by clarifying the facts. But we may disagree about what are effective remedies and how far individuals have the power to deal with their insecure circumstances. Is it morally outrageous for a government/individuals to take little action in relation to chronic unemployment? It is if you believe that there are a variety of effective remedies that governments/individuals can take. It is not disgraceful if you think there is little that governments and/or individuals can do.

Was there a golden age of security?   We worry that we will be plagued, poisoned or plunged into poverty, and all this may leave us more apprehensive than our ancestors. Is this because we really are more at risk than our great-grandfathers? In many respects the evidence suggests otherwise, though simple generalisations do no justice to the subtleties, complexities and varieties of human hazard, peril and uncertainty. Equally varied is the range of human expectations, beliefs, assumptions, patterns of meaning and morale that themselves greatly influence our sense of overall well-being and security.

Technology and insecurity   There is no call for complacency, but average life expectation on this planet is increasing. Technology has vastly expanded human capacity to deliver goods and services. It has produced toys, comforts and distractions that our ancestors could not even have imagined. In some respects, even the lifestyle of the relative poor would leave a medieval king wide-eyed in envy; one thinks of anaesthetics, for example, along with many other modern conveniences. Technology has also made us much more interdependent, and this can engender feelings of helplessness and powerlessness regardless of the real risks of power failure. In a medieval village the risk of famine was far greater than it may be now; but villagers felt like bigger fish in their smaller, and more familiar, pond. We may find it hard to feel anything other than insignificant fry in our impersonal global village of billions of people.

Technology may both improve the opportunity for some while undermining that of others. It may, in other respects, both improve and undermine *everyone's* security. We can now, quite literally, move mountains. Consequently, we have a capacity to solve problems that was quite outside even the imagination of our ancestors. In their eyes we would, quite literally, seem like gods. But technology also provides the capacity to *create* problems on a scale that could not previously be imagined. We can catch all the fish in all the oceans. What power, and what folly. We are not haunted at nights by fear of tigers; instead, we fear that there may soon be no tigers, along with literally tens of thousands of other species. Nonetheless, for all our current fears and uncertainties, would we swap them with the insecurities of our ancestors? If we could enter a 'time machine' and go back to any, supposedly more secure, place and time in history, how many locations would we actually choose?

Human assessment of insecurity This does not always bear much relation to objective mathematical analysis of threat. Death by road accident is a far greater hazard than a plane crash, yet the plane frightens many far more than the car. Why? Partly it is familiarity, which may breed not so much contempt as confidence. A familiar risk becomes less frightening. The monster we have seen several times becomes ever less of a shock. We know how to drive cars, we know something about how they work and we probably know the driver if we are not actually driving ourselves. Here is a danger over which we have some control. This makes it less frightening. Familiarity also allows us to learn how large the risk is. It thereby becomes easier to bring our fears into line with the real extent of the danger. Indeed, familiarity may then engender recklessness. Cars are comfortable, we have never had an accident, we feel confident that we can get out of trouble; then we drive too fast, and discover that we have been *under*estimating the dangers.

A statistician will say that a risk of, for example, a nuclear accident or food poisoning incident is very low but that its exact size is unknown. We hear the word 'uncertain' more than 'very low' and we see that, like passengers on a plane, we have very little control over the outcome. In addition to familiarity, our sense of justice, our explanations and notions of contextual meanings and purposes all influence our attitudes to, and feelings about, risks. For example, if you believe that nuclear power is essential for a comfortable and secure future, then you may decide that the risks are part of the price to be paid. The risk is 'acceptable' and therefore does not disturb you too much. If, on the other hand, you think that non-nuclear technologies are preferable and that we should not in any case be so energy-dependent, then your discomfort and anger about the dangers are likely to be much greater. This risk is 'unacceptable' and 'unnecessary'. Therefore, however small, it is irritating.

Actuarial assessment of insecurity Risk and insecurity can be measured relatively objectively by statisticians using a wide variety of measures. For example, we can attach probabilities to our health and employment prospects and correlate these with social class. The patterns and the social class differences are significant and important. Less easily, we can attempt historical comparisons. When we do so we find that, in many respects, we have never had it so good. We are more likely to

die of cancer simply because we are less likely to be caught by plague or
starvation. Reducing the risk of one threat allows the one behind it to loom over
us. Reducing risk also allows our expectations to rise. We thereby become less
tolerant of that which, yesterday, seemed unavoidable. From an objective
standpoint, therefore, risk is relatively easy to define and measure. It is essentially
a question requiring numerical analysis. From a personal point of view, however,
risk is only partly determined and defined by the objective circumstances. More
so, it is constructed by meanings, purposes, narratives, expectations, self-image,
values and assumptions that we make in relation to ourselves and our lives.

Insecurity and expertise   Our assessment of risk is greatly influenced by the
perceived status and expertise of the would-be 'expert' who is advising us. For
example, in the 1960s, scientists promised that, thanks to nuclear power,
electricity would soon be free. The risks were almost unknown, the benefits
seemed enormous and the status of the scientists was high. Now, however
confident the nuclear scientist may be, we are more inclined to be sceptical, less
likely to feel reassured. Even less believed are economists: if they advise that they
know how to solve economic problems and we must not worry unduly about
unemployment, few are likely to feel reassured.

Relative insecurity   Feelings about insecurity will also be dependent on the baseline
from which we are making comparisons. There is no 'absolute' conception of
insecurity. We are more or less insecure only compared with some other defined
time and place. Currently, Europe and America tend to compare insecurity at
work with the 'golden age' of the postwar 1950s and 1960s (see Chapter 5 for an
analysis of this comparison). We are, it is claimed, less secure than we were
during this postwar period. The claim is in any case challenged, and who is this
'we' that is being compared? Surely not everyone's security has improved or
declined in the same way?[1]

   Since this supposedly 'golden age' (which included the Cold War terror of
nuclear annihilation), average living standards have risen substantially. Inequality
seems also to have widened very considerably. Are we more or less insecure?
Compared with what place and time? Which 'we' are 'we' referring to? If you
are a postwar baby boomer with socialist leanings, then the present time may
seem to be one of disappointment and growing uncertainty. If you are a part of
New Labour then (at the time of writing!) you may be feeling much more
optimistic. If you are younger, with lower or different expectations and
assumptions, then the world as you see it may well be different again. Your
education and class background will be crucial. Some graduates moving into
professional life may decide that life can be negotiated, and even enjoyed. An
unskilled male from a depressed region may have good reason to feel pessimistic
about the opportunities in his locality.

Age   Age is another factor determining our experience of security. People may
reach middle age and imagine that thirty years previously their lives were

brighter, safer and more golden. Much of the brightness of youth arises from the superior eyesight of youth; the sensitivity of all our senses become literally and substantially less sharp with age. The past could feel safer because we did not have to stand on our own feet as adults. The past may have felt golden because our expectations and assumptions had not yet become tarnished and weatherbeaten by the years. The present may feel more threatening if we, quite literally, feel less secure on our feet, less certain in our grasp, less clear in our perception. 'Be careful', the old advise their young, as they have always done. The youngster, as always, is sometimes wise, and sometimes foolish, to downplay the advice.

History and literature History is full of writers bemoaning a deteriorating present, an uncertain future and a supposedly golden past. The consequent moral panics recur on a regular basis. In the 1860s the London press stirred up widespread fears about being garrotted. 'The mob' has been a source of terror for centuries. In the 1950s, flying saucers were spotted regularly. Currently, many in the USA claim to have been abducted by aliens.

'Great expectations' Our interpretations and expectations substantially determine our feelings about, for example, job insecurity. If you think that government can, and should, protect the poor and vulnerable, you will be likely to have strong negative feelings and views about the painful consequences of global restructuring. If you believe that, on balance, free trade is a liberating influence that creates the best of all possible worlds, then the pain and discomfort suffered will be seen as an unavoidable part of the price of change. You will assume that we must cope rather than complain.

If my expectations outstrip achievable reality, then I will feel insecure however comfortable my circumstances. Growing security may feed my expectation, making me feel more fragile. People, and nations, in comfortable circumstances are prone to panics about ever more (historically) trivial dangers. Even a run of good luck may leave us feeling uneasy. We may feel haunted by the fear that this good fortune simply cannot continue.

Forms of insecurity

Within social policy debate, the form of insecurity uppermost in people's minds is *material insecurity*. Within psychology, not surprisingly, the discussion of insecurity concerns its *psychological and existential* dimensions. One dimension does not exclude the other, of course; psychologists will readily agree that material insecurity can promote a chronic experience of personal unease. However, there are other, possibly more important, dimensions to psychological insecurity. Over the past century, the most significant progress in our understanding of existential insecurity has been made by Jean-Paul Sartre and, even more, Martin Heidegger, building on the writings of Kierkegaard and Nietzsche. It is impossible to do justice to their work within the agenda of a social policy textbook, but it is

64   *Alex Howard*

important at least to note that much insecurity can arise from the way we apprehend our identity.

Existentialists criticise the notion of self as a commodity, an object to be bought, sold, promoted and adorned. We buy others and sell 'ourselves' and our portfolio of skills just like any other commodity. Yet in a world that, we imagine, is a purely material economy, many of the goods and 'lifestyle' commodities that we accumulate are often more to do with making 'personal statements' than with material survival. Advertisements seek to imply that, by buying the commodity on offer, the customer will satisfy the non-material needs that really are primary among those who already have food and shelter. Buy the chocolates and you will have fun, serenity, respect, comfort, peace-of-mind, sex, status, self-regard or whatever. The poor are victims of this false consciousness/bad faith as much as, or more than, the rich. A significant proportion of a very limited budget may go to buying £85 designer footwear that, from a purely material perspective, is completely irrational and irresponsible. When you already have shirt and shoes, what you may really be after are the designer labels, with all the psychological connotations that go with them. Even in Third World countries, such purchases of status symbols are an important component of consumer efforts for status and security. Does anyone *need* caramel fizz? It contains almost no worthwhile ingredients, and it is expensive. But if it is *Coca-Cola*, it signifies that you have joined the global economy. You are no longer just a backward peasant. You can say goodbye to fresh mango juice. Your status as village leader is reinforced.

What does such status-symbol purchasing suggest concerning our spiritual poverty and insecurity? What does real wealth actually consist in? What kind of self-esteem provides a genuine sense of security? The 'good life' can now be seen on TV. Advertisements show how to find the right 'image' by buying appropriate lifestyle commodities. You will then be popular, and you will live with the style, zest, serenity, security, fun, humour, happiness, love and respect that you deserve. However, this consumer lifestyle fetishism seems not to bring lasting peace of mind, love or wisdom. Our deepest insecurity may well be a primarily spiritual matter. How can this dimension of our existence be successfully integrated with the more mundane and material components of insecurity? Perhaps greater efforts should be made to integrate psychological/spiritual and material/secular dimensions of insecurity?

Philosophies of insecurity

Our underlying philosophy of life crucially influences the way we experience setbacks and uncertainty. For example, I may decide that 'this is God testing me, I must show that I am strong and brave'. Or, I may conclude that 'God is punishing me for my sins; I must make a sacrifice, suffer and feel contrite'. Alternatively, I may opt for a blaming strategy: 'this misery is all the fault of the Trade Unionists, the Bosses, the wicked West, fundamentalists, the Jews. We must go to war and rid ourselves of...' (whoever I have selected as scapegoat).

Currently, explanations of insecurity that invoke a deity and how best to relate to it have become less fashionable. Constructions that put all the blame onto some convenient scapegoat have however been as popular in the twentieth century as ever. They may well continue to prosper in the next millennium, especially if/when our circumstances, once again, make serious demands on us.

Our construction and interpreting of our circumstances is substantially influenced by whatever underlying philosophy we may have passively inherited or actively chosen. Philosophy shapes our basic beliefs and the values within which we locate and make sense of ourselves, our intentions and our expectations. It is impossible, therefore, to think and see independently of philosophy. It provides the building blocks, and the underlying organisation, to the very manner in which we perceive and reflect. However, the more all-embracing a philosophy becomes the more difficult it is to detect. When it gains hegemony in a society it can become completely invisible. It then provides the only way in which we can think about our world and ourselves. For example, social democracy as a political ideology has become difficult to detect. Its boundaries and shape, its strength and limitations become hard to assess because there is little serious competition against which it can be compared and contrasted. The options it suggests become not 'options' but 'inevitabilities'.

Consequently, when people say that they do not know any philosophy, what is really meant is that they use, without knowing it, only *one* philosophy, but they have no means of locating or assessing it. As a result, it structures everything they do and care about. It also prevents them from considering alternatives or placing immediate preoccupations into a larger perspective.

Our cup of good fortune can overflow depending, in part, on the size of the container we consider to be 'fair'. It can seem half-empty, or half-full, according to the expectations we have of the future. In the concluding section, I consider a sample of philosophical strategies for dealing with insecurity, illustrating them with the views of particular philosophers whose observations, however ancient, still deserve careful attention to this day:

Philosophy and coping strategies for insecurity

Confront change

Heraclitus (*c.*540–480 BC) advised that we felt insecure because we failed to understand the true nature of reality. We hoped and expected that people and circumstances would remain the same, or reasonably stable. But the underlying reality of existence was change. Everything was in a state of flux, of becoming something else, of transforming, interacting and interrelating. If we wanted to feel secure, there was no point in identifying with, attaching ourselves, or clinging onto the face in the mirror, the factory down the street, the (present) furniture of our lives. All would change, age, decay, move away and surprise us in ways we could not predict. Events and processes constituted the primary reality. Objects of attachment would ultimately prove to be events that arose, then passed away.

A wave in the river was an event. A mountain on the land was also an event; it took a little longer to pass on, since the processes of change moved slower on land than on water. But move they did, and you would have to move with them if you wanted to feel secure.

Of course, Heraclitus is himself long gone, but versions of his teaching have recurred down the centuries and remain influential. In particular, Oriental philosophies have regularly claimed that movement and process are more central than frames and objects. Consequently, they have offered strategies for coping with change and thereby gaining peace of mind. Within most of these teachings change is not to be feared since, underlying all this movement, is a harmonious and interconnected universe to which we belong and within which we are an inseparable part. Therefore, if we learn to live with change we can move beyond a sense of chaos and insecurity and thereby discover a deeper harmony and coherence within our ever-moving, ever-changing, existence.

The danger, of course, is that such philosophies can encourage a fatalistic attitude towards our own or other people's misfortune. They may engender a failure to cultivate and defend our own turf. In seeking to survey our lives with Olympian detachment from their ever-changing circumstances, we may become voyeurs on our own existence. It is possible to learn to avoid feeling insecure, however insecure we may actually be. But is this desirable? Surely not, if the result is that we do not look after our own security.

Confront tragedy

Sophocles (*c.*496–*c.*406 BC) explored the tragic dimensions of the human predicament. His dramas, unlike so many soap operas, popular fictions and nursery stories, did not provide happy endings or predictable outcomes. There was no necessary justice and fairness in earthly existence. The mightiest hero did not necessarily triumph over adversity but might, easily, effortlessly, and for no particular reason, be crushed. Human life was insecure, capricious and uncertain, and would remain so however hard we tried to establish control over our existence. Nonetheless, we would and should try to gain some hold over our circumstances, and we should attempt to avoid despair when our best efforts nonetheless resulted in failure. Our struggles to avoid failure and despair were admirable, but disaster and desperation would nonetheless remain frequent and common.

Come to terms with suffering

Two thousand years ago, Stoicism explored means of coping with the vision of existence as described by Greek tragedians. Our lives were insecure and would always remain so. We could seek to fashion our circumstances according to our preferences, but more often than not, circumstance would not be budged or, worse yet, would change to shatter whatever hopes we had about them. Consequently, a stoic attitude towards life required that we accommodate our preferences to suit our circumstances. Seneca, forced by his pupil Nero to commit suicide, said: *'Never mind, I leave what is of far more value than earthly riches, the example of a virtuous life'* (Russell, 1961: 267).

'I must die. But must I die groaning? I must be imprisoned. But must I whine as well? I must suffer exile. Can any one then hinder me from going with a smile, and a good courage, and at peace?' [2] These are ancient observations, but the stoic philosophy is still an integral part of our contemporary efforts to cope with stress, for example, within versions of psychotherapy. Rational emotive therapy and cognitive behavioural therapy attempt to show that *'people largely needlessly disturb themselves by, first, self-downing (SD) and, second, indulging in low frustration tolerance (LFT) or by demanding that their life absolutely must be easier and more gratifying than it is and by awfulizing and whining when it is not'* .[3]

The Stoic Epictetus even went so far as to suggest that the good man could find fulfilment even on the rack. It has been wryly observed that this would require a very good man on a very bad rack. Positive attitudes clearly help, but we are fooling ourselves if we think that positive attitudes can always triumph over negative realities, and that mind can reinterpret matter so as to abolish all pain and suffering. This kind of popular, get-on-your-bike, do-it-yourself psychology can be a way in which people in objectively miserable circumstances learn to blame themselves while government, and the more comfortably situated, look the other way.

Pray to God

St Augustine (AD 354–430), argued that insecurity and misery were inevitable as long as we sought to control our lives and circumstances without God. The saint's views were required teaching within Catholic philosophy right through to the end of the nineteenth century. For St Augustine, the secular approach to maintaining security could only lead to misery. Our self-centredness was sterile, barren, a hell on earth and ultimately self-defeating. We gathered goods around us like squirrels to ensure status and survival but security lay in letting go of all this and giving ourselves over to God: *'Sell what you have. Win a full harvest by giving to the poor, and the treasure you have shall be in heaven'* (St Augustine, 1977: 327). For Augustine, God was a lived and felt presence, the only light within and around. In his *Confessions*, Augustine is in continuous dialogue with his maker. This can seem difficult to grasp and archaic from a contemporary secular perspective, but it is salutary to remember that for many centuries the route to security, before all other strategies, lay in God.

Dance with the devil

Macchiavelli (1462–1527) explored the dark underside of the human condition in his advice to any would-be prince who wished to remain in power and retain security. To be secure, it was advisable to cultivate friends, allies and a reputation for honesty and integrity. If people loved you, that was all well and good. But fear was also a powerful incentive: '*...it is much safer to be feared than loved, when, of the two, either must be dispensed with*'. People were '*ungrateful, fickle, false, cowardly, covetous*'. You could not just rely on the power of love and trust: '*...that prince who, relying entirely on their promises, has neglected other precautions, is ruined*'. Similarly, honesty was not always the best policy: '*...and men are so simple, and so subject to present necessities, that he who seeks to deceive will always find someone who will allow himself to be deceived*' (Machiavelli, 1992).[4] We needed to learn to cheat, to deceive and to be ruthless while all the time developing a reputation for honesty, reliability and integrity. This way we would be most likely to find status and security.

Co-operate

Thomas Hobbes (1588–1679) believed that there could be no security for anyone, without the existence of a strong state: '*...men have no pleasure (but on the contrary a great deal of grief) in keeping company where there is no power able to overawe them all*' (Hobbes, 1998).[5] Without a strong central state we would be in a continuous state of war with our neighbours and our lives would be '*solitary, poor, nasty, brutish, and short*'. Hobbes was a Royalist during the Civil War and could therefore see that the notion that kings should rule by divine right was losing its hold over the populace. His arguments for the need for an organised society with a central authority were convincing but subsequent philosophers questioned that this central power should be of royal blood. For example, John Locke argued the need for checks and balances in a power structure based on property rights so that the central authority did not itself become arbitrary and oppressive: '*For he that thinks absolute power purifies men's bloods, and corrects the baseness of human nature, need but read the history of this, or any other age, to be convinced of the contrary*' (Locke, 1993).[6]

Get out of town

Jean-Jacques Rousseau (1712–78) saw no security or status within organised society. To find our identity, integrity, safety and peace of mind, we needed to escape from crowded human society and live more 'naturally' in rural withdrawal: '*Cities are the abyss of the human species. Men are not made to be crowded into anthills but to be dispersed over the earth which they should cultivate. The more they come together, the more they are corrupted*' (Rousseau, 1991: 59). Rousseau thereby began the tradition of withdrawal from urban affairs and instituted the romantic fantasy about rural life that has ebbed and flowed in Western societies ever since. His remedy was ultimately irresponsible, since he himself could see that we could not all manage to live a comfortable idyll in 'Rose Cottage'. He lived well off Western civilisation, condemned its uglier manifestations but provided inadequate practical social remedies to the social problems he observed. His notion of a 'general will' of the people, inadequately distinguished from the majority will, was a licence for wilful generals to claim that their own tyranny was somehow sanctioned by the masses. Some of his more personal strategies, however, deserve attention: '*It is by dint of agitating ourselves to increase our happiness that we convert it into unhappiness*' (1991: 81), and: '*He whose strength surpasses his needs, be he an insect or a worm, is a strong being. He whose needs surpass his strength, be he an elephant or a lion, be he a conqueror or a hero, be he a god, is a weak being*' (1991: 81).

Accept feelings of insecurity as part of our nature

Arthur Schopenhauer (1788–1860) also believed that the search for security could never end, but could only be transformed. As soon as one component of our lives was where we wanted it, we would move on to something else. Chronic dissatisfaction was part of the human condition because our will to achieve and control always ran ahead of our powers, abilities and achievements:

> *All willing arises from need, therefore from deficiency, and therefore from suffering. The fulfilment of a wish ends it; yet for one wish that is concealed there remain at least ten which are denied. Further, the desire lasts long, the demands are infinite; the satisfaction is short and scantily measured out. But even the final satisfaction is itself only apparent; every satisfied wish at once makes room for a new one; both are delusions; the one is known to be so, the other not yet. No attained object of desire can give lasting satisfaction, but merely a fleeting gratification; it is like alms thrown to the beggar, keeping him alive today so that his misery may be prolonged till the morrow.*
>
> (Schopenhauer, 1995: 180)

If we were fortunate we might achieve some control over our material circumstances, but: '*...just as want is the constant scourge of the common people, so boredom is the scourge of the fashionable world. In middle-class life ennui is represented by Sunday, just as is want by the six weekdays*' (1995: 199), and: '*no satisfaction is lasting, rather it is always merely the starting-point of a new striving*' (1995: 195).

Use, but do not be used up by, insecurity

Søren Kierkegaard (1813–55) saw insecurity as integral within both our circumstances and our very identity. We were intrinsically insecure in relation to ourselves because we could always sense that who we currently were was far less than what we wanted to become. We wanted to become someone, to make something of ourselves, yet there was insecurity about who we wanted to be and how to become that person. Where did we want to go? How could we get there? The questions were fraught with uncertainty:

> *The possibility of this sickness is man's advantage over the beast, and it is an advantage which characterises him quite otherwise than the upright posture, for it bespeaks the infinite erectness or loftiness of his being spirit.*
>
> (Kierkegaard, 1989: 44)

Despair was a part of the human condition, we could attempt to escape by withdrawal from daily life or by so immersing ourselves in day to day affairs that we lost contact with our own identity:

> *such a person forgets himself, in a divine sense forgets his own name, dares not believe in himself, finds being himself too risky, finds it much easier and safer to be like the others, to become a copy, a number, along with the crowd.*

(1989: 64)

For Kierkegaard, there were many who appeared secure and successful but who were gnawed from within by the feeling that they did not know who they were, that they lived a false life with a false self. There could be no real security within such existence:

> *They use their abilities, amass wealth, carry out worldly enterprises, make prudent calculations, etc., and perhaps are mentioned in history, but they are not themselves. In a spiritual sense they have no self, no self for whose sake they could venture everything, no self for God – however selfish they are otherwise.*

(1989: 65)

Change society

Karl Marx (1818–83) focused on the social and material bases of insecurity (see also Chapter 2) and saw these as the determinants of psychological and spiritual insecurity. 'Bourgeois' capitalism was the basis of our current collective and personal insecurity:

> *It has pitilessly torn asunder the motley feudal ties that bound man to his 'natural superiors', and has left remaining no other nexus between man and man than naked self-interest, than callous 'cash payment'. It has drowned the most heavenly ecstasies of religious fervour, of chivalrous enthusiasm, of philistine sentimentalism, in the icy water of egotistical calculation.*

(Marx and Engels, 1848: 52)

Capitalism was forever creating insecurity by its very nature: *'All old-established national industries have been destroyed or are daily being destroyed. They are dislodged by new industries, whose introduction becomes a life and death question for all civilised nations'* (1848: 54). Our employment remained continuously uncertain and this damaged our sense of self-respect as well as undermining our material security. Moreover the changing nature of employment was itself demoralising: *'Owing to the extensive use of machinery and to division of labour, the work of the proletarians has lost all individual character, and, consequently, all charm for the workmen'* (1848: 60).

Marx's descriptions of the problems were more powerful and penetrating than were his remedies. After the world revolution of the working class, we would all become more secure, productive, efficient, co-operative and caring: *'In proportion as the exploitation of one individual by another is put an end to, the exploitation of one nation by another will also be put an end to'* (1848: 85). History has not been kind to such utopian hopes.

Stop whining about insecurity

Friedrich Nietzsche (1844–1900) saw insecurity within and around us as integral to our existence. There was no escape, and why should there be? *'He who seeth the abyss, but with eagle's eyes, he who with eagle's talons graspeth the abyss: he hath courage.'* [7] We should not whine and complain; we should get tough with ourselves and with others. There was no stability nor security nor happiness to be expected in our existence: *'What is great in man is that he is a bridge and not an end: what can be loved in man is that he is an overture and a going under.'* [8] *'I have long ceased to strive any more for happiness, I strive for my work'* (Nietzsche, 1994).[9]

Nietzsche was contemptuous of his contemporaries' feelings of pessimism and insecurity. Modern man was endlessly worrying about suffering and setback because our lives had become too easy, too safe, too protected, insular and lacking in any spirit of adventure. We expected to be wrapped in cotton wool, and we whined about the smallest inconvenience:

> *these question marks about the value of all life are put up in ages in which the refinement and alleviation of existence make even the inevitable mosquito bites of the soul and the body seem much too bloody and malignant and one is so poor in real experiences of pain that one would like to consider painful general ideas as suffering of the first order.*
>
> (Nietzsche, 1974)[10]

Nietzsche was not alone in actively prizing a substantial degree of insecurity. Darwin's theory of evolution was adapted and applied to social, political and economic debates from the latter part of the nineteenth century onwards. Herbert Spencer (1820–1903) was a particular champion, himself coining the phrase 'survival of the fittest'. It was 'natural' that we competed, such competition was essential if the quality of the species was to improve. Conversely, it was inevitable that those who were not 'fit' would not, and should not, survive.

Classical economists, predating Nietzsche and Darwin, were similarly tough-minded and demonstrated why economics became known as the 'dismal science'. Thomas Malthus (1766–1834) argued that population would always tend to exceed the growth of production, and so many people were bound to remain insecure. Malthus's friend David Ricardo (1772–1823) was likewise concerned that overpopulation would depress wages to subsistence level. Both were prepared to accept that social casualties were unavoidable.

When you have 'made it', consider what to make of it

Carl Gustav Jung (1875–1961) centred on the concerns of those comfortably situated people who Nietzsche despised. He was not much interested in those seeking material security, identity and status in their lives. In our early years, we seek to secure a position in society and become 'normal', like others. But what is to be done when we have the house and job and car and all those other material accoutrements? *'About a third of my cases are suffering from no clinically definable neurosis, but from the senselessness and emptiness of their lives'* (Jung, 1995: 70).

Once we had 'made it' materially, we would start to wonder what to make of it spiritually and morally: *'Among all my patients in the second half of life – that is to say, over thirty-five – there has not been one whose problem in the last resort was not that of finding a religious outlook on life'* (1995: 264).

There could be no security for us in a world that made no sense to us. Hence the search for meaning, and hence the growth of psychotherapy as people sought substitutes to the Christian explanations that were losing their appeal. Jung, as a psychotherapist, might have been expected to welcome this new business. But he saw no future in a purely secular psychotherapy: *'The individual who is not anchored in God can offer no resistance on his own resources to the physical and moral blandishments of the world.'*[11]

Jung searched widely for ways in which we could make sense of our lives and thus find peace of mind. He was impressed with many Oriental theories and practical means of achieving peace of mind: *'Western man is held in thrall by the "ten thousand things"; he sees only particulars, he is ego-bound and thing-bound, and unaware of the deep root of all being.'*[12]

Notes

1 For example, analysis of UK Labour Force and General Household Surveys shows little evidence of a major change in job tenure in the UK. Also, Paul Gregg and Jonathan Wadsworth of the London School of Economics have analysed the available information not only on job tenure and turnover but also on the nature of vacancies available to the unemployed. This suggests that tenure and job security have changed only marginally for the majority, and pay levels have increased. See HM Treasury Labour Market Briefings, Graham Siddorn, http://www.hm-treasury.gov.uk/pub/html/econbf/eb10/art4.html.

2 From W.J. Oates, *The Stoic and Epicurean Philosophers*, in Russell (1961: 270).

3 Albert Ellis, in Palmer and Varma (1997).

4 Machiavelli (1992) ch. XVII, 'Concerning Cruelty and Clemency, and Whether it is Better to be Loved than Feared', and ch. XVIII, 'Concerning the Way in which Princes Should Keep Faith'.

5 Hobbes (1998), ch. X111, 'Of the Natural Condition of Mankind as Concerning their Felicity and Misery'.

6 Locke (1993), *An Essay Concerning the True Original Extent and End of Civil Government*, para. 92.

7 Nietzsche (1994), Fourth Part, 73, The Higher Man 4.

8 ibid.

9 Nietzsche (1994), Fourth Part, 61, 'The Honey Sacrifice'.

10 Nietzsche (1974), Book One, 'Knowledge of Misery'.

11 C.G. Jung, *The Undiscovered Self*, in Storr (1986: 360).

12 C.G. Jung, *Psychology and Alchemy*, in Storr (1986: 257).

Part II

Institutionalising insecurity

The four chapters in this section focus upon aspects of insecurity in contemporary society, with particular reference to Britain. Jane Wheelock explores issues about employment security, building upon her earlier chapter, to show how in the period since the end of the 'golden age' both unemployment and insecure employment have grown. There has been an abandonment of policies that provide security to workers, and an acceptance of a distribution of work opportunities in which many have too little work while some have too much.

Michael Hill develops some of the concerns of Jane Wheelock's chapter to argue that we are witnessing the progressive abandonment of a view – emergent earlier in the century – that state-promoted income maintenance policies can provide collective security. Social insurance policies are being undermined and replaced by a combination of much more individualised forms of insurance with the more residual approaches to relief from poverty which characterised the nineteenth-century 'poor law'. New Labour's preoccupations with expenditure restraint (influenced by a response to global economic developments of the kind criticised by John Vail in Chapter 3) mean that they will do little to reverse this trend.

Roberta Woods reminds us just how fundamental for our security it is to have a roof over our heads. She then charts how there have been, as with income maintenance, developments in government policy in the 1980s and early 1990s involving both a retreat from the provision of social housing and the encouragement of developments in the housing market that proved problematic for many people. The consequences have been a dramatic rise in homelessness, and even a diminution of the security of many in the hitherto privileged owner-occupied sector. She ends by tracing the slow and cautious moves by the new Blair government in Britain to deal with these problems.

Bob Simpson then takes us into an area of insecurity where, while the impact of both economic and political developments is still critical, attention must be given to changing social behaviour. Many contemporary writers are only too ready to inveigh against behaviour which reduces the role of the family as a source of security for its members (a theme taken up again by Bea Campbell in the third part of the book). Simpson suggests that this must also be seen as an area of social life where greater insecurity may have beneficial aspects. The crucial issues are about how individuals and the state manage transitions to a variety of new family forms and to the acceptance that marriage is now seen by very many as no longer necessarily 'till death do us part'.

5   Fear or opportunity?

Insecurity in employment

Jane Wheelock

The growth in insecurity

Modern life revolves around the labour market. For most of us, our livelihoods now and in retirement depend on earnings. Children are likely to live in poverty if their parents are not employed. Young people spend many years in and out of school training for the labour market, often subsidised by their household of origin. Those of working age who are not in employment either depend on other household members being in work, or they may be entitled to some form of income replacement from the state. People who are not in households, such as the homeless, are particularly vulnerable to poverty or even destitution. Children in lone-parent households, generally headed by women whose employment choices are restricted by scarcity of affordable childcare and breadwinning female wages, are also very vulnerable. This chapter is about the ways in which earning – or not earning – a livelihood affects the security and insecurity of people's lives.

It is because employment and non-employment have such far-reaching effects, because livelihoods and lives are so intimately intertwined, that the labour market is quite different from other kinds of markets analysed by economists (Polanyi, 1946). Unlike the general run of commodities – economists tradition-ally provide illustrations of guns and butter – labour is not produced for the market under the control of capitalists, but in family households (Himmelweit, 1995). When labour power (as Marx carefully called it) is purchased in the market, it is the capacity to do work that is being bought, but it is social relations in the workplace and the negotiation of a (fragile) balance between control and consent (Burawoy, 1981) that determines the quantity and quality of the work actually performed. The labour market, in other words, is quite clearly a socially constructed institution, incorporating asymmetries of power between its participants (Granovetter and Swedberg, 1992).

Labour market work determines, but is also determined by, the collective way of life. Family lives are structured around work, whether it be heavy manual work, migration of the family breadwinner, shift work or long hours in the office (Voydanoff, 1987). Communities, localities and regions have characteristics corresponding to the nature of the work available: dormitory towns and suburbs, the post-industrial countryside, ex-mining communities without employment and so on. Nor can unpaid work outside the labour market be disentangled from employment (Redclift and Mingione, 1985; Smith and Wallerstein, 1992). It is above all the reproduction process for labour that makes it different from other commodities. For people to be available for the labour market, they must be fed, rested, healthy and cared for, ready for work tomorrow, next week and in the new year. And as people retire, new entrants must be there to take their place. This means that the unpaid work that goes on in the household or in the social economy is *complementary* to paid work (Wheelock, 1992a). One cannot take place without the other.

What people work at, and the ways in which they work, have changed substantially over the last quarter of a century. The quantity – and the quality – of work available has altered as market-led change has brought about more flexible ways of working and fragmentation of the institutional context. In Britain and many other parts of Western Europe over the postwar era, an institutional framework for – largely secure – employment had been broadly settled until the mid-1970s (see Chapter 3; also Purdy, 1998). There was state-guaranteed full employment, income security through minimum (wages council) wages and a redistributive tax system, employment security through regulations on hiring and firing, work security through health and safety regulations, and job security through toleration of demarcation practices. As labour markets have been opened up to the operation of market forces, labour has steadily become more commodified. For some – the optimists – the shift in the character of labour markets has provided the opportunity for new, more independent ways of working, with more possibilities for self-fulfilment in a context of reflexive postmodernity (Piore and Sabel, 1984; Giddens, 1991). Pessimists observe growing contrasts between work-rich and work-poor individuals and households; between those who 'work all the hours that God sends'[1] and those condemned to idleness (Schor, 1992; Baily *et al.*, 1993; Wheelock and Vail, 1998).

There is not full agreement about the scale of the changes that have taken place in labour markets, but there is general consensus for the direction change has taken. What follows is a thumbnail sketch of how insecurity has been redistributed as the structure of power relations, the gender order, discrimination and state regulation have been modified.[2] Britain is taken as a paradigmatic example of these changes, for the UK has shifted from a relatively regulated labour market in the continental European mould towards the US model of a deregulated and flexible labour market, and the US remains a potent example for Britain's New Labour government despite some recent modifications to policy.

The first main trend affecting insecurity is to mass unemployment and the growth of workless households. In Britain, three million out of a labour force of twenty-four million were regularly unemployed during the 1980s, a figure that remained at two million even in recovery phases of the business–electoral cycle until the late 1990s. In 1975, a fairly disturbing 6.5 per cent of non-pensioner households had no adult member in work, but by 1995 3.3 million, or one in five households, were workless (Wells, 1998). Since that time, full employment for men has no longer been a reality in many of the advanced capitalist economies, while during the 1980s state policies of full employment were increasingly modified or even more or less abandoned. In continental Europe, overall rates of unemployment remain high as the millennium approaches. Indeed, changes in the structure of the economy and increasing internationalisation of competition have led to the institutionalisation of mass unemployment, particularly amongst unskilled and blue-collar workers in the developed economies (Godfrey, 1986). The only apparent exception to this rule is the US (possibly joined in very recent years by the UK), where rates of unemployment are lower.

Labour market trends affecting insecurity

1   Mass unemployment and the growth of workless households

2   Gender-based redistribution of hours worked

3   Differentiated intensification of men's and women's work

4   Shift from full-time waged work to full-time self-employment

5   Contrast between time-burdened poor households and time-poor harried rich

---

The shift to mass idleness in the advanced industrial economies has hit some groups particularly hard, such as the youngest and oldest age cohorts, and other groups who have traditionally suffered discrimination in labour markets including black and disabled workers. In some countries of the European Union such as the Netherlands and France, less than 40 per cent of the active male population aged 55–59 and less than 20 per cent of the 60–64 age group are now at work (Reday-Mulvey, 1998). Unemployment rates, even for the 20–24-year-old grouping of young people, are roughly twice the national average for many national economies, and in the European Union, people up to the age of twenty-four account for more than one-third of the total unemployed (Hollands, 1998). In the UK, the employment rate of disabled people is only 32 per cent, compared with 76 per cent for non-disabled people (Lunt and Thornton, 1998).

A second notable trend is a gender-based redistribution of hours worked. In Britain, for example, the number of women in paid employment (11.5 million) has gradually converged on that of men (14.1 million), so that men's share of total hours has fallen from 67.8 per cent in 1984 to 64.5 in 1996 (Wells, 1998). It is because the increase in women's employment has largely been part-time that women's share of total hours has not risen more. Indeed, throughout OECD countries, the growth of part-time employment has gone on alongside rises in women's activity rates. In all OECD countries, less than 12 per cent of men worked part-time (Bruegel *et al.*, 1998). Unfortunately, there is declining transparency of working time in Europe thanks to growing discrepancies between agreed hours per week and the number of hours usually worked (Fajertag, 1998). It is nevertheless clear that in Britain the proportion of male employees working long hours has increased. Nearly 40 per cent (39.2) of men worked 46 hours or more in 1996, up from 33.9 per cent in 1984 (Wells, 1998). This may take the form of overtime, where in Britain approximately half of full-time male workers worked overtime either periodically or regularly. As Bruegel *et al.* (1998) point out, men also tend to have longer basic working weeks than women, and longer travel time. This limits the possibility of men contributing to domestic work within the household, and in turn restricts women with domestic responsibilities to part-time employment at most.

It is unsurprising that the growing insecurity attributable to mass idleness also results in the intensification of work for those who are employed. There is in fact a trend towards intensification of both men's and women's work. For men, this takes the form of pressure to undertake more hours in the labour market. There is also some evidence for a very limited increase in the hours of unpaid work that men contribute within the household, but it is not sufficient to offset the increase in the hours that women are working in the labour market (Anderson *et al.*, 1994). For women, work intensification therefore takes the form of an increasing double burden of paid and unpaid work, and the pressures that arise from juggling two major roles. Juliet Schor's study of overall hours of work in the United States (Schor, 1992) confirms that workloads of both men and women have intensified since the end of the 1960s. She shows that hours of paid and unpaid work have risen by 163 hours – the equivalent of an extra month a year – even after taking into account those who are idle through unemployment. The struggle for security represented by over one hundred years of campaigning for shorter hours appears to have been decisively reversed. The fact that Britain has just signed up to the European Social Chapter's forty-eight-hour working week directive is unlikely to make any substantial dent in a well-entrenched long hours culture.

The third major trend is a shift from full-time waged work to full-time self-employment, which has occurred throughout the OECD economies (Mason, 1991). Even Britain, which started from a relatively low base at the end of the 1970s, now has one in eight of the labour force in self-employment. For the optimists, this trend represents a shift towards more independence and self-reliance in obtaining a livelihood. Policy makers in almost all the developed economies have seen the growth of small business as an important element of endogenous growth strategies, though not all have evinced the missionary enthusiasm for stimulating an 'enterprise culture' of the successive British Conservative governments of the 1980s and 90s (Ritchie, 1991; Hutton *et al.*, 1991; Keat and Abercrombie, 1991). Yet historical evidence indicates that growth in self-employment and growth in unemployment go hand in hand (Steindl, 1945; Foreman-Peck, 1985). The pessimistic view is that rising insecurity of employment pushes people in to self-employment as a next best way of obtaining a livelihood (Wheelock and Baines, 1998). That pressures remain for those who have taken this route is evident from the hours they work. The full-time self-employed work longer hours than their waged counterparts: in Britain, over half (51 per cent) of self-employed men worked over forty-six hours a week in 1996, while 22.5 per cent of self-employed women (compared with 9.3 per cent of employed women) did the same.

Optimists would argue that the trends in the growth of non-standard, atypical employment just charted can provide opportunities for those who do not necessarily want full time Fordist labour contracts. Women or men with caring responsibilities may wish to combine two roles in and out of the labour market, young people may wish to finance their training or education with part time employment, the disabled or older workers at the end of their career may prefer to work shorter hours. The desirability of a range of employment options is not at issue, but the ways in which they come about is, and this is the concern of the next section. A pessimistic interpretation of employment trends asserts that we are seeing a return to bad old ways of working. Long hours for those in work, punctuated by periods of complete idleness, combine with sufficiently low rates of pay to force a return to family-based income strategies with women (and children?) working in the labour market as well as working in the home, reinforcing traditional gender divisions of labour. But does not labour market mobility overcome such a vicious spiral? *Individuals* may indeed seek out better employment opportunities in other regions, even other countries. But the growth in migrant and away working undermines the co-operative basis for the family, as individual family members seek to better their individual position (Beck, 1992).

The next section hopes to provoke the reader with an attempt to schematise the ways in which the growing insecurity in labour markets (brought about by the commodification of labour) fragments and reconstructs patterns of power and powerlessness in ways which may consistently constrain choice in the use of time.

The sources of the problem: working all the hours God sends

At the risk of oversimplifying, it is possible to distinguish between what Alain Lipietz calls the high road and the low road to flexibility (Lipietz, 1992), or what Jill Rubery calls positive or long-term flexibility, in contrast with short-term or negative flexibility (Rubery, 1996), and Tony Killick sees as responsive versus innovative flexibility (Killick, 1995). I hope to indicate how each can take the form of a gendered social-political construction, which actually constrains the time options available to individuals and families (see Table 5.1)

Let us follow the low road to flexibility first of all, and see where it leads. Global competition and the structural shift to services put downward pressure on the wages of the unskilled, wages which are already at the lowest end of the market. The expansion of personal services associated with tourism and leisure, or with cleaning and catering in state education and health services, for example, draws in groups with limited training, such as women, youth or ethnic minorities (Baily *et al.*, 1993). The decline in relatively well-paid manufacturing jobs means

Table 5.1 Forms taken by insecurity

High road insecurity	Low road insecurity
	Either:
Pressure on paid work time: time bravado	Threat of unemployment
	Time-burdened poor
	Or:
Time-harried rich	Time pressure on whole household: women work due to low wages
Caring deficit	Caring deficit

that there are fewer alternative forms of employment, blocking off possibilities for career progression (Albo, 1998).

Responsive flexibility is characterised by particular industrial and occupational characteristics which mean that employers can readily offload any risk and uncertainty in their final goods markets onto employees, by hiring and firing as needed (Thurow, 1992; Bernstein *et al.*, 1998). There are of course minimal requirements for training for those groups that comprise the source of this workforce whose hallmark is insecurity of employment (Albo, 1998). Strategies of 'numerical flexibility' make solidarity between workers harder to maintain, and their encouragement of individualism undermines the social basis for trade union organisation and activity. Insecurity on the low road takes the form of a constant threat of unemployment in the face of short-term (economic recession) and long-term (technological) market forces.

The high road to flexibility, in contrast, relies upon employment based on sophisticated technology and innovation to keep abreast of international competition. Those employed in this sector – in high-tech industries such as petrochemicals, computing, biotechnology and so on – must be highly trained. They must be prepared to be 'functionally flexible', in the sense that they undertake a range of tasks and learn how to do new ones. In contrast with trade unions, the professional organisations representing such employees are often able to maintain a relatively powerful presence by, for example, restricting access to practising law, medicine or accountancy. In a deregulated and privatised market situation, relationships between employers and employees are individualised, but in a very different way to the low road. The managerial discretion that fragmentation facilitates is likely to be based on strategies to retain and upgrade expensively trained professionals, and avoid poaching by competitor firms. This means the development of promotion and career paths internal to the firm, in what have been called internal (as opposed to external) labour markets.

There are of course risks also for those on the high road. Internal labour markets are particularly likely to encourage longer hours of work as a means of establishing that the individual is worthy of promotion in an orgy of 'time bravado'.[3] Nor are those in highly trained labour market positions immune to what is euphemistically called 'corporate downsizing'. If developments in technology do not secure a market position, then redundancies for managerial and professional personnel can reduce costs. Those who remain after such cuts will be expected to take on the work of former colleagues. Insecurity in the upper echelons of the labour market tends then to take the form of pressure on paid work time.

Let it be recognised that strategies of short-term and long-term flexibility are not gender-neutral, but rely upon strategies of gender differentiation which take advantage of socially constructed gender roles (Wheelock and Mariussen, 1997; Bruegel *et al.*, 1998). The low road to flexibility is only feasible if society has institutions which can pick up the living costs of individuals who lose their jobs. The family is very important here. Married women are seen as the ideal work force where short-term flexibility is concerned. Some try to argue that the kind of temporary or part-time work found on the low road is 'family friendly', but they fail to see the likelihood that mothers will become exploited. The fact that women may also be forced into employment to supplement family incomes hit by falling wages is not so generally remarked upon. Of course the main argument for the low road to flexibility is that lower wages encourage higher rates of job creation, protecting people from unemployment, but lower wages undermine livelihoods, and can only be tolerated if more people work for more hours in more jobs within each family household (Bernstein *et al.*, 1998). Insecurity on the low road, then, also takes the form of time pressure, but it is time pressure on the whole household. This time pressure – or caring deficit – may be somewhat relieved in Britain, for example, by the combination of the Labour government's modest minimum wage which will be implemented for adults in April 1999, and by its national childcare strategy.

The high road to flexibility involves a very different experience for women. The time bravado demanded of those employed on this route tends to favour women without domestic responsibilities; indeed, it is noticeable that the age at which women are having their first child is rising relentlessly (Haskey, 1996). Unlike their male counterparts, fast-track mothers retain responsibility for organising child care (Gregson and Lowe, 1993). But unlike their sisters on the low road, mothers on high salaries can afford to purchase childcare; indeed it is often available at a knock-down price from those very sisters (Folbre, 1994). Whether it be the high road or the low road, insecurity will thus be offloaded onto our children, the next generation, in the form of an acute lack of time with their parents. What has aptly been called a 'caring deficit' is a feature of both short-term *and* long-term flexibility. Can this deficit be made good by such policies as the British national childcare strategy? Will it be possible to avoid the conundrum that (low) paid, commoditised childcare – almost always employing women – raises for equal opportunities? Has the New Labour pendulum swung too far back to old communist arguments first put forward by Friedrich Engels (1940) in *The Origin of the Family, Private Property and the State* that the only way to ensure the liberation of women is for them to devote their time to labour market activity? Do we not need to look at how men as well as women can be encouraged to take on the burdens – and the rewards – of caring?

Market forces have most notably failed to break down the institutional barriers between the high and the low road. The difficulty and expense of obtaining the education and training that could allow those on the low road to climb to the high road is actually reinforced by the very trends that are supposed to free up markets. Privatisation makes education more of an individual choice – for those who can afford it. Deregulation pushes training into the hands of individual firms, who will then want to establish internal labour markets to retain those they train, making it more difficult for outsiders from the low road. The problem for market-led policies is that education and training are by their nature public goods to a large extent: it is to the benefit of the economy and society as a whole that there should be a sophisticated workforce, but individual firms that offer training cannot guarantee that they will be the beneficiaries (Albo, 1998).

If this is correct, the tendency for the low road to flexibility to be unfenced and to allow all passers to eat whatever grass is left, while the high road to flexibility is carefully hedged off superior grazing, means that there is a tendency for inequality in wages to increase. It is particularly in countries that have pursued policies of deregulating labour markets most enthusiastically, notably the United States and Britain, that wage differentials have risen most sharply (Wells, 1998; Bernstein *et al.*, 1998; Baily *et al.*, 1993). Baily and his colleagues point out that American men have fared worse in this regard than women. Real earnings for young unskilled men, those responsible for supporting most of the nation's children, have been especially hard hit. Women have experienced greater gains in part because they are putting in more hours, but also because advantaged women are doing better than in the past.

When it comes to household, rather than individual incomes, the situation is rather different, though again there is a gender element. In the USA in the 1950s and 1960s, it is probable that the household distribution of income remained relatively egalitarian because women from the least affluent households were most likely to enter the labour force. More recently, as wages for well-paid women have increased most rapidly, women's earnings have contributed to a widening of household income differentials (Baily *et al.*, 1993). In the USA, growing inequality between households has gone alongside households in all income groups working longer hours over the period since 1979 (Bernstein *et al.*, 1998). These empirical data confirm the theoretical points made earlier that insecure households must intensify their work efforts to stand still.

In Britain, the structure of state welfare regulation makes for an additional set of inequalities, between work-poor households, where no household members are in employment, and work-rich ones, where husband and wife are both working. For households whose members can at best only command low wages, unemployment of one household member means that the other is not able to earn a wage which will take the household above state benefit levels (Wheelock and Mariussen, 1997; Morris, 1990). Low wages can therefore structure the whole household into unemployment. Insecurity under these circumstances takes on the further guise of a contrast between time-burdened households, which have no money to help wile away the hours in any socially meaningful way; and 'the harried leisure class' (Linder, 1970), time-poor households which may have so little time to spend their earnings that they make thoughtless purchases of luxury goods.

Market competition and opportunity

The economic argument for allowing or encouraging insecurity in labour markets is that it is only when labour markets – along with other markets – are 'competitive' that the incentives ensuring efficiency and economic growth can operate. This is the crux of the neo-liberal argument for deregulation. Let me look at the arguments through the eyes of one who is far from being a neo-liberal, Arthur Okum of the Brookings Institute in Washington. Writing in 1975, Okum provides a studiously reserved advocacy of an inevitable trade off between equity and economic growth, a subject on which the majority of economists are notably bullish.

Okum starts by acknowledging the contradiction between equal rights and the inequality of income in the USA, arguing that economic equality can be distinguished from equality of opportunity. The problem with rights – in contrast with economic assets – is the lack of incentive to economise in exercising them. Some degree of inequality is necessary to promote efficiency. This is the theory of the market as the invisible hand, where greed is harnessed to serve social purposes in an impersonal and seemingly automatic way. In following self-interest, efficiency – in the sense of producers getting the most out of given inputs – is achieved, based on the verdict of consumers. 'By some standards', posits Okum, 'rights in the market place represent equal rights to earn unequal incomes' (Okum, 1975: 35). Both in theory and in practice, the market has done very well as Okum sees it, and had he been able to see forward to the fall of communism at the time, he would no doubt have been even firmer in this assertion. Although he very openly accepts the price to be paid in terms of inequality, Okum is confident that it is a price worth paying, as he makes clear in the title of his book *Equality and Efficiency: The Big Trade-off*.

With the benefit of hindsight, we may nevertheless have reservations about the validity of these arguments, neo-liberal ideology notwithstanding. For Okum was writing at the end of an era of historically unprecedented rates of economic growth for the advanced capitalist countries, a period which also coincided with strong reductions in income inequality. In the two decades since then, we have seen a sharp secular deterioration in both economic growth rates and income equality (see Chapter 2). One possible explanation for this anomaly in economic theory is that market forces do not actually make labour markets competitive – they do not for instance break down the fences between the high and low road to flexibility – so that efficiency cannot be guaranteed. But a stronger argument – the foundation for which has been laid in Chapter 2 – is that market forces actually have an impact which economic theory ignores: they make labour markets *insecure*. And insecurity in turn has wide ranging micro- and macro-level effects which are likely to undermine economic growth.

Fear of failure: the impact of insecurity

Let us start at the micro level. How is individual behaviour likely to be influenced by insecurity? Chapter 3 argued that the standard economic argument carefully avoids talking about insecurity. It essentially takes a jaundiced view of human nature when people are at the bottom of the heap: if the poor are not forced to work, they will prefer to remain idle. If the unemployed are entitled to state benefit, policy analysts must look closely at 'replacement ratios' to be sure that 'high' benefits do not inhibit them from taking jobs. Nor should those at the lower end of the income scale be 'unrealistic' about the wage levels that the unskilled can command: it is important that minimum wage regulations, for example, should not contribute to aspirations, and organisations like trade unions which lead resistance to such realities are essentially undesirable. Inappropriate expectations will simply lead to higher levels of unemployment, chimes in economic theory.

So, does the economic system really require insecurity to make people work harder? Even a little insight into the way people are likely to respond to insecurity suggests that it may have just the opposite effect. Let us take each of the effects of insecurity identified in the last section in turn, starting with the threat of unemployment. We have already seen that this threat has contributed substantially to a growth in inequality. It is conceivable that society could decide to accept the negative effects of insecurity – in terms of loss of social cohesion, growing social disruption, rocketing child poverty and so on – if there were clear evidence that this could be offset by positive trends which could reverse the trend to inequality in the longer term. Unfortunately, there is not reliable evidence that inequality and insecurity have been offset either by substantial levels of job creation or by greater upward income mobility. Commentators in the USA are sceptical that there has been any job miracle, even if unemployment rates are lower than in Europe (Bernstein *et al.*, 1998), while in Britain those who are unconvinced by official unemployment figures pointed out during the 1997 general election campaign that there were one million fewer jobs than when John Major became Prime Minister in 1990. Nor, according to a report from the Centre for Economic Performance at the London School of Economics, have men been compensated for starting at the bottom of the heap with later high income rewards (Gregg, 1997).

This failure to compensate for the scourge of economic and social inequality is scarcely surprising. There is considerable evidence that men who have lost jobs through unemployment or redundancy are following the patterns already established by women who return to the labour market after a period spent caring: upon return they obtain lower wages, are placed in less skilled jobs, and are more likely to become unemployed again. There is a cycle of periods of low pay interspersed with periods of no pay for those subject to insecure employment (Gregg, 1997; see Chapter 11 for the case of youth). The vicious circle is further reinforced at the micro level by employers, who will be less likely to train or innovate if they are relying on cheap disposable labour of this sort. Nor is it surprising to find older workers in particular discouraged from seeking employment, even in the face of greater disincentives from state benefit systems (Jahoda, 1982).

The time pressure arising from greater insecurity is likely to have a number of insidious effects. While some pressure may be beneficial and encourage harder work, time pressure can easily translate into stress, and people suffering from stress are likely to work badly on their own tasks, and to make it more difficult for those above and below them in the hierarchy to work well into the bargain. Stress may give rise to absenteeism, as people find themselves coping badly at work, and stress-related illnesses will increase sick leave (Wilkinson, 1996). Pressure of time, and the pressure of expectations of performance that go with it, can lead to lack of self-confidence and to lack of morale. In the public sector, poor morale has had a destructive effect in both teaching and the health services, for example. Early retirement is not only a reflection of the financially rewarding packages that have been available to many of our most experienced public sector professionals, but is also a sign that they are literally sick and tired of coping with the many manifestations of employment insecurity.

Insecurity also puts pressure onto households' private time, and this reduces the time available for either parent to care for children and restricts the time available to look after the sick or the elderly. Time pressure – and stress – can have a destructive effect on personal relations, and may contribute to relationship breakdown. The risk of family breakdown affects men, women and children very differently. For fathers, the greatest problem is likely to be loss of contact with their children, while continuing financial responsibility will also impose pressures (see Chapter 8). For women, the major risks are not only a short-term loss of income, but long-term financial problems arising from their inability to maintain a double burden of childcare and employment alongside pension entitlement. Michael Hill shows that separation is likely to result in women facing substantially increased disadvantage, due to the gendered preconceptions of welfare state provisions (Hill, 1997). However amicably their parents manage to separate, the experience remains deeply traumatic for children of whatever age.

The growing contrasts that insecurity highlights between work-poor individuals and households with time on their hands, and the work-rich facing continual pressure on their time, leads to invidious comparisons. On the one hand, households 'working all the hours God sends' are likely to be intolerant of those who hang around all day. J.K. Galbraith describes a 'culture of contentment' amongst the middle classes, who want to retain their material advantages; fearful of insecurity for themselves, they also want to maintain the gap that divides them from those who are worse off (Galbraith, 1992). However, at the bottom end of the income scale, it is likely that what economists call the 'demonstration effect' will mean that the desire for the material comforts available to the better-off leads to aspirations that are out of line with low-paid work (Veblen, 1912). For example, young people who have been accustomed to the standard of living available in their household of origin may expect to be able to achieve these standards when they set up an independent household. The perceptions of unfairness or exploitation that arise from inequality can also undermine pride in work, as people ask themselves why they should care about producing a good product if they are neither decently rewarded nor secure.

Turning now to the macro impact of insecurity, let us start once more with the threat of unemployment. The economy-wide impact on skills and on innovation is potentially quite severe here. Thus a stable workforce facilitates accumulated knowledge, and the reproduction of skill through the passing on of on-the-job training and learning-by-doing (Fukuyama, 1995; Tomer, 1987). A competitive labour market is not conducive to either firms or individuals to develop skills, given that it is unlikely that the individual actors who bear the costs will be able to reap the full returns. Indeed, given the substantial external social benefits that result from training, firms in competitive markets may be fearful of developing the skills of a labour force which is then used by its competitors. As already pointed out, why should either employer or employee think about training if the job is insecure and the person filling it disposable? Insecurity is also an obstacle to innovation because it discourages the commitment essential to concomitant changes in working practices. Insecurity undermines long-term relations between employers and employees and makes a vicious circle of mutual distrust and antagonism likely (Thurow, 1992).

The insecurity arising from the threat of unemployment has had unforeseen and unintended impacts on important macroeconomic variables leading to greater economic instability, and potentially far-reaching effects on future generations. Insecure employment affects contributions to state pension schemes, while hopes of making up the shortfall through private arrangements are rendered problematic by uncertainty over levels of income and its duration (see Chapter 6). Britain has provided a by no means unique example of heightened macroeconomic instability over the last two decades. Policies of encouraging incentives through promoting owner-occupation in housing began to go badly wrong in the mid-1980s as rocketing house prices encouraged house owners to borrow extensively in newly deregulated financial markets (see Chapter 7). The consequent dramatic fall in the savings ratio had not been anticipated in macroeconomic models of the economy, and the consumer boom went unchecked until too late. When higher interest rates at the end of the decade burst the speculative bubble, people's jobs and the houses their families were living in came under threat together. House purchase had been necessitated by job moves, but jobs then did not last. Unemployment rocketed, house prices plummeted and consumer spending remained cautious for a number of years as people revised their government-encouraged risky behaviour and cut back on borrowing.

The time pressure of insecurity acts in two arenas at the macro level. Firstly, the micro impact of stress on employees has a collective impact on efficiency, as it undermines performance and collaborative and team working and the smooth running of organisations. Time pressure on households collectively affects social reproduction through the destabilisation of social reproduction within the family household, as mothers and carers face an increasing double burden and men are unable to make good the caring deficit thanks to the pressure on their own hours of work. As a number of commentators have suggested, this has a knock on effect on the macroeconomy through the processes which reproduce the labour force, including skills and attitudes to work assimilated in the home (Folbre, 1994; O'Hara, 1995).

The contrasts between time-burdened/work-poor and work-rich/time-poor individuals and households also act at a macro level, in undermining societal values of decent rewards for toil and people's expectations of fair dues. A sense of being taken advantage of is divisive and destructive of societal moral values. This may mean that people try to take ensuring fairness into their own hands, encouraged by the 'winner takes all' selfishness that underpins market competition. There is a fine line between selfishness and dishonesty which any widespread perception of unfairness in rewards is likely to blur. Industrial relations experts have long been aware of these dangers, codified in theory as the need to 'manufacture consent' amongst any workforce (Burawoy, 1981). Yet a set of moral standards is a prerequisite for markets, where it is impossible to codify all elements of transactions in legally enforceable contracts, as the theory of transaction costs recognises (Williamson, 1987). Insecurity undermines the trust that lies at the heart of effective market functioning, giving rise to the possibility of markets dominated by the Mafia, local warlords or other forms of gangsterism (Fukuyama, 1995).

The wider costs and benefits: self-exploitation or self-fulfilment?

This chapter has been concerned to indicate how the forms that power takes in conditions of insecurity in labour markets can undermine the choices that optimists see opening up in a more flexible climate. It is difficult, though not impossible, to find self-fulfilment in employment when competition enforces particular forms of economic behaviour. It may well be the case that there is more choice for more groups in more flexible labour markets. Students, those with children to care for or with other caring responsibilities, creative artists, those nearing retirement and the disabled are all groups who spring to mind as potential beneficiaries of new and more flexible patterns of working. Men too will want shorter hours if they are to be able to share the work and participate in the rewards of family life. However, it is no good if these advantages have to be traded for poor pay and bad conditions, and if they result in these groups being exploited.

The solutions to the problems posed in this chapter require a radical rethinking of time. In order to transform power relations and at the same time facilitate variety of lifestyle, we need to think again about how we as a society should distribute our time between ourselves so that we can all – men and women, young and old – have a share in paid work, unpaid work and free time to do with as we wish. The relationship between family, market and the state that was established in the advanced capitalist nations in the aftermath of world war half a century ago needs recasting. We need a new social settlement on hours of work and forms of employment. A good starting point would be to develop a blueprint for the redistribution of work and employment.[4]

Notes

1   This phrase came up many times in interviews with men who had become unemployed as a result of economic restructuring during the mid-1980s in northeast England. They were referring to the period while they were still in work (see Wheelock, 1990).
2   This analysis has also been presented as part of the introduction to *Work and Idleness: The Political Economy of Full Employment* (Wheelock and Vail, 1998).
3   Robert Hollands suggested the use of this term (Hollands, 1998).
4   The arguments for such a blueprint are developed in Wheelock and Vail (1998).

6 Insecurity and social security

Michael Hill

Introduction

The argument of this chapter is that increases in insecurity in society have been accompanied by decreases in the availability of social security. While this is not surprising, it involves a reversal of a significant development through the first three-quarters of the twentieth century. During that period, one of the objectives of social security was to try to reduce the impact of other forms of insecurity, particularly those deriving from the working of markets. It is important to explore the way in which contemporary reductions in security in society and in social security are linked, and to examine the way in which a negative dynamic is being reinforced.

Defining social security

Searches for definitions for terms can often seem to be rather boring academic exercises. However, in the light of the particular concern of this chapter with the relationship between social security as part of a social policy system, and security in society, the author felt that some exploration was necessary, not so much of dictionary definitions *per se*, as of common usage. That exploration was prompted by an understanding that British and American usage of the term differed.

In 1966, the British government passed the first piece of legislation using social security in its title, the Ministry of Social Security Act. That Act created a Ministry which was 'to take over responsibility for the existing schemes of War Pensions, Family Allowances, National Insurance and Industrial Injuries, and to administer a new scheme of Supplementary Benefits to replace National Assistance' (Ministry of Social Security, 1967: 1). What was clearly happening here was that the government was using social security as a generic term to cover all the income maintenance schemes for which it was responsible, comprising both social insurance and social assistance. The author's suspicious mind wondered at first whether there was here a piece of political sleight of hand, to obscure the distinction between the two at a time when political pledges to minimise the latter were being neglected (see Townsend and Bosanquet, 1972). However, it was then noted that Beveridge repeatedly described his pathbreaking report of 1942 as a 'Plan for Social Security'. While Beveridge was clearly putting social insurance as the central plank in his proposals he spoke of 'unified social security' to embrace social insurance and social assistance, advocating a single ministry (Beveridge, 1942: para. 30). Hence when Richard Titmuss, writing about social security in the *International Social Security Review* in 1970, saw the need to define social security as embracing '(1) cash benefits provided without a means or needs test and (2) cash allowances, provided after such a test' (Titmuss, 1987 [1970]: 222), he may be taken to be following standard British usage.

Exploring the use of the term 'social security' in the United States, we find an apparently similar starting point, a piece of legislation which seemed to take American usage in the same direction. The Social Security Act of 1935 established both insurance-based and means-tested programmes, and the Social Security Board (later the Social Security Administration) took on oversight of both types of schemes. Yet somehow American usage has evolved to make a distinction between social security as 'social insurance' and social assistance as 'welfare'. Skocpol speaks of US policies since 1935 as characterised by 'sharp bifurcations between "social security" and "welfare" '(Skocpol, 1995: 12). While Skocpol's book highlights the implications of that division for the politics of American social policy, the distinction in usage is common in the American literature.

The potential confusion between British and American usage leads writers to adopt other terminology to describe the programmes outlined above, in particular the expression 'income maintenance' (Heidenheimer *et al.*, 1990; Hill, 1996). While in this chapter, social security will be used in the British sense, it is acknowledged that American usage draws our attention to an important distinction, in as much as it seems reasonable to suggest that in most countries (Britain included, but with the possible exception of Australia) social assistance provision can be seen as the successor to the 'poor law', as not providing security but offering instead last resort poor relief, under conditions which can neither be regarded by workers as a promise of security when labour market participation is terminated, nor be regarded by its recipients as an income which they are guaranteed so long as they are in need of it.

The twentieth-century notion of social security seems to offer something more than minimal subsistence; this is what seems to make it different from what was available before. But in this chapter, it will be argued that this 'social security' deal has always been a fragile one, and that it is particularly under threat today. Social insurance-based provisions are under attack, and inasmuch as some social assistance arrangements may offer a measure of security superior to that offered by the 'poor law', they too are vulnerable.

Social security: replacing morality by mathematics?

The special nature of the security ideal embodied in social insurance is brilliantly enshrined in a memorandum Winston Churchill wrote to his permanent officials when he was working on the first British unemployment insurance scheme in 1909:

> I do not feel convinced that we are entitled to refuse benefit to a qualified man who loses his employment through drunkenness. He has paid his contributions; he has insured himself against the fact of unemployment, and I think it is arguable that his foresight should be rewarded irrespective of his dismissal, whether he lost his situation through his own habits of intemperance or through his employer's habits of intemperance, I do not like mixing up moralities and mathematics.
>
> (Churchill, quoted in Fulbrook, 1978: 137–8)

In that comment, the aristocrat Churchill was voicing what may be seen as the aspiration of those working people who saw the state as offering, through social insurance, a measure of security against loss of work which would be preferable to the poor law because contributions established entitlement. Socialised collective security was, furthermore, to replace or supplement personal security bought through private insurance and contributions to friendly societies.

However, the British social insurance scheme, like most others, did in fact mix 'moralities and mathematics'. Churchill's justification for the new legislation in a later Parliamentary speech, which Fulbrook suggests was in the same vein as his memorandum, may in fact give a clue as to why. He spoke of 'bringing in the magic of averages to the aid of millions' (see Fulbrook, 1978: 138). That is the rationale for social insurance as opposed to commercial insurance; it involves a very special pooling of risks across society. In this sense, social insurance is more than the Provident Fund established in Singapore, and widely offered as a future model for social security, in which individualised accounts are set up, which once drawn upon for whatever reason, profligate or not, are dissipated for future use. The founders of social insurance found it necessary by the very nature of the collective and potentially redistributive security they were offering, to take into account 'moral hazard' and guard against unjustifiable claims.

Social security policies are not designed under Rawls's veil of ignorance (1971), in which decision makers are unaware of their current interests and unable to predict their future needs. The politics of social security in the real world involves suspicious and reluctant assent from those who see themselves as more likely to be contributors than beneficiaries. Social security measures have been cautiously brought forward and have been regularly open to challenge. Contrary to the idealistic view that they should be at their most important at times of widespread social and economic insecurity, that is accordingly when they come under attack. This has been particularly true of Britain, as we shall.

Social security policies need to be seen as, in many respects, very conditional contributions from public policy, whose existence needs to be explained by the concerns of state elites with security in society in general. The continued support of those elites depends very much upon the identity of their main beneficiaries. These issues are explored further in the next two sections.

Social security and the security of the state

The provision of social security must be seen as subordinate to other state concerns. Primary amongst these are:

- Security through a system of defence against external enemies
- The maintenance of law and order

Poor law measures have been seen as having their origins in worries about the 'dangerous poor' (Piven and Cloward, 1972) needing to be controlled and perhaps appeased. Later concerns, in the emergent nationalism of the nineteenth century, went beyond this to look to the need to breed a healthy nation supported loyally by those who would be required to occupy the front line in wars. The creators of new nation-states, perhaps above all Bismarck, saw the contribution social security measures might make to the unification of the nation-state (Hennock, 1987). Hence we see, around the end of the nineteenth century, the development amongst political elites of a case for social security, independent of the demands of working-class political parties (who were indeed very suspicious of social insurance).

However, social security development must also be interpreted in the context of the emergence of state roles in respect of the regulation of market activities. By the end of the nineteenth century, various state responses to labour market insecurity began to be on the agenda. This was partly because of the increasingly effective political organisation by workers, aided by the emergence of democratic franchises. The workers were able to frighten the defenders of the *status quo* with an alternative 'classical economics', offering a model of the logical end to which the free market was leading (the economic analysis provided by Karl Marx). But the rise of the issue of unemployment on the political agenda was also affected by massive economic fluctuations. It is literally true to say that 'unemployment' was discovered towards the end of the nineteenth century, as it became recognised that the processes by which labour markets 'cleared' (particularly during the downturn in the 'trade cycle') were necessarily protracted (Harris, 1972). In other words, it became increasingly clear that workers willing and able to work, actively seeking work and not putting a high price on their labour, often had to wait a long while before they were re-employed. It also became increasingly recognised that labour forces were differentiated, not only in terms of skill, but also in terms of physical capacity. Workers who would face particular difficulties in a tight and competitive labour market were the old and disabled. The model that all adults could easily find work if they wanted to, enshrined in the 1834 Poor Law in Britain, began to become discredited.

Four alternative but interrelated ways in which public policy might combat economic insecurity began to reach the political agenda at the end of the nineteenth century: assistance with the working of the labour market, the protection of workers from the unbridled exercise of the power to hire and fire, the direct provision of work and the provision (on a basis rather more satisfactory than the niggardly role of poor relief) of financial support for those without work. This discussion is, of course, primarily concerned with the last of these, but it must be seen as (a) interacting with the other three and (b) in some respects assuming particular importance because of difficulties with, or political reluctance to use, the others (particularly the direct provision of work).

During the twentieth century, states have found the first of the responses outlined above, the development of techniques – the use of labour exchanges, advice and social work programmes for the unemployed, training programmes for those between jobs – to assist the working of the labour market comparatively uncontroversial. There have been important differences of response, of course. These have varied according to the extent to which it is believed that private activities along these lines can be encouraged rather than private ones and according to the extent to which these responses can be linked with others

The second response, important for trade unions in the twentieth century, has varied very markedly from society to society. Comparative studies of state policies have drawn a distinction between those states where 'corporatist' responses designed to draw trade unions into the management of the economy have become accepted (Austria, the Netherlands, Germany, Scandinavia) and the liberal *laissez-faire* societies where measures of this kind have been seen as illegitimate activities for the state (Britain – with a little 'wobble' in this respect in the 1960 and 1970s – and the United States) (Mishra, 1990; Esping-Andersen, 1990). Issues of this kind are now, of course, debated in the context of European Union social policy. It is arguable that inasmuch as there have been measures to protect job contracts, they have operated to favour the more secure rather than the less secure in the labour force. Perhaps the striking example of this is in Japan, once hailed in the West as the country of the 'secure' life-long labour contract, but subsequently discovered to be a society in which the security of some is underwritten by the insecurity of others. It is also argued that as jobs have disappeared in the 1990s, there are significant differences between societies where the state response has been to continue to protect the jobs of the more organised workers and those where a more general driving down of wages and work protection has been accepted (Esping-Andersen, 1996).

In many respects, the states that have been more prepared to accept the 'corporatist' approach described above have also been the ones that have been more willing to adopt the third way to combat economic insecurity and become themselves additional providers of job opportunities. But in practice, there is little evidence anywhere of states being prepared to be long-term job-providers simply as a response to unemployment. Rather, there are important distinctions to be made between states in which the development of services (in particular welfare services) has been recognised as something to be justified in terms of its job creation effects and those where services have simply developed as responses to other demands. One result has been that distinctions can be made between the end results. Sweden stands out as a key example of the former: state employment has been seen as very important in the pursuit of both full employment and high female labour market participation. It is thus widely argued that the most comprehensive social security systems have emerged in those societies where there have been comprehensive and relatively effective efforts to maintain full employment. Britain does not belong to that group.

Who benefits from social security?

Measure to relieve poverty predated the new efforts to develop 'social security' at the end of the nineteenth century by several centuries. These earlier measures were crafted to try to offer minimal relief to workers compelled to remain in (or return to) their own parishes at times when jobs were not available. By 1834, when the British government – influenced by utilitarian philosophy and market economics – endeavoured to reform the system, the preoccupation was still with that relief as an exceptional measure for the workless, designed to try to ensure that there was no impact upon the working of the labour market. However, the reformers of that time also paid some attention to the possibility that worklessness might have other causes, less directly connected with the labour market. The new workhouses were expected to segregate the old and sick poor.

In the years after 1834, the recognition that poverty might have other causes increasingly influenced policy. The poor law became more involved in the care of the sick, in some cases seeing them as appropriate recipients of indoor rather than outdoor relief. Private insurance-based schemes also offered workers protection against the impact of ill health. Out of the latter activity grew agitation for the state to make separate provision for the elderly, identifying a new phenomenon of retirement from the labour force for which neither the traditional poor law response to worklessness nor specific provisions for illness were appropriate (Gilbert, 1966). Income maintenance schemes began therefore to become differentiated and the poor law obsession about the need to control and deter 'sturdy beggars' became a much less direct influence on policy. The process of differentiation was heavily influenced by the emergence of social insurance, identifying various contingencies against which workers might be protected.

Today, a range of social security needs is identified. Only social security measures for unemployed prime-age adults, without direct caring responsibilities, are generally accepted as involving an unambiguous need for the co-ordination of relief with labour market policies. While in this sense, policies for the unemployed are quite explicit about the need to 'mix moralities with mathematics' using the need to enforce labour market attachment as the crucial concern, those issues are more implicit in relation to other benefits. Previous labour market attachment as a qualifying condition for insurance-based benefits is given varying degrees of importance in different schemes. Issues about continuing attachment arise at the margins, in relation to determination of pension age or test of fitness for work.

The issues about family policy – about support for children and about support for women as carers – are more complex. Child support policies are tax-funded and unrelated to social insurance in many societies. Here, the issues of concern to politicians have been a combination of nationalistic anxieties about the slow growth of the population and the fitness of future generations with a desire to prevent trade unions using the need for a family wage as a yardstick in wage bargaining (Pedersen, 1993). Clearly, issues about whether wage rates should be seen as for individuals or for families have played their part in determining social security responses.

With regard to the roles of mothers as carers for children, a distinction may be made between those societies in which mothers have become expected to be labour market participants (particularly the Scandinavian countries) and those where they have been expected to remain at home (the Continental European countries, at least until recently). In the former countries, benefit entitlements have been largely individualised; in the latter, benefit schemes have had to take into account the needs of female partners. Britain and the United States sit, often confusingly as far as their social security arrangements are concerned, between the two.

The whole issue of support for mothers has increased in importance on the social policy agenda with the growth of the single-parent family. The Scandinavian schemes have accommodated to this development most easily, but with some obvious inequalities between one-parent and two-parent households, because they are individualist schemes presuming female labour market participation (see Hobson and Takahashi in Lewis, 1997). Widowhood posed no problems for the designers of the older familist social insurance schemes; it was a contingency which could be regarded as covered by insurance. Family breakdown, other than by death, was another matter. Interestingly, Beveridge explored the idea that insurance coverage could be extended to family breakdown, but a 'moral hazard' perspective that such breakdown could under some circumstances be something deliberately sought by the potential beneficiary led him to reject this. Accordingly, outside Scandinavia the whole issue of social security support has been the subject of a continuing moral debate about the respective responsibilities of the absent father and the present mother (it is nearly always that way round) as providers, with the state benefits available (particularly in the United States) providing minimal security. (In Chapter 8, Bob Simpson explores aspects of British policy responses on this issue.) As far as the mother's role is concerned, a marked inconsistency has emerged in the United States (and increasingly now in Britain) between the willingness to see mothers as 'dependants' in the social security provisions relating to two-parent families and the expectation of labour market participation where they are the 'heads' of one-parent families. This is discussed further below.

Who does not benefit from social security policies?

The last section has explored the ways in which social security policies have been extended to various potentially insecure groups in society. The answer to the question as to who does not benefit from these policies requires the identification of two radically different groups. These are (a) in the upper echelons of society, those who do not need or have chosen to make their own arrangements, and (b) at the other end of the social scale, those who have been deliberately excluded from support.

Looking at these two groups together highlights the extent to which the politics of twentieth-century social security can be characterised as the acquisition of a measure of social security by the middle of three groups in society, winning political concessions from dominant elites who expected to protect their own security privately but also marking themselves off from the 'undeserving poor'. The political arithmetic regarding the sizes of these three groups is important. The universalist ideal endorsed in much writing about social policy is of a large middle group, perhaps ideally comprising much of the political elite, which provides substantive political support for policies that incorporate most citizens. Full employment is also important in uniting the interests of the middle and lower groups. Without these two conditions, a society's social security system is likely to be much more fragile. It will be argued below that this has widely been the case.

An awareness of the continuing importance of the 'social divisions' in many societies lead on therefore to a much less optimistic view of the prospects for social security than that which stresses the way in which benefits became extended to cover many categories of need earlier in the twentieth century. This is explored further in the next section

The insecurity of social security

The earliest of the social insurance initiatives were very much targeted at better-off manual workers, those who were represented by the trade unions and social democratic political parties. The insurance approach to this task – invented by unions, voluntary associations and municipalities in various parts of Europe during the second half of the nineteenth century – was taken up as a way of providing 'security' for this group in a form superior to the residual poor relief systems for those more marginal to the industrial labour force (Flora and Heidenheimer, 1981; Heclo, 1974). Attempts to generalise these schemes – perhaps both upwards to white-collar workers and downwards to the poor – and to see this as a more universal incorporating strategy came rather later. These ideas have been given particular recognition in Marshall's (1963) argument that there has been a movement from legal citizenship through political citizenship to social citizenship. Is it too unkind to suggest that this is rather more an intellectual attribution of meaning to the process than an actual explanation of what went on? Certainly most social security systems (with the salient exception of the Scandinavian ones) remained highly stratified. Either, as in the case of Britain and the United States, the public and private systems developed side by side and the social insurance system remained weak, or social insurance itself was highly stratified (as in Germany). These distinctions are the bases of Esping-

Andersen's influential typology of welfare states (1990), contrasting the 'decommodified' social democratic system of Scandinavia with the corporatist systems of much of continental Western Europe and the liberal systems of the 'Anglo-Saxons'.

It is interesting to note that the origins of the expression 'welfare state' lie in efforts during the 1930s to identify a new role for the state: to see the need to establish welfare states as opposed to warfare states. But, as has been shown, social policies predated that ideological labelling. There is a substantial literature on the reasons why social security policies have been developed by industrialised states (Mishra, 1977; Gough, 1979; Higgins, 1981; Ashford, 1986; Hill and Bramley, 1986; Hill, 1996). The rhetoric of the 'welfare state', of 'social citizenship' and of 'decommodification' conjures up a culmination of Elias's civilising process (1982): a benign process of social amelioration and a role for the state in which equality could be pursued without attacking capitalism directly.

However, many writers have shown how important it is to recognise that governments see social security policies as subsidiary to economic policies. The aim has been to compensate when economic processes fail. At the same time, policies have been very influenced by labour market status, as was shown above. The Scandinavian exception to this rule, it may be argued (see Sainsbury, 1994), only evolved because labour market participation was so high as to be near universal in those societies. In any case, Esping-Andersen's analysis of the Scandinavian case (1990) rests heavily upon the view, explored briefly above in relation to labour market interventions in general, that the demands of the organised working class were important for social policy development in those societies. Social policy may be seen as part of the corporatist compromise between capital and labour, which occurred in various degrees in most societies.

Equally, however, the poor law concern with labour market regulation has not been abandoned. Social security policies have been strongly regulated by governments to try to ensure that they do not interfere with labour market processes. Benefits for the unemployed have, of course, continued to be strongly influenced by the same principle which dominated nineteenth-century poor relief, that of 'less eligibility'. Unemployed people must be prevented from securing more money out of work than in work, regardless of their needs. They must also be continuously reminded that state support (including social insurance) is contingent upon making efforts to get work. In Britain, we now see this argument being extended as well to single parents and disabled people.

The welfare-state ideology sought to clothe these efforts in higher ideals. In doing so, it linked the development of welfare policies with efforts to combat economic insecurities. This is, of course, a connection that has been made by many writers on social policy, one which has been expressed pithily (though inaccurately if ones looks at the actual ideas of these two thinkers) as a marriage of the ideas of Keynes and Beveridge (Pierson, 1991). Like all ideologies that gain official acceptance, it led to the over-selling of the policy changes that had actually occurred. We were told that a system of welfare had been established which provided security from the 'cradle to the grave'. For most countries – and certainly for Britain – that was an exaggerated claim. Social policy had little impact upon social divisions in society (Le Grand, 1982). Indeed it can be seen as containing its own system of social divisions (Titmuss, 1958; Sinfield, 1978; Hill, 1996). Equally, its record with respect to the elimination of poverty has been seen to be deeply flawed (Townsend, 1979; Mack and Lansley, 1985; Gordon and Pantazis, 1997). While that over-selling did not alone lead to the backlash against this role for the state in the combating of insecurity, it has provided significant fuel for the arguments of those who want to 'turn back the clock'. We now therefore turn to the changing role of public policy in relation to insecurity.

The contemporary attack on social security

The attack upon the enlarged role of the state which has been led by the New Right involves many arguments about public policy: about the burden of its costs, about its distortion of market forces, about its limitations upon individual freedom, and about the extent to which it is deemed to provide too much security for citizens (Pierson, 1994; Waddan, 1997). It is obviously problematic to try to disentangle the various points. For many, the arguments about security are rather about the extent to which it is purchased at too high a cost, or with too many limitations upon entrepreneurial freedom, rather than that it is undesirable *per se*. Nevertheless, that theme does enter into the arguments of some writers, with particular reference to social policy and to a lesser extent in relation to some aspects of regulation. It certainly does not involve a quarrel with the state's role in the provision of defence or law and order.

The arguments against the welfare state from the 'New Right' have been given increasingly serious attention over the last twenty years and have contributed, above all, to a changed public policy stance in relation to social security. However, that change is very closely related to a changed stance on issues about employment. These two interact very strongly. Given what has been said already about the relationship between labour market issues and social security, that will come as no surprise.

In trying to analyse that interaction, we are faced with a complex spiral. It may be foolish to try to set out schematically what causes what, but any description of this phenomenon has to start somewhere. The starting point, acceptable from most ideological perspectives, is a need to increase the productivity and capacity for growth of the private sector. The right's response to this – now accepted also as appropriate by the centre (Waddan, 1997) – has been seen as involving a need to reduce the burden of taxation upon the private sector. But the problem is that the move away from a tax-and-spend approach to public policy has increased unemployment and insecure employment, and has thus increased the demand for social security expenditure. This has then led to efforts to cut that expenditure. Where that is difficult, an alternative target is other forms of public expenditure, with knock-on consequences for levels of public employment. This then further increases social security needs, and so on (see, for example, the analysis of Margaret Thatcher's efforts to cut public spending in

Hills, 1990). Of course the first of these moves, or any of the subsequent ones, were not seen as efforts to reduce employment security; but this has been a consequence, which was then treated by 'the hawks' as a good thing and by 'the doves' as hard to avoid.

The perspective of the 'doves' on social security goes back to what was described above as the marriage of the ideas of Keynes and Beveridge: that high levels of social benefits enable firms to restructure (shed workers) without causing serious suffering. The problem about this, it is argued, is that it contributes to an alternative version of the vicious circle to that outlined above. As Visser and Hemerijck put it in their analysis of this process in the Netherlands:

> Firms in high-wage economies can only survive if they are able to increase labour productivity. This is most commonly achieved through labour-saving investments and by laying off less productive workers. Under the principle of traditional breadwinner family dependence, increased inactivity drives up taxes and pay-roll social security contributions. This, in turn, puts pressure on wage costs, which provides new ground for reassessing the remaining workforce in terms of their level of productivity, most likely leading to another round of dismissals. A vicious cycle of high wage costs, low net earnings, exit of less productive workers, rising social security contribution ... intensifies the spiral of welfare without work.
>
> (Visser and Hemerijck, 1997: 137)

This analysis goes on to justify the Dutch attack upon disability benefits in the early 1990s in a book which argues that the Netherlands has been able to move out of the 'corporatist' prison described by Esping-Andersen (1996) in which good protective measures for the mainstream labour force are seen as leading to severe reductions in labour force participation overall.

To evaluate fully all aspects of the argument just cited would require exploration of matters far from the brief of this chapter. It has to be recognised that the whole issue of labour costs is influenced by the way in which social security is funded. Bismarck-style social insurance, as in the Netherlands and much of continental Europe, has particular direct implications for labour costs. Subsidy of social security by less direct forms of taxation may not have as strong an effect. The whole issue also needs to be seen in an international context. It is not so much an issue about the social security bill in general as one about its implications for an individual economy exposed to global competition.

However, what is particularly pertinent to this discussion is a need to examine these developments in terms of their specific effects upon the 'life chances' of various groups. It was suggested above that the idealisation of the welfare state was too ready to exaggerate the gains made by the most marginal people in society. Poverty has not been abolished, less eligibility rules continue to contribute to the formation of a class who could be regarded as a 'reserve army of labour'. As things have got tougher for this group it has become very convenient – as a device to try to disarm criticism – to 'blame the victims', talk of them as an 'underclass' and suggest that they are able to use the niggardly offerings of the social policy system opportunistically.

Diminishing job opportunities have tended to increase the numbers falling into this group (see Mann, 1992, on changes in the so-called 'under class' over time). The other significant development here is that as this group grows in size, so another state role must also grow; that is, its role as a maintainer of law and order through policing and the criminal justice system.

This goes to the roots of the conflict built into the role of social security as a protection against insecurity. The concern about labour market protection, which may be described as a concern about the maintenance of a 'reserve army of labour' willing to operate flexibly in the labour market, has tended to involve the expectation that this protection will be minimal, with workers moving in and out of marginal work as need arises. Twentieth-century social security policies may then be seen as to some extent involving moving beyond the reserve army concept in response to demands made by the organised working class (Castles, 1985; Esping-Andersen, 1990). Inasmuch as protection from incorporation into the 'reserve army' has been a political concession principally offered to skilled and organised working-class males there are particular tensions at the boundaries between the secure and insecure group. Changes in the economy are then contributing to the erosion of the secure group. At the same time, the security which has been provided is seen as preventing flexibility in the labour market, as in Visser and Hemerijck's argument quoted above. Critics of social security are, therefore, in the name of economic progress, arguing for the reduction of protection in order to enlarge the reserve army.

Thus, if one of the reasons why the social security system was developed in the first place was to incorporate the working class politically and to reduce the threat posed by a large reserve army, the question arises: how much can that process be reversed without creating a serious threat to the state and the dominant social order? That is a difficult question. Clearly the mid-twentieth century 'order' rested upon distinctions being made between the secure – socially incorporated group – and the insecure workers. It helped that there were distinctions of both gender and race which could be used to reinforce this division (Ginsburg, 1992). To the extent, therefore, that the enlarging 'reserve army' is still female and is likely to contain many members of minority ethnic, linguistic or religious groups, the answer to the rhetorical question may be that there is considerable scope for reversing the process since the potential opposition is very divided. On the other hand, two trends – the increasing political involvement of women and the diminishing job opportunities for male manual workers – offer evidence against that assumption.

The social security system is under attack. Some of that attack comes in an impersonal form inasmuch as it is being damaged by changes in the labour market. Social insurance was, generally speaking, designed to function in a secure labour market. Indeed it functions best, as the Scandinavian case indicates, with full employment including high female labour market participation. Its funding through contributions is undermined by unemployment, part-time work and low pay. All of these mean that the state has either to increase the solidarity aspects of social insurance, under which the contributions of the secure are used to support the insecure, or increase its own contributions. These are options that governments have been reluctant to accept. That reluctance has been reinforced by arguments that social insurance is damaging to economic institutions, imposing too high costs upon enterprise and undermining the flexibility of the labour force (Visser and Hemerijck, 1997).

Of course there is a need to recognise that the security element in many systems, particularly those of Britain and the United States, has always been limited (Esping-Andersen, 1990). Nevertheless, the attack that has been mounted against social security emphasises (a) costs with their economic knock on effects and (b) labour market deterrent effects. That attack has involved direct attacks on beneficiaries of both social insurance and social assistance schemes.

Changes to the provisions for unemployed people in Britain have very largely eliminated insurance, have imposed very strict job-seeking conditions upon claimants, and have made it impossible for many young people to get cash benefits. It might be expected, bearing in mind the observations above about the weak connection between the labour market and social security for other groups of people, that the attack upon the social security system would end there. But we have also seen, from the last Conservative government, a related attack upon benefits for the long-term sick (or partially disabled), forcing people in this group back into labour market participation and off insurance benefits (Hill in Dorey, in press). Despite that, the Labour government has still argued, in its Green Paper *A New Contract for Welfare* (HMSO, 1998, Cm. 3805), that higher levels of labour market participation should be expected from disabled people.

It is worth pointing out that in this case, disability benefits had been seen as a way of supporting people who were *de facto* prematurely retired. Could we see a similar attack upon retired people? Clearly, the introduction of a rise in the British female retirement age to sixty-five (to be phased in early in the next century), introduced without regard to whether or not work will be available, points in the same direction. So, in a more indirect way, will any measures adopted to increase the privatisation of pension provisions, if this is done without regard to the difficulties faced by marginal groups of workers in making contributions.

But, at the time of writing, it is another group of social benefit claimants who are most evidently under attack in Britain: single parents. In this case, the Secretary of State has justified changes in support for single parents on the grounds that labour market participation is in *their* best interests (see Hill in Atkinson *et al.*, forthcoming). It is hard to challenge that assumption, particularly as the benefits available to single parents are very limited. But forcing people to become labour market participants when few secure or well-paid jobs are available to them, is just another way of reinforcing the 'reserve army'.

In sum, in as much as the main policies designed to make more secure the broader body of working people – as described above – have been undermined by diminishing job opportunities, so the cry has gone up that social insurance based pensions, unemployment benefits and invalidity benefits can no longer be afforded. Hence we have seen public policy changes which, by their very nature, increase the size of the insecure group in society.

Despite the fact that their employment policies are very much oriented to influencing the supply of labour (training, help with job search and threats to those whom they regard as 'too secure' on benefits) much of the thrust of the Blair government's approach to social security reform has been that, in the words used in the 1997 election manifesto and echoed in the Green Paper, 'Labour's welfare-to-work programme will attack unemployment and break the spiral of escalating spending on social security'.

Amongst the arguments for attacks upon mainstream 'social security' is one that it is better that we provide for our future security ourselves through private market arrangements. So, while those in a weak labour market situation drop down into the insecure group described above, others more advantaged are invited to try to join the well-off group in society who have long expected to make private provisions for their security (not albeit because of any necessary hostility to state provision, but just because private arrangements are better).

The well-off have always tended to answer the question, 'who do you best trust for your long run security, the state or the market?' by indicating that they prefer the latter. This confidence has of course been influenced by the role the state plays as a regulator of private market activities. Here, then, we encounter some ironies. The more the state withdraws from social security, the more justified it becomes not to trust the state. On the other hand, the private devices available to fill the gap left by the state become increasingly more risky the further 'down market' they are required to go. In order to offer a deal to new lower income participants, private pensions and insurance ventures have to increase their risks. These new customers can only afford lower contributions, are more likely to default (because of a lack of employment security) and are more likely to become premature claimants where this is possible (this last particularly applies of course to health and disability insurance).

In a situation in which the state is withdrawing from social security and encouraging private entrepreneurs to take its place, while at the same time the risks are high, less scrupulous entrepreneurs will be likely to enter the market. They will be attracted by the front-ended nature of pensions and long-term insurance schemes: the contributions flow in before the claims. These may be companies whom the well-to-do private customers will approach with caution. But *caveat emptor* is a principle more easily practised by those who have many choices in the market than by those who (by virtue of their low contributions and high-risk status) have few. There are parallels here outside the social security field, with for example car and house contents insurance.

The result is that the state's role as regulator becomes more important. In Britain, many people are still trying to secure redress from the consequences of public policies like those described above, for example, when the Conservatives (under the 1986 Social Security Act) made state pensions less attractive and provided incentives for people to purchase private ones, while at the same time not imposing an effective regulatory structure which would prevent unscrupulous selling of pensions by companies offering poor prospects to investors. The regulatory structure has since been tightened up, but 'money purchase' pensions remain an unrecognised 'bad buy' for many low-income workers, and future prospects are very uncertain (Lynes, 1997). Despite this, the Labour government sees private 'stakeholder' pensions as the way forward for pensions for lower-paid workers. Such a policy will only work if the state will take its ultimate protective role so seriously that it will do more than regulate to prevent unfair practices. Since the long-run prospects for many private schemes are far from predictable, the only way the state can make private pensions schemes quite secure is to undertake to pick up the responsibility if there is market failure. Furthermore, if pension contributions are not to be large and regressive 'taxes' upon low incomes, ongoing subsidy will be necessary too. Will these be forthcoming? It seems unlikely. At the moment, therefore, many poor people could reasonably answer the question about whether they have more trust in the state than in the market with the answer 'neither'.

Conclusions

To sum up, it has been shown that employment and social security issues are inextricably, and probably perversely, entangled. Rather than being prepared to enhance their social security role, states are tending to fall back on merely regulatory responsibilities as more individuals look to the market for security. The ensuing argument has then tended to put the prospects for a more regulatory state rather negatively. Clearly there is an alternative view – put very strongly in a World Bank report (1997) – that a strong state role as stable regulator of private markets is the model for the future. In the social policy field – given the difficulties in sustaining full employment, the importance of global competition and the attack upon taxation – it is arguable that this is a model easier to recommend than sustain.

To end on this global theme, is it not perhaps pertinent to look at the very first of the ways in which states contribute to security: defence against external enemies? How much can we attribute the changing of the social security agenda to the fact that as the integrity of the state has become less threatened, so social security has become emphasised rather less by elites than was the case when they worried about the commitment of the German workers to the new nation or the falling French birth rate or the capacity of the British working class to fight to protect the Empire. That is admittedly a Western European view and not necessarily a universal proposition, as residents of Taiwan, South Korea or Croatia might want to say, let alone people in much of Africa. However, in many of the more politically secure countries, elites have become international in outlook and thus committed to free worldwide trade. They thus see choices of labour supply as global ones. At the same time they have lost their fear of the 'dangerous classes', who are often a long way away, and in any case can be contained by new ways of maintaining internal security (I owe some of this argument to Zsuzsa Ferge, 1997). Alternatively we may argue, first, that 'the growing gap between the world's rich and the poor could unleash a popular backlash against global free trade' (report of a United Nations report in the *Guardian*, 16 September 1997) and second that, as Jane Wheelock shows in Chapter 2, economic insecurity is becoming an issue for the rich as much as for the poor nations. In this case, the issues about social security have relevance not only for national but also for international security.

7 No place like home?

Insecurity and housing

Roberta Woods

The security of housing?

The idea of home has a special place in our conception of security. The loss of one's home is therefore a particularly acute manifestation of the global experience of insecurity considered in the introduction. When young children are asked to draw a house, they often depict something that is detached with pretty curtains, garden and gate; the sun is often shining and the happy residents smiling. However, much research now exists to tell us that homes are not always safe or secure (Bull, 1993; Logan, 1986). Despite this there is a general mythology that the home is a haven from outside pressures (Saunders and Williams, 1988; Saunders, 1989; Darke, 1995). It is therefore particularly threatening both materially and psychologically when housing problems become a source of insecurity.

One particular assumption, which has dominated British political thinking about housing, is that owner-occupation offers particular security. This chapter will show that, in addition to policy developments which have undermined security in the rental housing sector, increasing economic insecurity has also undermined the security of owner-occupation, at least for some of the less secure participants in the labour force.

This chapter is concerned with issues about housing policy in contemporary Britain. It will consider the relationship between housing and insecurity, and will seek to examine how this became such an issue for many people during the 1990s. The analysis will start by reviewing the main tenets of housing policy since 1979, its interaction with social security and the effects on housing consumers and providers.

The chapter also briefly explores the housing policy agenda of the new Labour government. The extent to which proposed policy changes will add to or weaken the experience of insecurity in housing that developed during the last decade is considered.

The recommodification of housing

Housing policy under the period of Conservative governments between 1979 and 1997 encompassed two interrelated trends: the expanded provision of housing as a market commodity, and the residualisation of the non-market arena of the underfunded local authority and housing association sectors (Malpass, 1990). Both changes greatly exacerbated feelings of insecurity and profoundly damaged the fabric and cohesion of local communities.

The ideological agenda behind Conservative housing legislation is well documented (Malpass and Means, 1993; Cole and Furbey, 1994; Lund, 1996). Much of this analysis focuses on the Conservative commitment to upholding the primacy of the market in providing goods and services with individuals purchasing from the market according to their means. The social rented sector was to exist, if at all, only for those who were not able to avail themselves of owner-occupation and a stake in Britain's property-owning democracy. The assumption implicit in the ideology was that those who could not purchase for themselves should as a last resort have access to a residualised social housing sector.

Another key aspect of housing policy under the Conservative administration was that the linkage of housing to the booms and troughs of the wider economy became more intensified. This was particularly pronounced in the period 1982–9 when house prices rose year on year corresponding to growth in the general economy. Housing output across all tenures, with the exception of local authorities, also rose during this period. Similarly, when recession hit the wider economy house prices fell.

When house prices were rising steadily, little consideration was given to the consequences of recession in the housing market. When it came, mortgage default, repossession and negative equity literally brought home to hundreds of thousands of people the insecurity of commodified housing. During 1994, more than 60 per cent of owner-occupiers who became tenants had done so because of losing their previous home through mortgage arrears (Morris, 1997). However, people in the decommodified social rented sector were often no more secure, with a series of policy measures residualising their communities and driving up homelessness.

Residualisation

The term 'residualisation' in housing refers to the process whereby social housing has increasingly found itself catering for those on benefits or very low incomes rather than 'general needs' (English, 1987; Malpass, 1990). It is a term that has increasingly been identified with social exclusion, whereby people living on estates in the social rented sector are set apart physically and economically from the rest of the population (Malpass and Murie, 1994).

Figures from Wilcox (1994) show that employment levels of household heads in the council housing sector fell from 43 per cent in 1981 to 25 per cent in 1991. Levels of economic inactivity (including not just unemployed people but also the sick, retired and disabled) rose from 42 per cent in 1981 to 59 per cent in 1991. A similar pattern has emerged for those living on housing association estates. In 1981, 42 per cent of housing association tenants were employed, but this had dropped to 29 per cent by 1991. The unemployment rate in the housing association sector rose from 43 per cent in 1991 to 56 per cent in 1991. By 1987, the council sector housed 61 per cent of all income support claimants.

In large part, the residualisation of social housing has been caused by the gradual move into owner-occupation that had been taking place in Britain. The best of council housing stock was sold to tenants under 'right to buy' legislation introduced in 1980 and thus converted into owner-occupation. Local authority funding for building new housing fell to virtually zero, and budgets for maintaining the existing housing stock were slashed (Le Grand and Robinson, 1984). Ironically, Conservative government policy was to keep pushing up council rents so that tenants found themselves paying more each year for what was often a deteriorating service. For waged tenants, this was an incentive to take up the right to buy and move into owner-occupation. Increasingly, remaining tenants had incomes so low that they received housing benefit to pay their rents. Thus, as direct subsidies to council housing were cut and rents increased, the social security bill rose.

In 1985, changes to the use of capital receipts from the sale of council housing meant that local councils could only use a small proportion of these for reinvestment in the housing stock. Those authorities with the highest income from sales did not necessarily have the most pronounced housing need (Malpass and Murie, 1994). Moreover, resources were taken away from general housing investment allocated according to indicators of need and recycled into one-off projects based on competitive bidding through initiatives such as Housing Action Trusts and City Challenge that promoted partnerships with the private sector and 'tenure diversification' (Cole and Furbey, 1994).

The concentration of low-income families in council housing estates produced problems for local authorities in management terms as well. Housing managers and tenants had to contend not only with a deteriorating physical environment but also rising levels of crime and record levels of unemployment. Crime rates have risen in general in inner city areas (*Social Trends*, 1997). Rising crime and fear of crime have led many local authority housing departments to respond by improving security for individual dwellings, diverting spending away from other types of maintenance and improvement. Other initiatives have included supporting neighbourhood watch schemes or employing security guards to patrol estates. Such measures can be very physically unattractive, and the use of security guards and closed-circuit television, while helping residents cope with the actuality and fear of crime, can also stigmatise these areas as unattractive and unsafe places in which to live.

Reports from Coleman (1985), Power (1987) and Page (1994) document the problems of community safety faced on large housing estates. The remedies vary from the estate redesign approach associated with Coleman to the need for more management-oriented approaches associated with Power. While it is important not to overdramatise life on such estates, it is worth pointing out the difficulties that can be faced by residents. Elderly people in particular and single parents may be anxious about gangs of youths, and the threat of burglary is a very real one (Woods, 1995). Physical housing improvements alone have been shown to be ineffective (Tunstall, 1995; Holman, 1995). In Power's 1995 study, antisocial and disruptive behaviour did not reduce with physical improvements; many tenants were much more concerned about crime and social breakdown in 1994 than they had been in 1987. Over half of resident groups were concerned about what they saw as the disruptive consequences of 'care in the community', with people who had once been institutionalised because of mental health problems now apparently being concentrated on local authority estates. Power (1995) suggests that crime prevention policies could be based more soundly on a community reconstruction approach that recognises the need for longer term investment in social and economic development (see also Passmore and Brown, 1997).

Power's conclusions point to the need to have a more wide-ranging strategy to deal with problems experienced in such areas, including tackling unemployment and improving education. This is in some ways a depressing finding, as the Home Office-funded Community Development Projects had concluded some twenty years before that a strategic approach to tackle the broad ranging nature of inner city problems was sadly missing from housing and regeneration strategies.

Power (1995) also makes the point that as far as estate improvement is concerned, the answer in policy terms was seen in the 1980s to lie with one-off flagship initiatives such as City Challenge, Estate Action or schemes funded by the Single Regeneration Budget. This, however, meant that resources were often unavailable for ongoing planned maintenance and incremental improvements. To qualify for funding, estates had to demonstrate that they had reached the top of the ladder with regard to their social problems; they had to enter a deprivation contest in order to secure resources for improvements.

In addition to having concentrations of low-income people, local authorities have also had to contend with greater movement in and out of local authority housing. A study commissioned by the Rowntree Foundation found that the annual turnover of properties had risen sharply in the previous ten years (Centre for Housing Policy, 1997). A high turnover of stock makes it more difficult to develop community spirit and identity and makes it harder to achieve sustainable and supportive communities. The report also noted that those moving out of the sector were generally couples aged under forty-five where one or both people were working. On the other hand, those moving in to the sector were in the 16–29 age group and unemployed.

Not all tenants have been equally affected by the problems facing social housing, and many estates represent vibrant and stable communities. Nevertheless, problems of neighbour nuisance and racial harassment have been increasing, leaving ethnic minority communities and individuals at particular risk of attack or abuse (Henderson and Karn, 1987). This creates a powerful resonance of insecurity for black tenants. It has traditionally been the case that local authorities have moved families to a 'safer' environment when they have been subject to racial harassment. This has partly been a response to the difficulty of securing evidence against the perpetrators. More recently, local authorities have sought to take action against perpetrators by obtaining injunctions or seeking eviction. The Housing Act (1996) has strengthened the legislative basis for such action and indeed makes it easier for all social landlords to address the issue of antisocial behaviour amongst tenants.

Ward (1991) notes that a disproportionate number of people from ethnic minorities experience homelessness. Housing conditions are also poorer, with black people living in the worst accommodation, often in the private sector. Black households have also been particularly affected by the process of residualisation given the reliance of this population on the council sector (Karn, 1991). Bowes *et al.* (1997) note the increasing importance of the social rented sector to the Pakistani community. They document the vulnerability, fear and sense of isolation felt by many on local authority estates and highlight the need for local authorities to effectively tackle this problem.

Studies by Bowes *et al.* (1997) and Cameron and Field (1997) have demonstrated that black people experience similar problems in the housing association sector, and note that more needs to be done to support black housing associations in the development of housing and environments that specifically recognise the needs of this population.

Tenant participation

It would be erroneous to create the impression that the residualisation of council housing was not contested or challenged by the tenants who were affected by this process. As the studies carried out by Power (1995) and Page (1994) demonstrate, tenants have been active in resisting the imposed decline of their areas. The type of action that tenants took did of course vary depending on what they were trying to achieve: in some areas it was opposition to a landlord change, in others it was actively working with City Challenge or SRB schemes to participate in the management of regeneration. Many others established or maintained community development programmes to offer support and services to their local community.

Tenants were able to get advice and support from the Tenant Participation Advisory Service and/or their local Federation of Tenants Associations. Gaining advice was important where tenants were putting forward different plans for their areas than those being suggested by their local council or central government. An example of this would be tenants resisting the imposition of a Housing Action Trust.

Grayson and Walker (1996) brought their history of tenants' organisations up to date by listing recent actions taken by tenants under the heading of 'Protecting Council Housing'. This was indeed the outcome of tenant action in some areas such as when a transfer of stock was resisted. However, tenants' organisations have gone further to rebuild their communities, sometimes in conjunction with community partners. They have also demonstrated a commitment to their areas when others wanted to leave them to decay. A full discussion of what can be achieved is considered by Young and Lemos (1997). It is possible to argue therefore that action by tenants in support of their areas can moderate the effects of insecurity faced by the process of residualisation.

Homelessness

There can be no greater type of insecurity than homelessness. A number of specific policies have contributed to the rise in homelessness between 1978 and 1992. This period was also characterised by a growing amount of 'rooflessness', evidenced by a rising number of people on the streets. It is notoriously difficult to estimate the number of people who may be roofless at any one time, but estimates based on local surveys place the number at between 2,000 and 3,000 (Lund, 1996: 93).

In the immediate sense, homelessness may be precipitated by relationship breakdown, the loss of sharing arrangements, mortgage default, benefit problems and unemployment (Greve and Currie, 1990). However, two more deep-seated issues account for homelessness: the lack of investment in social housing, and the issue of affordability. Some measures were taken by the Conservative government to reduce the numbers of homeless people and numbers have been falling, but a significant problem of homelessness still remains (Ginsburg, 1996). More resources were directed towards social housing by increasing the resources made available to housing associations and a series of initiatives was implemented aimed at reducing the number of people sleeping on the streets.

Local authority homelessness acceptances show the numbers who were homeless and deemed to be so by local authorities rising steadily from 63,003 in 1978 to 172,946 in 1992, then dropping to 150,501 in 1994. Such figures should always be treated with a degree of caution, given the different ways in which local authorities interpret the legislation. For example, some local authorities will accept all 16–17 year-olds as vulnerable and therefore entitled to rehousing and others will not. The percentage of applicants accepted as homeless was 49 per cent in 1991 and 43 per cent in 1992, but had dropped to 34 per cent in 1995 (Lund, 1996: 92). Data from *Social Trends* (1997) show that the number of homeless households in temporary accommodation rose sharply between 1982 and 1992 (see Figure 7.1). Since then the number has fallen but remains at around 50,000 households.

The most significant response to homelessness made by the last Conservative government was the introduction of the 1996 Housing Act. The right to permanent accommodation for homeless households was removed under Part VII of the Act. Under this legislation, local authorities only have a duty to house homeless households in temporary accommodation for two years. In order to secure permanent accommodation, homeless people must be placed on the general waiting list (Cowan, 1997). The loss of the right to permanent accommodation has greatly added to the insecurity faced by homeless households. The Labour government has indicated its wish to review this aspect of the 1996 legislation (LGIU, 1997).

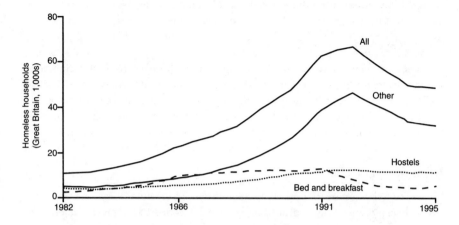

Figure 7.1 Homeless households in temporary accommodation

Source: *Social Trends*, 1997, Table 10.20, Office for National Statistics, © Crown copyright 1999

The nature and quality of temporary accommodation that is on offer can vary enormously. In addition to facing insecurity about accessing permanent accommodation, those in temporary accommodation often have to face poor housing standards and unsuitable conditions. The most unsatisfactory type of accommodation available is bed-and-breakfast hotels and boarding houses. Numerous reports have commented on the unsuitability of bed-and-breakfast accommodation for families and young people: there is a lack of safe play space for children, difficulties may be experienced in settling children at school, poor diets are common given the lack of facilities for food preparation, and parental stress is common. Residence in temporary accommodation has been linked to a number of health problems (Connolly and Crown, 1994).

The last Conservative administration also presided over the largest recorded increase in street homelessness. This has been a particular problem for young people, and is one that has been exacerbated by changes to benefits. From 1988, sixteen- and seventeen-year-olds have only been able to claim benefits in exceptional circumstances. The introduction of the job seekers' allowance also meant reduced rates of benefit for those under eighteen and for those between eighteen and twenty-four (Dennehy *et al.*, 1997). Homeless young people have usually been forced to leave home and are caught in a poverty trap; they include disproportionate numbers of care leavers. Currently, the number of young people who are homeless is estimated to be 250,000, with many living in hostels and bed and breakfast accommodation (CHAR, 1996). Labour's 'welfare to work' policy targets young people, but it is likely that many will still have problems gaining access to secure and affordable accommodation.

Changes to policy regarding asylum seekers also contributed to growing insecurity for this group of people. The Asylum and Immigration Act (1996) removed asylum seekers' rights to benefits and council housing. Subsequent court rulings have, however, established that under the National Assistance Act (1948) local authority social services departments have a duty to house and 'provide for the basics for survival' to those seeking asylum in the United Kingdom. The level of support offered can be very inadequate, and local authorities lack the resources to meet the demand (Ellery, 1996; Yeend, 1996). Asylum seekers can spend long periods of time faced with an uncertain future in detention centres while their cases are being assessed. The way in which this Act is being implemented is being reviewed by the Labour government, but the outcome is likely to fall short of repeal (West, 1996).

Housing agencies

Insecurity has also affected major agencies involved in the production, financing and delivery of housing and housing services. Perhaps the biggest challenge in this respect was directed at local authority housing departments. The first such challenge came with the Housing Act (1980) and the introduction of the right to buy for council tenants. Between 1980 and 1992, approximately 1.4 million dwellings were removed from the housing stock of local authorities (Wilcox, 1994, quoted in Lund, 1996). This had the effect not only of reducing the amount of stock available for letting, it also reduced the quality of stock that was available as much of the best stock was sold (Malpass and Murie, 1994).

Local authorities were also subjected to measures aimed at reducing their role as direct providers of social housing. Opportunities for tenants to opt for other landlords, voluntary transfers of stock, rent to mortgage schemes and regeneration measures including privatisation and tenure diversification were designed to further reduce the role of local authority housing (Murie, 1997). In fact, while the right to buy has been popular among those tenants able to participate, opting for an alternative landlord has been considerably less popular and relatively little housing has been removed from authorities in this way.

Local authority housing management staff also faced an insecure future with the extension of Compulsory Competitive Tendering to white-collar services under the Local Government Act (1988). The Act requires local authorities to invite tenders to manage their stock. Although 89 per cent of contracts have so far been won by in-house teams, local authorities have been subjected to a time-consuming and disruptive process (Williams, 1997). As yet, it is unclear whether Labour's proposals to replace CCT with a 'best value' policy will reduce the insecurity of housing management staff.

Housing associations have also undergone change. For a period under the Conservatives, housing associations were very much championed as the organisations which would in the future be the main agents for the production and management of social housing. However, housing associations have been encouraged to emulate the private rented sector rather than local authorities: in effect, a recommodification (Randolph, 1993). Policy changes introduced with the Housing Act 1988 ushered in a new financial regime that encouraged housing associations to finance more of their schemes from private funding. Rents were to move towards market levels and subsidy for each unit was cut (Best, 1997). In addition, rents for new tenancies were decontrolled and all new housing association tenancies were assured tenancies or shorthold tenancies and were subject to more market orientated rents. These changes created new opportunities for funding but brought in a more difficult financial regime for housing associations. Changes introduced under the 1996 Housing Act affected tenancies further, requiring that all new tenancies be shorthold unless specified otherwise by the landlord. This has undermined the security of tenure of housing association tenants and further moved housing associations towards the private rented sector.

Mortgage default, repossession and negative equity

The clear direction of Conservative housing policy was to promote owner-occupation wherever and however possible and to privatise as much of the public sector stock as could be achieved. To a large extent this policy has been successful, with over two-thirds of the population being homeowners by the end of the 1980s (Forrest and Murie, 1994). This rise had been gradual since the Second World War, but was accelerated during the 1980s by the selling of council properties to tenants and the expansion of low-cost home ownership.

The recession in the late 1980s revealed the weakness of policies that moved so many people into owner-occupation. Building society changes under the 1986 Building Societies Act and financial deregulation in general led to a loosening of the criteria under which loans could be achieved. This had the general effect of increasing the size of loan relative to the borrower's income. As unemployment rose and people lost jobs, mortgage default increased leading to record levels of repossessions. The situation was exacerbated by high interest rates, which peaked at 15.4 per cent during 1990 (Forrest and Murie, 1994). Those who had initially borrowed with high multipliers on their income found repayments hard to sustain. For others, the slump in property prices led to a situation of negative equity with their houses worth less than the mortgages secured on them. Both of these factors contributed to insecurity in owner-occupation that led to many people losing their homes. Figure 7.2 shows how, between 1988 and 1992, repossessions rose dramatically.

Estimates of those caught in negative equity amount to 1.5 million house-holds (Lund, 1996). Dorling and Cornford (1995) demonstrate marked regional variations. The size of the initial mortgage as a percentage of the purchase price was important in producing these variations. Dorling and Cornford conclude that the borrowers who were most likely to be affected lived in the Southeast and had purchased between 1988 and 1991. In every region, negative equity was most likely to affect borrowers who were under twenty-five at the time of purchase. In addition, most of those affected were skilled manual or junior clerical workers with relatively low incomes. Many people were therefore not able to move house, and this led to further stagnation in the housing market.

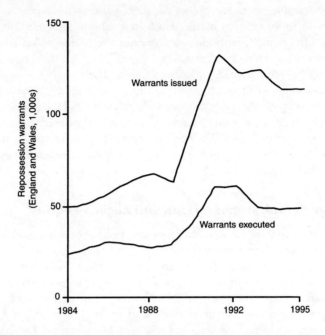

Figure 7.2 Repossession of properties: warrants issued and executed

Source: *Social Trends*, 1997, Table 10.26, Office for National Statistics, © Crown copyright 1999

This number of repossessions and the degree of negative equity had never been witnessed before and led to a questioning of the rationality of some lending policies. As McLennan comments, the rosy view that housing investment would always lead to capital gains was shattered by the collapse in the housing market in the late 1980s:

> The severity of the 1989–1992 housing market downturn has created adverse household circumstances for particular groups which have still not unwound and, at the same time, changed more general expectations about the riskiness and returns to housing investment.
>
> (McLennan, 1997: 24)

The downturn in the housing market intensified the recession in the economy in general and produced a slump in housing output in the early 1990s (see Figure 7.3).

The downturn in output by the private sector was not counterbalanced by higher levels of building in the public sector. Local authority housebuilding had virtually ceased and new building by housing associations did not compensate for the loss of private sector output. The recession in the country at large was further affected by a loss of jobs in the building industry and allied trades (Nother, 1995).

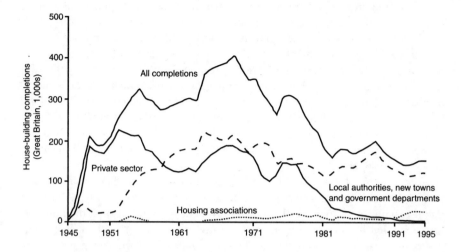

Figure 7.3 House-building completions: by sector

Source: Social Trends, 1997, Table 10.11, Office for National Statistics, © Crown copyright 1999

An insecure future?

A key question for the present and future is what are the chances of this situation happening again? The experience of the last recession and housing slump and the very slow pace of recovery has led to considerable academic and policy debate about the possibility of creating sustainable home ownership in the future (Williams, 1997; Chartered Institute of Housing and Joseph Rowntree Foundation, 1997; Perry and Ayriss, 1997). The forecast for owner-occupation is that it will level off at between 68–70 per cent of the total stock and, if the right to buy declines, may even fall (Chartered Institute of Housing and Joseph Rowntree Foundation, 1997).

Contributors to the debate about sustainable home ownership recognise the changed nature of the labour force and employment patterns in Britain. The effects of global restructuring of the labour market, with a need for a more flexible labour force, are now evident (see also Chapter 5). Some of the worse effects of this restructuring in terms of low wages and poor working conditions may be offset with the Labour government's commitment to a minimum wage and the adoption of the Social chapter of the Maastricht treaty. Nevertheless, it is likely that the shift to part-time working and flexibility in employment will continue. Dwelly (1997: 1) states that there are now 9.5 million workers in flexible employment, an increase of 2.1 million since 1984. This now amounts to 38 per cent of the workforce (see also Gibb, 1995). This may mean people having to plan for periods of unemployment or reduced working hours. A central feature of the discussion of sustainable home ownership is about reducing the housing insecurity of these groups.

During the present parliament, the number of workers in flexible employment will reach ten million. While the majority of these who own their own homes will not be at risk of losing them, a significant minority will. Add to this the part of the full-time workforce who may lose their jobs, and the numbers for whom owner-occupancy is at any one time at risk are very substantial (Perry and Ayriss, 1997: 7).

There is also a recognition that mortgage products have to become more flexible to deal with vulnerability to unemployment or lower pay. Flexible payment methods, flexible repayment periods and a greater availability of fixed interest rates are all ways in which the issue could be addressed. Rent to mortgage schemes and the designation of flexible tenures would be an innovative policy response.

A key feature of this discussion is whether the recovery in the housing sector that is now underway is another boom-and-bust cycle (Briscoe, 1997). A crucial question with the change to a Labour government is, to what extent the housing insecurity that has been felt by many so many will continue? McLennan (1997) points out that the recovery of the housing market is based on an economic policy that supports low inflation and that demographic trends may reduce the number of young people entering the housing market. This may therefore be an indication that, while the housing market will improve, it will not experience the booms and the busts of previous decades. Another related key factor which is extremely relevant to the discussion in this book is the change to the labour market structure and patterns of employment in the UK (see Chapter 5 and Hutton, 1995). More people are working on short-term contracts which may influence the demand for long-term mortgage commitments. McLennan (1997) further argues that fluctuating interest rates may compound this problem, thus leading to more circumspection in the future about the suitability of owner-occupation for certain groups. Finding an alternative to owner-occupation will only be possible if renting is feasible, therefore increased investment in rented accommodation is necessary.

The Labour government has already started the release of local authorities' capital receipts for reinvestment in housing, and there may be further changes in capital spending (Armstrong, 1997a). The development of local housing companies has also remained high on the agenda and a few local authorities have already established housing companies (*Guardian*, 25 March 1998). However, what will be necessary in order to reduce insecurity in housing products and environments is a multi-faceted approach to tackle poor housing, unemployment, urban decay and unhealthy environments. The Labour Party is aware of this (Armstrong, 1997b); whether they manage to achieve it is another matter. It is now very likely that there will not be a housing bill in the next parliamentary period (1998–9), and it looks as though any ideas for a change in housing policy will have to await the outcome of the Comprehensive Spending Review (*Roof Briefing*, February 1998). A Housing Bill has, however, been promised before the next general election. In the meantime the issues that have concerned this chapter – such as homelessness, residualisation, mortgage default and the commodification of housing – are changing.

Figures for homeless households in priority need are now in decline, and have been since 1993 in England and 1994 in Wales and Scotland (Wilson, 1998). The absence of legislation to replace the homelessness sections of the 1996 Housing Act has led some people to begin to press for new homelessness legislation that provides for the needs of single people as well and not simply a restoration of rights to the previous priority groups (Holmes, 1998). With regard to street homelessness, the government is spending £23 million in London and twelve other areas to alleviate this problem, with a further £8.1 million to focus on the specific needs of young people (Wilson, 1998).

The debate in terms of residualisation has moved to a consideration of social exclusion. The government has made the tackling of social exclusion on estates of social housing one of the priorities of its newly established Social Exclusion Unit in the Cabinet office.

Debates about the provision of housing have moved to addressing the need to provide new houses across all tenures and the balance between the use of greenfield and brownfield sites to achieve this. There is also a concern about the need to provide affordable housing across tenures (London Pride Partnership, 1998). The affordable housing issue is closely allied with the need to have a housing subsidy that is tenure neutral and creates less of a poverty trap than the current operation of housing benefit.

As mentioned earlier, it still remains to be seen whether the government's proposals for best value to replace Compulsory Competitive Tendering in housing management will alleviate the insecurity felt by many housing staff.

Conclusions

It has been the argument of this chapter that housing policies developed under the previous Conservative governments created a situation of insecurity in housing. Insecurity increased across all tenures, but was experienced in different ways. For those in owner-occupation, a slump in house prices led to negative equity, and rising unemployment contributed to record levels of mortgage default and repossessions. In the public sector, the process of residualisation and underinvestment created a climate where the very tenure itself was threatened and where tenants constantly faced a change of landlord through transfers or regeneration initiatives. Many tenants faced a deterioration in the state of their overall environment and neighbourhood even if their own property was improved. Housing association building did not expand sufficiently to plug the gap that was emerging between the demand for affordable housing and the provision of it, and this contributed to a rise in the levels of homelessness.

The final sections have sought to examine whether such experiences of housing are likely to be addressed by the Labour government. The picture that is emerging is that change is taking place but it is slow and incremental. The government are putting further, if limited, resources into council housing. Additional resources have been made available to counter homelessness. A wider range of mortgage products are being developed. However, the big issue of creating sustainable communities for the future remains to be tackled and legislated for.

8   Nuclear fallout

Divorce, kinship and the insecurities of contemporary family life

Bob Simpson

In his account of the tribulations of self and identity under the conditions of 'high modernity', Giddens (1991) introduces, by way of Eriksonian psychology, the notion of ontological security. He defines ontological security as 'a sense of continuity and order in events, including those not directly within the perceptual environment of the individual' (Giddens, 1991: 243; see Lash and Urry, 1994: 38–44 for a critique of this position). In all human societies, one of the fundamental contexts in which a sense of ontological security is established is that of kinship. In its most general sense, kinship refers to the social organisation of human reproductive activity but also includes the system of values and attitudes which structure and regulate relational possibilities in society. One of the key points at which kinship and ontological security cross is in the notion of time. The sense of security or insecurity generated by growing up within this or that arrangement of family and kin is not simply a spatial phenomenon, but one capable of bringing order and predictability over time: kinship systems structure relationships as they extend into the past but, more crucially, as they might extend as unrealised potentialities into the future. During a period when the apparent certainties of public life such as employment, community, environment and economy are subject to turmoil, fragmentation and unpredictability, the ability to locate oneself in an actual past and an imagined future is indeed an esteemed resource.

The main point I wish to develop in this chapter elaborates upon this basic observation regarding the temporality of kinship and its role in creating the very possibility of security, ontological or otherwise. Thus, even though in the late modern age we may no longer be able to talk of regularised life cycles and must necessarily think in terms of more open-ended life courses, these are still structured in important ways by the broader dictates of kinship or what Schneider has characterised as 'a diffuse and enduring solidarity' (1968) of kinship relations and what Bloch has referred to as their 'long-term' morality (1973). Relationships can be active or dormant, strong or weak, marked by daily co-residence or separated by continents; but regardless, the fact of kinship, as defined through blood, law or some fictive connection, is integral to questions of how persons locate themselves psychically, emotionally and socially in the world. In trying to understand the continuing importance of kinship in contemporary life and the novel forms it is currently taking, I have focused on divorce and the circumstances of men, women and children who find themselves living in post-nuclear families. Particular attention is paid to the way in which these circumstances are currently being shaped by recent legislative changes in family law in the United Kingdom. The Children Act (1989), the Child Support Act (1991) and the Family Law Act (1996) each constitute legislative measures to preserve and extend individual rights while at the same time affirming the ties of dependency and obligation upon which collectivities such as the family are built. Consideration of these developments is crucial if we are to understand the way that insecurities are generated and mitigated in the late twentieth century.

Personhood, place and family life

In the English language, to speak of security is to evoke ideas of protection, shelter and defence, which are in turn linked to states of material and economic well-being. Its antonym, the notion of insecurity, evokes a different and not merely opposite set of ideas and concerns. To speak of insecurity is to raise concerns more directly linked to the psychic and emotional state of the individual and indeed extreme forms of insecurity are taken as signs of neuroses, phobias and obsessions. Throughout most of this century, the broad aim of economic and social policy in Britain has been to maximise securities of a material kind while minimising insecurities of a more emotional variety. The institution most fundamentally implicated with this process in practice has been the family: a complex, but above all durable, ensemble of caring and work arrangements which have been regularly asserted by politicians, academics and social commentators alike as the foundation of a stable society. Indeed, in the last century and for the early part of this century, gender, family affiliation, descent, blood ties and ethnic identity rendered a person's place within the world predictable, ordered and to a large extent beyond doubt or questioning. The family was the main institution within which these building blocks of personhood and identity were ordered and orchestrated. Marriage was the seminal rite by means of which co-habitation, sex and parenthood were socially legitimated and, in many cases, spiritually affirmed. Along the powerful tramlines of marriage and family life also rolled intimacy, friendship, reciprocity and support, as well as more negative forms of sociality such as oppression and violence. As Harris has suggested, the households that were formed by such arrangements took on a 'natural' appearance (Harris, 1981) and, during the period of rapid social and economic change characterised as modernity, to be aligned with 'nature' was to gain some respite from the turbulent and unsettling consequences of public life. Durkheimian anomie, Marxian alienation and, more latterly, Giddensian anxiety could all, to some degree, be mitigated through the translation of outer predictability and continuity into inner certainty.

In more recent times, however, the social structures which ensured the practical, day-to-day delivery of predictability and certainty would appear to be dissolving and, with their dissolution, what were previously taken as inner certainties have given way to doubts and insecurities (Beck, 1997). Individuals find themselves subject to a rapidly changing world in which the key reference points for personhood and identity are changing and increasingly open to self-conscious revision (see also Giddens, 1991, 1992). Under such conditions, it appears that 'instead of individuals being resources for families, families are becoming resources out of which individuals construct their selves' (Gullestadt, 1996: 37). Projections of the family as the archetypal collectivity are thus brought into conflict with personal experience. Flexible labour markets and the 'enterprise culture' increasingly propel individuals towards economic and emotional autonomy in ways that run counter to the obligations of family and kinship. In short, domestic and interpersonal arrangements have become increasingly characterised by instability and unpredictability; the family would appear to be less and less a haven of affective certainty and more, as old securities diminish and new insecurities arise, a site for the creation and negotiation of risk (Beck, 1992).

Evidence of changes in the sequencing and structure of family life in Britain is now abundant. Utting (1995) identifies the following: a fall in marriage rates as more people defer or reject marriage, deferred child-bearing, declining fertility, a rise in births outside marriage, an increase in the numbers of lone parents and more mothers in paid employment. All of the above signal a switch away from what were hitherto well-trodden pathways of domestic and family arrangements. Moreover, they signal the emergence of new possibilities for choice and voluntarism in key aspects of personal life and interpersonal relationships (Strathern, 1992: 132–5). Each of these changes could be explored for what they might tell us about security and insecurity as mediated by experiences of home and family in the late twentieth century. Clearly, this enterprise would be beyond the scope of a single chapter, and for the remainder I turn to what has been perhaps the most far-reaching change in family life of recent years, the rise in divorce rates.

Marital breakdown on the scale witnessed over the last two decades has profound implications for our understanding of the role of family as a place in which individuals might find an antidote to the insecurities of the modern world. Over the past two decades, divorces in England and Wales have doubled, rising to an all-time high of 171,000 divorces in 1991 (*Social Trends*, 1994). This unprecedented rise in the breakdown of marital relationships has some important consequences. First, it is estimated that by the year 2000, some three million children in the United Kingdom will be growing up in a step-family (Haskey, 1988). Second, the number of lone-parent families has doubled since 1971, reaching 1.3 million in 1991, and the vast majority of these are headed by women (Haskey, 1993). Third, the proportion of second marriages has increased substantially, and a third of all marriages each year are remarriages for one or both partners; thirty years ago the proportion was one in ten (*Marriage and Divorce Statistics*, 1992). What the above catalogue of statistics represents is nothing less than the fundamental transformation of one of the key institutions of Western society and the emergence of families which are reconstituted, blended, recombinant, step- or otherwise 'unclear' when measured against the former certainties of the nuclear family (Simpson, 1994). The implications of these new arrangements for the way that men, women and children might look to one another for care and support in the longer term are profound; what was previously characterised as a 'haven in a heartless world' (Lasch, 1977) is itself becoming a place of insecurity or where security may be short-term at best. Before going on to look at these novel and emergent forms of family and kinship in more detail, it will be useful to look at the ideology of familism upon which they are built.

Nuclear fallout

The word 'family', despite having a multiplicity of meanings in practice, is still for many cast in the mould of the nuclear or conjugal family. The nuclear family, as the metaphor borrowed from physics would suggest, was taken by those of a functionalist persuasion as a basic building block of society (Linton, 1949; Murdock, 1968). This elemental unit comprised a co-resident man and woman who were, as a result of some religious or civil ceremony, also husband and wife and would in turn become the legitimate father and mother of their offspring. Thus, like a series of Chinese boxes, home, marriage, sex and parenthood fitted one within another in conformity with the dominant ideology of familism. Successive governments have identified this arrangement as the key to stability in patterns of production and reproduction, and indeed this ideology lay at the centre of the British Conservative government's 'back to basics' campaign of the early 1990s. The arrangements associated with the nuclear family were not however merely spatial; they also incorporated crucial temporal dimensions. Implicit in the notion of the nuclear family were assumptions about regularised life cycles which unfolded according to the natural inclinations of those brought together by such arrangements and kept men, women and their children together in long-term, affective relationships. Typically, men would be husbands, fathers and breadwinners, whereas women would be wives, mothers and fulltime home-makers and carers. Particularly in relation to bringing up children, the nuclear family was seen as deeply implicated in the way bonds, fundamental to the formation of adult personalities, were formed and developed through time. In accounts of socialisation, such as those put forward by Parsons (1955) and Bowlby (1953) the nuclear family, with the domains of motherhood and fatherhood clearly mapped, was taken as the self-evident backdrop against which the drama of particular relationships would unfold. Deviations from the norm were readily identifiable as the cause of all kinds of social pathology. The character of these powerfully normative arrangements is captured in Fletcher's definition of the Western family as:

> a small relatively permanent group of people, related to each other in the most intimate way, bound together by the most personal aspects of life, who experience amongst themselves the whole range of human emotions...who

experience continual responsibilities and obligations towards each other;
who experience the sense of 'belonging' to each other in the most intimately
felt sense of the word.

(Fletcher, 1973: 26–7)

According to Seccombe (1993), in the period following the Second World War,
domestic arrangements entered a brief but golden age in which the shape and
function of families in Britain did, by and large, conform to this powerful
stereotype. In the late 1940s, marriage rates were high and divorce rates were
low; male employment rates were rising and women were getting back to the
business of producing and looking after children following the disruption of the
war (Morris, 1990). The ideal-type family was celebrated in film and television
and eventually became a key site of burgeoning economic consumption. For
example, the Oxo adverts of the 1960s saw Katie, the iconic housewife,
conveying gravy from the kitchen to the family table, at which sat her husband
busily carving a large piece of roast meat while two fresh-faced children looked
on in eager anticipation. This was the 'cereal packet norm' as Leach (1968) once
described it; a vision of stability and security against which the varieties of
family life were to be compared and measured. However, throughout the 1960s,
the dominant ideology of familism and the actual experience of family life
began to undergo some spectacular divergences, particularly for women and
children.

During the 1960s, the dominant paradigms of family sociology and psychology began to prove less and less adequate to encompass the emerging complexities of family life. Critical accounts of the family drew attention to the way that
this celebrated institution was failing to meet the emotional and economic
aspirations of its individual members, and went on to question whether these
needs had ever been met in the way that classical sociological accounts of the
family had so neatly and eloquently described. A series of powerful polemics
against the nuclear family emerged attacking the central tenets of the prevailing
functionalist orthodoxy, namely that the family was an effective agent of
socialisation, that the world was neatly divided into the private world of families
and the public world of work and commerce, and that women's destinies were to
be accounted for solely in terms of a comfortable sexual and domestic
subordination.

The image of the family as a haven providing a supportive, nurturant coun-
terbalance to an impersonal world which lay beyond its walls was strikingly
challenged by a series of 'anti-family' writings which described how the family
had become emotionally isolated and overloaded to the detriment of its
members. In his Reith lecture of 1967, Leach was moved to comment that 'far
from being the basis of the good society, the family, with its narrow privacy and
its tawdry secrets, is the source of all our discontents' (Leach, 1967). Children in
particular were seen as primary casualties of the modern family, crippled by its
conformity and starved of their natural inclination to creativity and individuality.
The emphasis was on the self-centred securities that individuals might find

through liberation from family and society rather than passivity in the face of their strictures and hierarchies. Laing and Esterson (1970) described how the nuclear family was a site for the cultivation of madness. For children, caught up in the confused and contradictory messages of their parents, schizophrenia was not an aberration but a logical response. Cooper, famous for his pronouncement of 'the death of the family', spoke of paranoia as a 'poetic protest' against the tendency of parents to invade their children with their own anxieties, insecurities, fears and alienation (Cooper, 1971: 11).

But the haven was not simply collapsing from within, it was also under attack from without. Throughout the 1960s, functional accounts of the family were superseded by structural accounts which drew attention to the way in which family forms were not free-floating but deeply tangled in the skeins of history. The impermeable line drawn between private, family life on the one hand and the public world on the other was presented not so much as a scientific fact but as an ideological construction. The family was not simply a device to keep the world at bay but a deliberate product of social engineering in which social, health and education services, aided and abetted by an army of social scientists, had all colluded (Lasch, 1977). For Lasch, the modern family was far from isolated, being 'besieged' by the state with individuals left unable to see their problems in anything other than psychological and individualistic terms. In similar vein, Donzelot describes a pervasive psychologism which protects the state by identifying problems in families rather than at broader structural levels (Donzelot, 1979). Donzelot describes a systematic pressure on individuals to bring their children up according to the objective criteria and values which circulate in the discourses of health professionals, counsellors, educators and mass-circulation magazines. In an ambitious attempt to bring a Marxist perspective to bear on questions of private versus public life, Zaretsky (1976) brings into question the division of family and economy into separate realms, seeing the distinction as 'illusory'. The significant change which the emergence of capitalism had brought was the separation of 'work' and 'life'. The distinction was readily demonstrated in the dichotomy between valorised, male occupation and trivialised, female housework. To present this distinction in terms of private and public domains, according to Zaretsky, was to focus on relationships within the family rather than to bring into focus the ways in which these relationships are influenced by the wider economy and in turn play a role in shaping it (also see Zaretsky, 1982). Such accounts begin to reveal the faultlines which lie beneath popular and academic representations of the nuclear family. However, the greatest faultline was to be the one surrounding issues of gender.

The feminist critique of the family, which gathered pace and momentum through the 1960s, ultimately came down to a recognition that traditional ideologies of the family concealed deep discrepancies of power and influence within it. In response to the assertion that the family functioned well, feminists were inclined to ask, for whom? They were quick to point out that beneath the ideal-type projection onto modern family life of the qualities of harmony, love and devotion to the tasks of nurturing and home-making lay a rather more desperate world of entrapment and oppression. Drawing attention to economic and political dimensions of housework and motherhood feminists highlighted power discrepancies within the conjugal family (Barrett and McIntosh, 1982; Ehrenreich and English, 1979; Oakley, 1974). The patriarchal structure of the conjugal family restricted women's access to the labour force and reinforced control of sexuality and reproduction. Women were exploited, limited and confined, the human equivalent of battery hens, servicing capitalist production by reproducing the next generation of male workers and female housewives. The development of feminist analyses over the last thirty years has been instrumental in irreversibly rupturing the gendered division of labour upon which the nuclear family was originally founded (Beck and Beck-Gernsheim, 1995). This can be seen in the fact that opportunities for employment and education have taken women out of the home and into the labour market in increasing numbers. By 1991, almost three-quarters of women (71 per cent) were active in the labour force either as full-time or, as was increasingly the case, part-time employees (*Social Trends*, 1994).

Whereas fifty years ago the social, legal and economic possibilities for women to escape from marriage were extremely limited, the improving position of women over recent decades has made the option of exiting from marriage a realistic possibility. Leaving behind an unhappy marriage was given further impetus by the fact that, unlike in earlier times, a woman could expect to retain custody of her children. However, liberation for women in terms of domestic and employment options has been at a price. A major cost has been a serious overburdening as women take on multiple roles. As working wives, women might well work the 'second shift' (Hochschild, 1989), that is, they simply add domestic work to their daily paid employment. After divorce, the burden may extend even further with women under pressure to work, keep house and, as numerous informants put it, 'become mother *and* father' to their children. For men, on the other hand, the problem is rather different. Threats of redundancy in social, emotional and economic terms can bring a stunning loss of predictability of role which, for increasing numbers of men, spells crisis for traditional models of paternal masculinity (Simpson *et al.*, 1995: 78–81).

The means to unambiguous identities structured through family thus appear to have been shaken; the mould which was so widely responsible for shaping expectations about role, identity and personhood has been cracked. However, to assume that these developments opened the floodgates to personal insecurity is to underestimate the momentum which earlier family forms carry into the present, and indeed the future, as the following sections begin to illustrate.

The unclear family

For many individuals, divorce is a turning point or, to use Denzin's term, an 'epiphany' (Denzin, 1989) in the life-course in which the parties to a marriage set about disentangling biographies which are deeply entwined. Dismantling the edifices of home and family life and the renegotiation of new economic and emotional relationships between former family members is far from being painless and routine but is marked by distress, disruption and uncertainty. The resulting sense of insecurity can be glimpsed from the fact that marriage breakdown is associated with higher rates of admission to psychiatric hospitals and higher suicide rates; divorced women report increased incidence of depressive illness, and divorced men suffer higher than average rates of physical and mental illness (Dominian *et al.*, 1991). Whether actively sought or accepted as an inevitable consequence, divorce represents a major departure from anticipated patterns and pathways. The quest for greater individualism, personal choice, gender equality and economic independence brings with it high levels of risk and uncertainty which carry costs, not only economic but physical and existential in nature.

Children in particular are identified as vulnerable when their parents undergo separation and divorce; they rarely want their parents' separation, and often have little control over the disruption to their lives that is set in train when it occurs (Emery, 1988). Even the most sensitively handled divorce generates anxiety and uncertainty for a child, and it is hardly surprising that the children of divorced parents are singled out as being of particular concern by the state. Indeed, continuous care and guidance provided by family arrangements which differ significantly from the nuclear form are far from trusted by the state and those it appoints to exercise professional concern for the welfare of children. The experience of growing up in single-parent or step-parent families is thus identified with a host of impediments which manifest in the lives of children. Disruption of nuclear family arrangements is readily equated with inadequacy of parenting and an insecure emotional environment, which is in turn causally linked to a variety of social problems including juvenile crime, antisocial behaviour, drug abuse and underachievement at school.

For some, these changes in the structuring and sequencing of family life and their apparent consequences readily translate into concerns for the present and future well-being of society in general. Dire consequences are believed to follow each time the threshold of escape from marriage is lowered. It has been argued that with the demise of traditional family forms, the last bastion of resistance to the predations of market capitalism is removed (Dennis and Erdos, 1992; Mount, 1982) and the social fabric unravels yet further as individuals begin to lose their sense of belonging together (Skolnick and Skolnick, 1971: 376–86). The future of our most intimate social life appears to be a grim and alienated affair.

However, more recent empirical researches into contemporary family and domestic circumstances might lead one to question the atrophy of human sociality implicit in the above accounts. In the not too distant past, divorce was a relatively isolated and anomalous incident in a world of 'normal' families. As such, divorce was perceived as evidence of deviance and pathology and invited attention of a therapeutic kind (Dominian, 1965). Today, however, divorce and family reconstitution are an increasingly distinctive weft running through the fabric of society. It is relatively common to find households linked in novel and distinctive ways through the movement of children and property from former marital relationships. My own contribution to understanding these emergent family forms has been by way of a focus on what I have dubbed the 'unclear family' (Simpson, 1998: chapter 2). In this analysis, emphasis is placed on conflict and contradiction in post-divorce family life, not as a source of ending and termination but as a means of continuing relationships which are, in terms of intimacy, defunct. Accounts by divorced people of their relationships reveal that they find themselves continuing to be bound to their former partners, and indeed their relatives, by negative but nonetheless ongoing ties and obligations as well as by the more positive relationships typically associated with kin. Former partners maintaining communication around issues of contact and financial support for their child would be a case in point. However, the dialectics of identity are complex and unclear in such circumstances; the confusion of boundaries, rights and obligations are apt to be a source of anxiety and insecurity. The refiguring of kinship, residence and family economics which is implied in these post-marital dialogues have also begun to come into focus in the work of a variety of researchers.

Stacy (1990), in her account of family change in contemporary United States, describes the 'post-modern family'; a fragile, fragmented but ultimately democratic structure which she discerns from the tangled biographies of white working-class families in Silicon Valley. The educationalist David Elkind has coined the term 'permeable families' to describe the flexible and fluid arrangements which have displaced those formerly centred on the nuclear family; his work focuses on the stress that these arrangements cause to those who find themselves living in them (Elkind, 1994). Beck and Beck-Gernsheim, addressing more specifically the experience of divorced men and women in Europe, speak of the 'post-familial family' and the 'post-marital family' to describe the networks of relationships that develop when a marriage ends (Beck and Beck-Gernsheim, 1995). In their account, the emphasis is on the continuities in arrangements and not merely their transformation. Divorce and what follows is accounted for within a wider socio-historical framework and presented as a logical consequence of gender, economic and social relations rather than as some postmodern aberration which is wholly new. In one of the few pieces of research to focus specifically on this aspect of social relations, French researchers Buisson and Mermet (1986) have coined the term 'familiality' (*familialité*) to refer to the arrangements that parents make for their children after divorce. Familiality is used to characterise relationships which differ significantly from conventional family relationships but which carry within them aspects which are family-like. In their analysis, they highlight two forms of post-divorce familiality. In the first, the private sphere is dismantled but parents maintain the public appearance of a functioning family by participating in wider networks of kin and friendship beyond the former nuclear family. In the second, little attempt is made to sustain overlapping networks between former partners and their communication is limited to projects which focus on the child. In each instance, significant social continuities are carried on from former family arrangements.

What each of these studies reveals is the changing constitution of private life, and with this the emergence of new forms of insecurity. However, they also reveal clues as to how new forms of personal security are also being fashioned. The retrocession of traditional social structures does not simply leave an existential void, but gives way to new forms of kinship, agency and identity. Thus, from the perspective of any one individual, several layers of kin may have to be fitted together to accommodate economic and emotional continuities from earlier relationships. New constellations of relatives are created by the formation of new long-term associations. For children caught up in these changes, the discrete family residence may become radically de-centred as they pass through multiple family spaces in which they might well also have their own private spaces. Resourcing the family may be similarly fragmented with household income a patchwork of wage, state benefits and the formal and informal inter-household transfer of money, labour and commodities. As we have seen, the models for how to organise these complex entities are not formalised and to a considerable extent people must rely on their own efforts to ensure that these novel and often fragile communities of interest survive but, more importantly, survive to fulfil some of the functions previously carried out within the compact sociality of the nuclear family.

Parallels can thus be drawn across a number of societies which have undergone the 'divorce revolution'. In each, there are new and often complex arrangements for managing the business of care, support, resources, dependency and obligation in the aftermath of divorce and as these extend into the future. Detailed empirical knowledge about the broader implications of these new patterns of family and kinship are still relatively meagre. However, such evidence as exists points to the development of novel yet meaningful relationships across the conjugal divide (see Simpson, 1994, for case studies). However, although similar, it would be mistaken to assume that arrangements made for life after divorce in France, for example, are the same as those in Germany. In each case, the particular relationship between family life and economy, law and culture needs to be taken into consideration. In this final section, I turn to a consideration of some of the particular underpinnings of post-divorce family arrangements in contemporary Britain. Without such a discussion, it is impossible to begin to characterise the way that these new forms of family and kinship impact upon the experience of insecurity.

Managing continuity and transformation in the late twentieth century

Divorce is a mechanism for terminating relationships that have been established in civil or religious law. Putting asunder, however, does not have the dire consequences that it had in the nineteenth century when divorce brought shame and ostracism, particularly to women. Nowadays, divorce is more likely to be cast in an idiom of journeying, growth and self-discovery: 'an acute version of the process of "finding oneself" which the social conditions of modernity force upon us all' (Giddens, 1991: 12). However, divorce is not entirely the unfettered quest for personal freedom and individual autonomy which such comments imply. On the contrary, personal destiny and the networks of relationships within which a person is located are just as likely to reproduce continuities in social relationships as to establish discontinuities: typically, these continuities centre on relationships between parents and children, ex-husbands and ex-wives, grandparents and grandchildren, and also wider circles of kith and kin.

The terminologies applied in popular discourse to the divorce experience tend to mask such continuities while emphasising the discrete households and family forms that emerge. Categories such as 'lone' or 'single' parent, 'second family' and 'absent parent' all emphasise the separateness of persons rather than the ways in which they retain connections economically, socially and emotionally after divorce. Just as marriage generates a universe of kin who are like one's consanguineous or 'blood' relations but who are related 'in-law' (for example mother-in-law, father-in-law, etc.), divorce converts these relatives into 'ex' relations. People will thus talk of their 'ex-mother-in-law' or 'ex-sister-in-law'. In practice, the continuities that are preserved are complex and unpredictable. In terms of the wider network of kin, separating couples undergo a process which has been referred to by Finch as 'working out' (Finch, 1989: 194–211) in which relationships are evaluated on the basis of shared histories and future expectations rather than rigid role prescriptions. However, there are, as yet, no clear patterns as to how such 'working out' ought to be done. For example, how should one treat an ex-husband's new wife, or what should one's attitudes be to affines who were, prior to divorce, close and supportive relatives (Finch and Mason, 1990). 'Working out' relationships entails considerable confusion over the meaning of relationships and the manner of their expression.

Where such confusion is particularly problematic is when it comes to parental relationships after divorce. Divorce is a reversal of adult conjugal relationships. What it cannot reverse, however, are ties which are founded in the bio-genetic connection of parenthood and conceptualised in the West in consubstantial terms as 'flesh and blood' (Pitt-Rivers, 1973). In conventional nuclear family arrangements, marriage, procreation and parenthood come together. What happens at divorce, amongst other things, is that these contrasted elements – the legal and the natural, the conjugal and the cognatic, the affinal and the consanguineal – have to be unpacked from one another (Schneider, 1968, 1984). Conjugal relationships are sanctioned by law and are therefore capable of reversal; that is, the married can return to being unmarried. However, these must be disentangled from those relationships which are seen as essentially irreversible, that is, the set of *natural* relationships which are brought into being by the birth, or indeed the adoption, of a child.

Efforts to achieve continuity while at the same time effecting discontinuities of one kind or another is a difficult process, not least because there is often disagreement over precisely what form such continuities should take. The shape and form of familial relationships is often the subject of disputes between parents after divorce: where children will live, how they will be financially supported and by whom, appropriate levels of contact between a child and the non-resident parent, the role of the non-resident parent in the child's upbringing are just some of the many questions which have to be addressed once the issue of continuity is relocated beyond the nuclear family. Given that in the majority of instances children continue to reside with their mothers rather than fathers after divorce (Simpson *et al.*, 1995: 4–7), the form that such questions take is deeply gendered. Mothers who live with their children are mostly concerned about the contact that their ex-husbands have with the children. Fathers on the other hand are likely to be concerned about restrictions on the amounts and quality of their own contact with their children. The high levels of conflict and concern over these issues would suggest that the fact of large numbers of mother-centred or matrifocal households does not sit easily with an ideology of patrifiliation which reinforces the links between a father and his children (for example, in terms of surname, property, economic responsibility and so on). Furthermore, parents, children and the state are currently far from clear as to what the relationship between a non-resident father and his children from a former marriage ought to be. What is clear, however, is that maintaining relationships with children across the conjugal divide is often stressful and unsatisfactory for all participants and indeed significant numbers of fathers simply give up or suspend relationships with their children (Simpson *et al.*, 1995: 4–7).

The 'official' solution to the continuity problem is a strong pro-access/contact ideology combined with an expectation of ongoing financial support from the non-resident parent. Thus, just at the point where a husband or wife might begin to feel relief at never having to deal with an ex-spouse ever again, there is a compelling expectation from counsellors, judges, solicitors and society at large that a former couple will co-operate practically and economically over their children, perhaps in ways that they had never done before. Advocacy of contact between children and their non-resident parent is legitimated by research findings which indicate that children who had retained contact with both parents coped better with the break-up of their nuclear family unit than those who lost contact with one parent (Hetherington, 1979; Wallerstein and Kelly, 1980). More recent research has suggested that it is the style and patterning of relationship with the non-resident parent and not simply the fact of contact that is significant for the child (Amato, 1994). Around such claims, a powerful consensus has emerged concerning the importance of maintaining regular and positive links between fathers and children after divorce. Arguments for continuing financial support are rather more pragmatic. The growth of lone-parent households carries significant costs for the state. In 1989, only 30 per cent of lone mothers received regular child maintenance from their ex-partner and the cost in real terms to the taxpayer of providing income-related benefits for lone-parent families was running at £3.2 billion (*Children Come First*, 1990).

Over the last decade, the maintenance of parental or more accurately paternal continuities has been enshrined in three major pieces of legislation: the Children Act (1989), the Child Support Act (1991) and the Family Law Act (1996). In different ways, each of these pieces of legislation aims to minimise the insecurities attendant on marital breakdown by mapping out and reinforcing particular continuities between parents and children after divorce. However, taken together, these pieces of legislation have two other important consequences. First, recent legislation surrounding the family represents a trend towards the privatisation and delegalisation of domestic life. Whereas in earlier times the emphasis was on scrutiny and investigation of the conditions of divorcing couples, and particularly in relation to children, today the emphasis is on private ordering and ongoing parental responsibility with public interest played down. A second consequence arising out of the first is that, even after divorce, the former nuclear family is more likely to be highlighted and preserved albeit within a much wider and more complex network of post-divorce association and dependency. Those divorcing today are thus much more likely to be made aware of the economic, social and emotional problems which accompany divorce and the ongoing moral and financial responsibilities arising out of an earlier marriage. By looking at each of these three pieces of legislation in a little more detail, we can begin to see the way in which issues of privatisation and relational continuity are reinforced at the level of legislation.

The two guiding principles of the Children Act are that the best interests of children are paramount and that in discharging obligations to their children, parents do not simply have rights but also have significant responsibilities. What is of particular significance in the divorce context, is that the notion of parental responsibility remains whatever the family circumstances. Thus, parental separation ought not to challenge the fundamental assumption within the Act that mothers and fathers are responsible for the well-being of their children. Furthermore, the thrust of the legislation is non-interventionist. Unlike under previous legislation, orders are not made in relation to children unless it is felt to be in the interests of the child to do so. In other words, considerable responsibility is expected to be exercised by parents in arriving at their own arrangements for their children in relation to residence and contact without paternalistic legal and welfare intervention (Bainham, 1990).

Whereas the Children Act has aimed to create a loose and non-interventionist framework for post-divorce arrangements, the Child Support Act by contrast is highly prescriptive. One of the main objectives of this legislation is to ensure that fathers, irrespective of whether they are in physical contact with their children, do not evade their financial obligations to them. Although couched in the moral imperatives of paternal obligation and duty, the legislation has a more fundamental aim of transferring costs which currently fall on the state back onto families in general and fathers in particular (Maclean, 1994). The attempt to achieve fairness (by the use of a formula rather than a judicial decision) and enforceability (by the setting up of a special agency to administer the calculation and collection of maintenance) has produced strong negative reactions from mothers and fathers alike. The Child Support Agency, set up to administer maintenance claims, appears to have been effective in getting more money out of those already paying maintenance regularly but rather less effective in getting money out of those who are set on evasion. A further problem with the way that legislation has been implemented is that it overrides many of the informal arrangements which former couples might have made in good faith. For example, it is not uncommon for a woman to have agreed with her partner to forego rights to maintenance in return for her husband's share of the equity tied up in the matrimonial home. Stable agreements which long predate the intervention of the Child Support Agency might thus be painfully unearthed once rules and regulations are applied.

The Family Law Act has as one of its major objectives an aspiration first mapped out in the 1974 Finer Report; namely, burying dead marriages decently rather than subjecting men, women and children to processes which simply exacerbate already painful situations. The belief that underpins the Act is that marriage and family life are central to a healthy society. The ideal form that this should take is one of life-long marital partnership. However, the Act acknowledges that this ideal may not be sustainable and many of its provisions seek to incorporate the consequences of relationship breakdown by seeking to preserve family life despite the occurrence of divorce. The way in which this is achieved is by seeking to minimise distress to the parties and their children should separation occur, and by promoting continuing relationships, particularly between parents and children. The emphasis throughout the legislation is on a conciliatory approach to marital breakdown and its aftermath. Parties to a divorce will experience a combination of information giving, marital counselling and mediation through which the pain of divorce will hopefully be assuaged and its unpleasantness sanitised. Divorcing under this ambitious piece of legislation means that the parties will be steered away from traditional, adversarial legal forums and encouraged to seek out the kinds of expert discourses which will enable them to fashion their personal and family relationships anew.

In each of these three pieces of legislation, laudable attempts have been made to create a legal framework which tackles the uncertainties and injustices of post-nuclear family life, while in recognising the inevitability of transformation there is also an attempt to ensure continuity in key relationships. The three main areas addressed in this regard are ongoing parental responsibilities after divorce, alleviation of poverty and the facilitation of consensual divorces. However, a common theme throughout the criticisms levelled at this important triumvirate of legislation is that in each case the law, however sensitively drafted, fails to take account of the burgeoning complexities of family life in the late twentieth century. Marriage remains a significant context in which parenthood is initiated, implemented and maintained, but increasingly there are other inter-personal contexts in which the business of bringing up children is being conducted. Family-based systems of control have given way to new possibilities in which old authorities are increasingly the object of conflict and negotiation. The law, hitherto a powerful arbiter in such conflicts, appears to compound the problem by trying to encompass fundamental contradictions: marriage should be preserved but divorce should be made less painful; individual autonomy must be preserved but within the gendered collectivity of family life; children are the responsibility of their parents but they are also increasingly in possession of rights which should be articulated, if not by them, then by experts on their behalf. The law is faced with the challenge of reconciling a deep-seated drift towards individualism and personal autonomy on the one hand, with the desire to be part of the powerful collectivity of family life on the other. Inevitably, the extent to which the law can resolve this contradiction in practice is limited. However, what is of relevance to the argument put forward here is that the legislation described above pushes back responsibility for creating and sustaining the conditions to ameliorate insecurity back onto the parents and children themselves. The difficult business of resolving these contradictions is carried out at the level of individual practice, and it is at this level that new patterns of interdependence are evolving. Solutions to the problems of changing family life are characterised by complexity, negotiation and a determination to manage the insecurities which family breakdown brings in its wake (Simpson, 1998). The strategies for doing this, however, are not simply individualistic but involve men, women and their children in the creation of new collectivities.

Conclusion

It is readily apparent that old securities centred on the traditional models of family life are eclipsed and with this process new insecurities arise. The project of family can no longer be relied upon to deliver structural stability and temporal continuity mapped across a predictable life cycle. Nowadays, it is divorce and not death which brings long-term conjugality to an end. Those who exit from marriage are likely to be faced with an arduous struggle to carve out new securities and to address the crises and anxieties which arise from these distinctive shifts in the organisation of personal and domestic life. However, these forms are not simply novel transformations of what went before but also carry with them significant echoes of earlier structures and experiences. Life after divorce is rarely a clean break, but is shot through with temporal continuities in which the family values, arrangements and expectations of one era are carried through into the next. Memories of caring, narratives of family and the transmission of knowledge and property carry through with considerable momentum into the projected futures of individual and collective life. Marriage, classically conceived, represents the merging of biographies, a determined effort to create and inhabit a relatively permanent fragment of the social order; divorce represents the opposite process, a deep despair on realising that stable, fulfilling and harmonious equilibrium can never be achieved, followed by the scramble to exit with dignity and whatever remnants of ontological and economic security can be salvaged.

In recent times, exiting with dignity has become as much about preserving relationships between men, women and their children as it is about ending them. The imperatives of kinship and the quest for security in a world where change and insecurity are all too evident are not totally undermined by divorce. Indeed, one should not underestimate the commitment and sense of responsibility that many divorced couples develop towards one another and towards their children.

Theirs is the task of making new networks and carving out new securities from the networks of potentiality which remain when long-term conjugality fails. As I have demonstrated, efforts to preserve family-like structures, albeit in radically altered form, are given considerable impetus by recent divorce law reforms which have encouraged privatisation of the domestic arena in relation to divorce and separation. Within this legislation, the transformation of family life, which is accepted as an inevitability for many couples, is subject to an expectation that important relationships will continue after marital breakdown.

Understanding the impact of relationship breakdown on individuals is well advanced. However, understanding the wider social implications of large-scale relationship breakdown is still at an early stage. Mapping the structures and processes that I, and others, have begun to describe will be a significant challenge for researchers well into the next millennium. This will entail a radical reconceptualisation of the way that 'public' and 'private' are articulated in personal and domestic arrangements as the task of bringing up children shifts from the 'compact household to the wider social domain' (Robertson, 1991: 122). It will also require new ways of thinking about how, if at all, the basic currencies of social life such as trust, amity, support, care, obligation and predictability might be located in new and emergent structures of family life after divorce. As Giddens suggests, this is a 'fraught and difficult enterprise' (1994a: 106); nevertheless it is one in which increasing numbers of men, women and children find themselves implicated, and ought to be the subject of theoretical and policy concerns.

Part III

Insecurity as lived experience

This section explores the complexity of security and insecurity in a number of settings. Peter Phillimore and Suzanne Moffatt's analysis of pollution on Teesside highlights the insecurity that occurs if our environment is unsafe. However, they also consider the problems of conventional political rhetoric which sees the need to engender employment through the encouragement of capitalist enterprise as the overriding issue concerning insecurity. The conflict between people's health, made insecure by pollution, and securing employment is not easily resolved by either local communities or political leaders.

Neil Ward and Philip Lowe likewise introduce new complexities into our consideration of insecurity by showing the way in which competing demands for greater security arise. In our predominantly urban nation we want agriculture, like industry, to refrain from poisoning us. Many of us want to live in the country, even though we do not secure our livelihoods from the country, and most of us want to enjoy the country as a place of recreation from time to time. But there are competing claims being made by those who want the country to provide them with a secure income and those who have their own traditional country-based recreations. They trace how the countryside has become a site of contestation between these competing demands.

Robert MacDonald takes us back to Teesside and back to the theme of employment security, exploring the very important issues about the insecurity facing many young people, particularly in deprived regions. He offers us an account of the limitations of the public policies that have been developed to deal with youth unemployment, reminding us again of the importance of the issues explored earlier in the book by Jane Wheelock. He highlights the inadequacies of government responses to the problem of unemployment which do not get to grips with the issues about the demand for labour.

Finally, Beatrix Campbell introduces us to another area of contested claims and inter-acting problems. Many accept explanations of youth crime which highlight the economic insecurity analysed by many of the chapters in this book. Others draw attention to the implications of changing family patterns for this phenomenon. There is then a group of writers, who have secured political and media attention, and who link these together with particular emphasis on the changed world in which the working-class male grows up. Campbell attacks this perspective, emphasising instead some deep-rooted problems about masculinity. In doing so, Campbell, like Ward and Lowe, offers a challenge to simplistic approaches to the phenomenon of insecurity. Do we want to see a more secure world created by a reversion to the patriarchal working-class world of the 'secure' mining communities of old, or are there not some rather more complex issues to be grasped? The same rhetorical question might be asked, in relation to Ward and Lowe's chapter, of those who demand a return to traditional rural communities; and, in respect of Phillimore and Moffatt's chapter, of those who want to see the return of polluting industry.

9 Narratives of insecurity in Teesside

Environmental politics and health risks

Peter Phillimore and Suzanne Moffatt

Introduction

In 1990, Langbaurgh Council decided upon the demolition of nearly one hundred houses in Grangetown, near the mouth of the River Tees, in northeast England. Few areas of housing in Britain stand as close to major industrial sites – in this case steel and petrochemicals – as Grangetown. The initial intention had been to refurbish much of the area; but this plan was modified after Langbaurgh Council decided that the more prudent action in the case of a portion of these houses was outright demolition and no subsequent rebuilding on the site. This decision was taken largely in the light of advice from the Health and Safety Executive (HSE) and the Inspectorate of Pollution (HMIP) in February of that year. Their joint concerns hinged around assessment of possible risks to residents from extending the lifespan of housing in the closest proximity to ICI Wilton and British Steel plants.

The decision by Langbaurgh Council to demolish the homes provoked a strong reaction. In particular, the confidential briefing to the council by the HSE and HMIP fuelled demands for wider disclosure about the nature of the risks involved. This demand was amplified by media reports that a 'very slight risk' of an explosion at ICI Wilton similar to that at Flixborough was one of the considerations raised in this briefing. Flixborough, further south down the North Sea coast on Humberside, was the site of a large explosion in 1974 at a major chemical plant which had killed twenty-eight people. In addition to public anxiety about the nature of the risk identified by the regulatory authorities, unease was also voiced about the rationale for demolishing nearly one hundred homes. This led one councillor to ask why one side of the street should be considered 'safe' if the other was not (*Northern Echo* 3 February 1990; 9 February 1990).

Yet at a public meeting held to 'allay fears and alarm in the area' (*Northern Echo* 14 February 1990), a majority of those present opposed demolition. A final decision by Langbaurgh Council was then postponed to await further risk assessment by the HSE's Major Hazard Assessment Unit. The conclusion of this further assessment was that the risk of an explosion at ICI's nylon plant was, after all, so small that it could be discounted, though as the *Northern Echo* noted (20 July 1990), no details were released 'about the degree of risk'. This advice made it easier for the council to respond to popular opposition to large-scale demolition, and Langbaurgh Council cut back from 93 to 27 the number of houses proposed for demolition (*Northern Echo* 15 August 1990). Soon afterwards, however, public pressure appeared to sway back the other way. A call for another public meeting followed petitions from some local residents urging that a much larger number of houses be demolished, one report citing up to 600 houses (*Northern Echo* 12 September 1990). In the end, demolition was restricted to 27 homes, while the housing in the remainder of the area was refurbished using central government funding (*Northern Echo* 27 March 1991).

The ebb and flow of this particular local controversy, as depicted in local press coverage, and the ambivalence reflected throughout it towards local authority intentions, brings together several themes: public insecurity in the face of environmental hazards, scepticism about scientific calculations of risk and official reassurance, the intangibility and uncertainty in assessing environmental risk and, coupled with such doubts, a desire to protect and keep together a community already weakened by the experience of high and long-term unemployment.

Such events, and the concerns they generate, have parallels in many places in the 1980s and 1990s. Across Europe, west and east, closure of old industries and contraction of employment in many of those that remain have taken place alongside the rise of environmentalism and new anxieties about the implications of pollution, both global and local. While the human costs of job loss and environmental damage have been far more severe in eastern Europe than anywhere else, in a British context, Teesside nevertheless stands out as one place where economic and environmental concerns have been both profound and potentially in conflict. An unenviable health record has amplified these concerns, for mortality in working-class areas of Teesside has persisted at unusually high levels: unusual, that is, even in the context of a region with high mortality (Townsend *et al.*, 1988; Phillimore and Morris, 1991; Phillimore and Beattie, 1994; TEES, 1995). We have been among those arguing that one factor contributing to this mortality has been air pollution from industry (TEES, 1995; Pless-Mulloli *et al.*, 1998). Argument and debate about jobs, prosperity, pollution and health thus provide the framework within which we explore themes of insecurity in this chapter. Although our interest is primarily in the recent past, we also suggest that arguments in Teesside over the economy and the environment go back to the turn of the century or even earlier.

The perspective we adopt here is that preoccupations about health issues in a city open a window on other aspects of that city's life. Public statements and private reflections about ill-health and its causes can be seen as elements of a larger discourse about a place and its identity, about what it has going for it and the drawbacks it faces. And in the ways that Teessiders have articulated their concerns about their own health prospects or the wider public health, we can discern the push and pull of two contending but unequal narratives: one of insecurity about the causes of ill-health, the other of reassurance.

Insecurity has been a theme of recurring interest to social critics and theorists ever since the time of Marx. But with Beck's characterisation of modern society as 'risk society' (Beck, 1992, 1996), reflection on insecurity has been transformed by an entirely new recognition of the *social* significance of environmental pollution in our lives. Beck's arguments – that the sense of impending crisis in our relationship with our environment, and the pollution that has triggered the crisis, lie at the heart of social theory – represent a novel departure. The pollution created by industrialisation has until recently been marginal or irrelevant to social scientists, in a manner which reflects its byproduct status. Implicitly, it has been regarded as a techno-scientific matter that was beyond the domain of social relations. But, through the writings first of Douglas (1975, 1985; also Douglas and Wildavsky, 1982) and then of Beck, this attitude has changed. Despite the different inspirations for their interest and their divergent conclusions, these writers share a perception that the ways we handle the pollution we produce – our cultural and political responses to it, the ways we define, assess and symbolise the risks it is seen to pose – are central, not marginal, to an understanding of the social world in which we live.[1]

Nonetheless, insecurity in Teesside is not only – indeed not even primarily – focused upon environmental pollution. As will become apparent, the insecurities and risks that find expression in Teesside relate as much to economic marginality and social exclusion. These two sources of insecurity compound one another, but are in many respects hard to compare. The insecurity generated by long-term exposure to air pollution, for example, revolves around uncertainty, expressible in the idiom of 'what if' and 'maybe', and has consequences that can often only tentatively be linked back to causes (Phillimore and Moffatt, 1994; Phillimore, 1998; Pless-Mulloli *et al.*, 1998). This contrasts sharply with the day-to-day insecurity associated with unemployment, in which problems of making ends meet, managing to participate socially and retaining self-respect and a sense of identity have an immediacy generally lacking in relation to pollution. This chapter provides an opportunity to explore the contrasting preoccupations with economic and environmental insecurities, viewed through the prism of perceived threats to personal and public health. In that respect, it touches on what has come to be called popular or lay epidemiology – people's understandings of the causes of ill-health (see Brown, 1992; Moffatt *et al.*, 1995; Phillimore and Moffatt, 1994; Popay and Williams, 1996).

These preoccupations are by no means new in Teesside. Despite Beck's insights about the qualitatively novel features of environmental risk and insecurity in the world today, the notion of the present phase of modern society as 'risk society' can easily exaggerate the departure from earlier phases of industrialisation, and carries with it the danger of overspecific periodisation. Even though the relative prominence of particular pollutants has changed over time, with the decline of smoke and sulphur dioxide, preoccupation with pollution and its effects on the urban environment has a long (if often muted) history in Teesside. Yet in a conurbation which through this century has known unemployment and pollution to an unusually severe degree, how have the insecurities thereby generated been conceived of and related to one another? This chapter presents an account of the argument and dialogue such insecurities have created locally: in some contexts compounding each other, in others (the majority) counterposed as alternative threats, the one immediate and real (unemployment), the other lying in the future and hypothetical or unprovable (pollution).

Teesside: historical background

Built first around iron and steel, and after the First World War around chemicals as well, the Teesside towns of Middlesbrough, Stockton, Thornaby, Billingham and Redcar were initially notable for their extraordinarily rapid growth (Beynon *et al.*, 1994; Briggs, 1968). The conurbation remains even today a patchwork of distinct towns, with Teesside the name used by planners or outsiders rather than a strong badge of local affiliation. Even so, all parts continue to share in the identification with steel and petrochemicals, with ICI the dominant corporation on the chemicals side and British Steel the present-day inheritor of a number of separate steel-producing companies. These industries are visible from almost every angle on the Teesside landscape, as dominating physically in their installations and the amount of land they take up as they are economically and figuratively in Teessiders' lives.[2]

At the same time, this dominance was even greater until around 1980 than it is today, at the end of the century. For Teesside has been an area of high unemployment at various periods in the twentieth century, but especially in the 1920s–1930s and 1980s–1990s. Even early in the 1960s, concerns were being expressed about disturbing pockets of unemployment, particularly in the old working-class neighbourhoods of Grangetown and South Bank, close to major steel and chemical sites (Eston UDC, 1962). Problems were relatively localised at that stage, however, and it was at the end of the 1970s that unemployment rates soared rapidly. For well over a decade, through two major recessions, Teesside was as severely affected as any area of Britain. At several times in the 1980s the county of Cleveland (of which Teesside formed the major element) recorded the highest unemployment in mainland Britain. At the 1981 and 1991 national censuses, a number of local government wards in Teesside had unemployment rates in excess of 30 per cent, with the peak of unemployment in the region occurring in 1986 (Townsend *et al.*, 1988; Phillimore *et al.*, 1994). The dramatic contraction of the steel industry, a smaller contraction in the chemical industry, and the disappearance of shipbuilding and repair on the River Tees, were the most visible features of a disastrous period in the area's economic fortunes, and one from which it has still to recover.[3]

Yet in local government and in academic writing, Teesside's economic problems have not been seen simply as typical of the Northeast's industrial decline. For one thing, this was an area of comparatively high investment. The 1950s and 1960s were not only times of economic growth but also of long-term optimism about Teesside's future development (Beynon *et al.*, 1994; Hudson, 1989a). Even in the 1930s, Hudson argues, Teesside was a place of 'comparative prosperity and economic dynamism in the North East' (1989a: 331), though it has to be said that any advantage the Tees towns had over Wearside and Tyneside is reflected in the most marginal differences in unemployment rates. Yet the post-1945 economic security may well have made the economic collapse of the 1980s all the more traumatic, because this was not an area obviously in decline. Beynon *et al.* (1994: 3) summarise Teesside's distinctiveness within its region when they state: 'While Teesside might be *in* the North, it was certainly not *of* the North' [original italics].

Two major patterns of movement have taken place over the last one hundred years. While industry has, in successive waves of development, tended to move downriver to the mouth of the River Tees,[4] the population has been rehoused in successive waves away from the river. Gradually, therefore, the population has been located further from the biggest industrial sites. Yet despite this, it is easy to exaggerate the separation. In several areas, particularly on the south side of the river, substantial blocs of housing still remain in close proximity to chemical or steel sites (at the 1991 census, approximately 12,000 people were living within one kilometre of such sites). That number would have been even greater in 1981, with further industrial sites still then in use.

Another kind of divorce between population and industry is also relevant to our discussion. One legacy of the job losses of the last two decades has been that few of those now employed in steel or chemical production are any longer also local residents, living alongside or in the vicinity of their workplace. In contrast to the period up until the late 1970s, those who live closest to the main plants are today unlikely to work there, weakening the former ties binding people to their main local sources of employment. These predominantly working-class neighbourhoods have always borne the brunt of unemployment. But in the last decade and a half, these have become centres of long-term unemployment where residents have less and less personal investment in the companies on their doorstep, as their prospects of ever being employed in one of them recede. The following quotation from a newspaper article reflects this bleak realisation: its arresting imagery of motherhood extends the common metaphor of an industry as a community's lifeblood, sustaining and nurturing those who depend on the work provided:

> They were born and raised to serve their steel mother. It was all they were taught and all they ever knew. And they believed she would keep their children…Grangetown, one time centre of the world's iron and steel trade, has indeed been abandoned by her steel mother.
>
> (*Northern Echo* 20 November 1991)

One consequence of this development is that the balance of costs and benefits is less in evidence in the immediate vicinity of the major works than it is elsewhere. Residents instead face a double set of costs, experiencing the drawbacks of proximity in the form of atmospheric pollution, without the benefits in terms of employment. Yet despite this uncoupling of work and neighbourhood, the industries on the doorstep are still seen as the lifeblood of the place, assisted by the absence of major new employers (such as Nissan at Sunderland). The hope of work in these industries remains ingrained in the collective expectations of these neighbourhoods, however unlikely the prospect for anything but short-term work for subcontractors of the big companies. This is perhaps hardly surprising: many of those out of work would once have worked in steel or chemicals, and would know those who still do so. Even if personal hopes of employment are slim, steel and chemical industries are still seen to personify Teesside, and to represent its future prospects as much as its past or present identity.

Environmental insecurity and environmental politics in Teesside

Pollution has been a recurring motif in Teesside's image of itself as a place, dating back to the end of the nineteenth century. 'If there is one thing more than another that Middlesbrough can be said to be proud of, it is the smoke. The smoke is an indication of plenty of work', responded the mayor to the visiting Prince of Wales at the opening of the new town hall in 1887 (quoted in Briggs, 1968: 263). Yet such pollution for long conjured up contradictory associations: it was the visible sign of Teesside's economic vitality, yet it was also a sign of the particular risks to which its population was exposed. Such ambiguity is well reflected in the following pair of quotations from annual reports by the Medical Officer of Health for Eston, downriver from Middlesbrough, in 1921 and 1925. Written at times of recession they reflect the two sides of economic inactivity:

> During the year the atmosphere has been very clear and the air pure, owing to the fact that the large industrial works have been standing most of the time. The absence of the clouds of black smoke which are emitted in normal times from the large chimneys have contributed to the favourable health statistics of the District.
> While we all deplore the fact that the trade of the District is so bad, yet I am of the opinion that with greater care when the industries are in full swing much of the polluted smoke may be prevented.
>
> (MoH Report, Eston UD, 1921)

> The health of the District is fairly satisfactory when one takes into consideration the privations suffered by many of the inhabitants through lack of work, as this has been one of the hardest hit districts in the kingdom.
>
> (MoH Report, Eston UD, 1925)

Despite such indications of concern with pollution in the early part of the century, Medical Officers of Health were articulating what was generally a minority point of view. There is little indication that environmental considerations were given much weight prior to the 1950s outside a narrow circle of public health officials.

From the 1970s on, however, a case can be made for a growing incorporation of environmental issues in politics and policy debate in Teesside. Conflict over the environmental costs of proposals to reclaim Seal Sands (an area on the north shore of the Tees estuary renowned for its wading birds) for chemical and oil-refining operations marks a watershed in this respect. On the one hand, Seal Sands provided the catalyst which brought into being new environmental groups in Teesside; at the same time, it generated a wider level of concern within local authorities than such industrial developments had provoked in the past. The trade-off between environmental quality and economic security informed the entire controversy. Critics of the Seal Sands plans were accused of damaging the prospects of new investment, and the counter-argument by those in favour of the development was expressed in the derisive terms of 'birds versus jobs', as if their case brooked no serious reservations. But the loss of jobs in both the main sectors of the economy in this period did not simply translate into a 'jobs at all costs' philosophy, as Hudson has pointed out (1989a: 341):

> The consensus on modernisation policies began to be questioned not simply by the 'green' politics of environmentalist groups but also from within the local authorities themselves, especially since these industries were increasingly associated with large-scale job-shedding....In this context the 'jobs at all costs' philosophy which had been used to justify policies supporting such industries was increasingly difficult to sustain.[5]

Yet there are two qualifications which need to be made about this interpretation of the post-1970 period. In the first place, it would be a mistake to overlook the limited concerns about industrial pollution which were being raised before Seal Sands became a local issue. It needs to be remembered that in the 1950s, air pollution was an issue of national concern in the wake of the catastrophic smogs in London and other cities, even if the policy response was targeted towards domestic rather than industrial smoke control measures. On the other hand, the national determination to do something to clean up urban air quality in the 1950s, with the introduction of smokeless zones and the first curbs on domestic sources of fuel, did not in Teesside completely overshadow the local concern with industrial emissions. Moreover, with the introduction of routine air quality monitoring during the 1950s, the evidence was inescapable for council (including public health) officials that the highest pollution levels were being recorded at sites close to industry. These data do not, however, seem to have had much impact on wider policy, nor were they a trigger for public concern. Particular pollution incidents sometimes led to council action, but they appear as isolated cases, not as part of a larger tide of public unease about pollution. Minutes of a meeting between representatives of ICI and Billingham Urban District Council, on the north bank of the River Tees, illustrate one such case in the mid-1950s, as well as the paternalistic response, with the 'little or nothing that could be done' attitude helping to pre-empt further action:

> The Chairman stated that complaints had been received regarding the increase in the atmospheric pollution in the Chiltons Area and the Council thought these should be investigated…
>
> Mr Blench [ICI] enquired whether there had been any increase in the number of complaints in the past year or so, and he was told that personal complaints had been increasing during the past two years. Mr Blench stated that he could not understand how there could be any increase during this period as there had been no change in working conditions in the factory during that time…
>
> One of the complaints was about fog conditions early in the morning and of a grey deposit. Mr Blench was asked whether any complaints had been received by the Company from their own tenants and he admitted that certain complaints had been received…Mr Blench stated that if the cause of complaint was the C.C.F. Plant there was little or nothing that could be done, as the Company had already taken all practical measures to minimise the dust nuisance from the plant.
>
> (Billingham UDC, 1955–6; parentheses added)

In the second place, it would be naive to suggest that the post-1970 era saw the emergence of a new consensus among local authorities in favour of acknowledging the existence of Teesside's pollution problems. Far from it: whatever the internal debates going on in local authorities and within the industries concerned, there are clear signs from the 1960s onwards of the strong institutional pressures to control and minimise debate about Teesside's environmental problems, playing down both the scale and the possible effects of *industrial* pollution (Beynon *et al.*, 1994; Gladstone, 1976). To some degree, such defensiveness may be taken as an indication of the growing environmental awareness alluded to earlier in that it reflects a reaction to new pressures and influences. On the other hand, this same defensiveness has certainly inhibited vigorous debate in Teesside politics on environmental issues (Beynon *et al.*, 1994; Gladstone, 1976; Sadler, 1990).

Taken overall, however, the development of Seal Sands introduced environ-mental campaigning to Teesside, providing the first alternative to official political channels for the expression of concerns about pollution risks. Three issues in particular have mobilised public responses and concerted opposition to new development plans. The first centred on proposals in the early 1980s by NIREX to bury low-level nuclear waste on ICI's Billingham site. ICI's support for these proposals set them at odds with the residents of Billingham, who campaigned under the acronym BAND (Billingham Against Nuclear Dumping). As one local participant and witness observed to us about the biggest public meeting, 'I've never known a public meeting like it in Billing-ham', adding, 'NIREX wouldn't have brought many jobs'. The campaign was in the end successful, assisted perhaps by ICI's discomfort at finding its own erstwhile company town up in arms against its support for the NIREX proposal.

In the 1990s, controversy has surrounded proposals for the building of a major toxic waste incinerator in northeast England. Two of three sites earmarked were on the north bank of the River Tees, one at Seal Sands, the other closer to the centre of Stockton, in Portrack. A Public Inquiry which started in 1990 became the focus of opposition, not only from local authorities but also from STINC (Stop Toxic Waste Incinerators in Cleveland), described by one newspaper as the most high-profile of the region's anti-toxic waste campaigning groups. One campaigner summarised their view: 'The concern for people is the additional risks from toxic waste incinerators, that they will add to already unacceptable levels of pollution in Cleveland' (quoted in *Northern Echo*, 11 September 1990). Around the same time, ICI formed a partnership with the American company Enron to recycle waste gas for electricity generation on the Wilton site, on the south bank of the River Tees. This also met considerable opposition in neighbouring parts of Teesside from residents groups, though they had no success in stopping the building of the new power station.

What all these cases have in common is that they revolve around opposition to the introduction of specific *new* industrial activities, raising concerns about *additional* pollution risks, in an area seen by campaigners as already having more than its share of pollution-creating industry. These have been single-issue campaigns, fought by groups assembled for the purpose. Pollution from existing industries has never mobilised people in a comparable way, however much there has been private unease, because people's jobs and the economic well-being of the area are seen to be at stake. Moreover, it is for precisely these reasons that there has been no distinct trade union dimension to debate over pollution in Teesside. Yet a sense of the different currents running through Teesside's unending conversation with itself about its environment may be gauged by the fact that the issues of the toxic waste incinerators, the Enron power station and the proposed demolition of up to one hundred homes in Grangetown with which we started this chapter – new and old sources of pollution risk alike – were all occurring simultaneously through 1990.

While the Teesside boroughs opposed new toxic waste incineration, they have also been assiduous in minimising the significance of air pollution from existing industrial activities. Several different strategies have been detectable in official efforts to deflect attention from industrial pollution, with the primary objective of creating a new image of Teesside as a 'clean' environment attractive to investment by high-tech industries. One line has been to emphasise the huge improvements that have been made in air quality in Teesside, highlighting the dramatic reductions in levels of sulphur dioxide and smoke, especially since the 1950s. A second, still emerging as important, has been to emphasise the role of traffic pollution and its enormous environmental significance. A third has been to lay stress on the role of air pollution from outside the region, whether imported from the power stations of South

Yorkshire or from across the North Sea. A fourth has seen local authorities and
industries taking a joint approach to both pollution control and public
education: although the objective has been to secure improved air quality, one
consequence has been to tie local authorities more closely to the industries'
interests and their own gloss on the improvements being made.

Something of the flavour of all these arguments comes across in the following
extracts from a recent leaflet circulated by the Teesside local authorities and
industries (funded partly by the Department of the Environment). Entitled 'Air
Quality Today' (1996), the leaflet has two photographs on its cover, comparing
Middlesbrough in the 1960s with the present day:

Smokey old Teesside?

Fact: Teesside used to be one of the most polluted places in Britain. In the
1960's it suffered from some of the worst air pollution in the country, due
partly to domestic coalburning.

Fact: it used to be – but not any more!

The latest analytical techniques available have shown that our air is as good
as other towns and cities in the country – and in many cases a lot better.
Take airborne particle pollution for example, which is the most significant
local pollutant nowadays. National statistics show that in 1994 Middlesbrough had the lowest reported levels...Our biggest air quality problem on
Teesside is one of perception.

So, do we ever get poor air quality?

Yes. On about a dozen occasions through the year. Sometimes these occur in
the summer when we get PHOTOCHEMICAL SMOG drifting into Teesside from as far away as Europe.

Despite great care being taken with industrial processes, there are occasions
when locally-produced short-term emissions of pollutants do occur...Thankfully these episodes are quite rare. You might also be interested
to know two things:

1   Peak pollution levels occur on 5th November.
2   Nowadays, much of our local air pollution comes from road traffic.

Do you get annoyed when people talk down Teesside?...If we have wrong
perceptions of our area, WE CANNOT BE SURPRISED IF OTHERS
DO AS WELL. A wrong perception could mean people do not invest in our
area...

The way forward involves everyone getting together to challenge wrong
perceptions.

This leaflet is ironically part of a strategy of increased openness and improved provision of information to the public. Ironic, because the tone of the

leaflet seems so defensive, with its exhortation to root out 'wrong perceptions'. Moreover, the reference to distant pollution sources recalls Beck's (1992) observations about the global, boundary-crossing character of pollution, the local authorities using this to deflect attention from more homegrown forms of pollution.

What is omitted from the picture of Teesside that emerges here is any possibility that notable spatial differences may persist between localities.[6] Air pollution is not evenly spread now, nor was it in the past.[7] Recent developments in methods of air quality monitoring have played a part in obscuring this salient detail. Today, modern measuring equipment permits continuous monitoring of a range of pollutants, and the emphasis has shifted away from the older pollutants such as sulphur dioxide, smoke and ferric oxide, to ozone, small particles (PM_{10}), volatile organic compounds (VOCs) such as benzene, and polycyclic aromatic hydrocarbons (PAHs), few of which were measured before 1990. However, cost means that monitoring is centralised in one or two locations, situated at some distance from the most important sources of pollution. Gains in the coverage of pollutants monitored, and the temporal sensitivity which allows any short period to be reviewed, must be set against the loss in geographical coverage of the 1960s and 1970s, when less sensitive equipment nonetheless allowed comparisons to be made between the different pollution burdens of different areas within Teesside. It has paradoxically become harder than formerly to tell how much heavier pollution is in some areas than others within Teesside, even if it is easier to compare how Middlesbrough (standing for Teesside as a whole) fares in relation to other British cities with similar data. One consequence is that it has become easier for the local authorities in Teesside to publicise 'good news' about the Teesside air, in an official 'narrative of reassurance', partly because some of the potential 'bad news' is no longer collected. Yet in areas close to industry, this reassurance is not wholly convincing as it flies in the face of personal observation, as comments from recent research suggest:[8]

> We tend to get a lot of dust in the house blowing through windows. I think it comes from nearby works such as ICI and British Steel.

> A lot more could be done to make the local atmosphere cleaner. We notice that the outpouring from ICI, Enron and BSC tends to increase at night-time.

We have looked at the parameters of debate surrounding air pollution routinely emitted by existing industrial operations in Teesside, and at the arguments over potential new sources of pollution from proposed developments. We end this section by illustrating the terms of debate when emergency pollution incidents arise. The concerns generated at times of accidents – fires, explosions or unintended releases of gas – of course have an urgency and immediacy which sets them apart from those associated with the routine, day-by-day emission of pollutants. Yet public concerns and official responses in the wake of accidents simply elicit a more vivid and dramatic variant of a familiar discourse around environmental risks. This can be illustrated by reference to an incident such as the major fire in 1995 at a BASF warehouse of plastics on the ICI site at Wilton. In that year alone, there occurred five chemical industry incidents of sufficient importance to involve the county emergency planning team.[9] By all accounts, this particular fire proved to be the largest in Teesside since 1945 (*Northern Echo* 10–11 October 1995). In its aftermath, described in images such as 'on the brink' and 'very nearly the accident we've always dreaded', one dispute centred on the toxicity of the fumes. The different perspectives were reflected in statements in *Northern Echo* news stories.

> ...last night BASF insisted it was always under control and as it was non-toxic posed no danger to the public.
>
> (*Northern Echo* 10 October 1995)

> A spokeswoman for Cleveland police said: 'If anything burns and gives off smoke then it can be said to be toxic. It wasn't a toxic cloud full of petro-chemical by-products. If we had told people to evacuate because the smoke was toxic there would have been panic.'
>
> But a spokesman for Friends of the Earth, in London, said: 'Polypropylene is toxic by ingestion and a respiratory irritant. It gets into the blood stream via the lungs. In such circumstances it is pointless telling people to remain indoors unless their homes are fitted with an air purification device.'
>
> (*Northern Echo* 11 October 1995)

Here also conflicting narratives – of anxiety and insecurity on the one hand and reassurance on the other – manifest themselves. The context in this case may have been one of near-disaster, but the concerns and disputes over the toxicity of fumes in this extreme instance merely echo those which recur throughout the persisting arguments about pollution and its effects in Teesside.[10]

Experiences of insecurity

While the last section looked at the ways in which pollution issues have emerged in local politics alongside concerns over job creation and preservation, this section returns to the experiences of insecurity of those living alongside industry. One version of what people in Grangetown, South Bank, Dormanstown and elsewhere are concerned about, frequently articulated by local authority staff or managers in steel and chemical companies during our research, stresses the overriding importance of unemployment, poverty and crime. These concerns are so pressing, it is suggested, as to push any anxieties about pollution and the urban environment well down the scale of priorities for a better life. It would be hard to disagree that economic insecurity is a far more potent force in daily lives than anxieties over pollution. Yet in suggesting what those who live in these areas think, a degree of convenient misrepresentation occurs: convenient because it helps to sustain a sense that local authorities and public alike are at one in placing jobs first, and legitimates the attempt to play down environmental questions.

It seems to us that people who live close to the main industries do not discount pollution as an issue. Instead, the prevailing attitude is more complex and ambivalent, one of being inured to pollution, seeing it as a necessary evil to be endured for the sake of the work associated with its production, and something to which people have long grown accustomed. This attitude has been reinforced, among men at least, by the concerns of trade unions in steel and chemical companies. Such resigned acquiescence is misconstrued if taken to mean that pollution risks are simply accepted, and regarded as merely a minor issue which pales into insignificance alongside concerns over unemployment or crime. Moreover, new local authority policies to offer environmental information, such as Middlesbrough's publication of daily measurements of air quality, do not necessarily change these attitudes. In the neighbourhoods closest to the main industries, people can judge for themselves and know that their experience is not necessarily reflected in readings from monitoring sites a few miles away. Such efforts by local authorities, although intended to reflect greater openness and willingness to share information, paradoxically end up by underlining the gap between local neighbourhood and town hall.

The remarks from our survey quoted below reflect something of this ambiguity about the risks of pollution. In effect, these are personal balance sheets of costs and benefits: the more diffuse risks for health associated with pollution weighed against the more immediate risks (for the wider community as well as for individual health) associated with redundancy, joblessness, social exclusion and low income.

> Common sense tells you that a cleaner environment is essential, but for jobs to be lost would also affect people's health. So which is the greater evil? I just honestly don't know.

> I think that the lack of employment is causing far more havoc than anything and in my mind even supersedes having a cleaner environment.

> I think it is ridiculous how industry in this area gets away with the amount of pollution they pump into the air and rivers. In my opinion it is industry that is to blame for the amount of chest problems people suffer from in this area.

> Health is not simply a physical thing but also emotional, mental and spiritual. Without jobs, people get depressed, vandalism and burglaries are rife because of lack of money and nothing to do. Everyone is stressed out and I think this is the reason for a lot of illness.

Fewer industries and a cleaner environment do not necessarily contribute to better health. The lack of regular work can give rise to psychological problems and mental malaise. From my point of view, it is preferable to have regular work and retain one's mental health. Increased pollution by industry can and should be contained or eliminated in the best way available.

Concluding remarks

> The proletariat of the global risk society settles beneath the smokestacks, next to the refineries and chemical factories in the industrial centers of the Third World....There is a systematic 'attraction' between extreme poverty and extreme risk.
>
> (Beck, 1992: 41)

While the extreme examples may come from Africa, Asia or South America, matters are not so different in Teesside or in some other cities in the richest countries. Beck's exploration of the politics of risk emphasises precisely what is ignored or obscured in Teesside's environmental politics. As several illustrations in this chapter have suggested, the dominant institutional voices in Teesside, in government and industry, have disconnected issues of poverty and economic security from matters to do with the urban environment and pollution. Treated as separate, it has been relatively easy to oppose them, to rank one as far more important than the other, and to stigmatise the articulation of pollution concerns as rocking the boat of economic stability (a tendency Beck recognises as all too typical).[11] Moreover, the demands of daily living can make such a separation seem self-evident. Yet, as Beck's remark at the start of this section suggests, that separation is not as self-evident as it may seem. Though these sources of insecurity may manifest themselves as distinct and separate, in many respects they compound one another. It is the relationship between the two, not the absence of any connection, that Beck emphasises, and that we have sought to examine in this case study.

It is against this background that a further twist needs to be taken into account. Specific concerns about health risks posed by pollution, expressed by residents or others, are all too readily dismissed as unfounded and unsubstantiated. Time and time-scales are crucial considerations here, as Barbara Adam (1995, 1996) and Veena Das (1995) have emphasised. In assessing health risks from exposure to environmental hazards, the long-term is relevant in three senses, each of which complicates judgements about health effects: first, the long-term exposure to pollutants; second, the long time lag often occurring between cumulative exposures and medical symptoms; and third the chronic nature of ill-health (terminal or not) once symptoms manifest themselves. Such extended time frames militate against confident claims about causation in environmental epidemiology: empirical data with measurements of pollution or exposure over long periods are habitually lacking, and there is inevitable uncertainty as to alternative factors which may have played a part in the causation of ill-health.

The upshot is a high degree of caution and qualification in epidemiological studies of pollution effects. Such caution can meet with ridicule from those whose personal experience leaves them in little doubt that they have suffered the health costs of exposure to pollution.[12] However, the uncertainties surrounding such work also do little to reduce the insecurities associated with environmental risks. At the same time, what is rarely acknowledged (particularly within epidemiology) is that a consequence of this caution has also been to benefit and lend arguments to those with a stake in minimising possible risks from pollution (see Phillimore 1998).

The example from Langbaurgh which opened this chapter provides as good an illustration as any of the push and pull of different considerations about local environmental risk. The twists and turns as this planning drama unfolded illuminate how perceived environmental dangers are agonised over alongside other threats, such as the possibility of final community fragmentation. It is not the irrationality or exaggeration of fears of an explosion (as the regulatory authorities saw it), nor the relative insignificance of pollution concerns alongside the more pressing problems of poverty and housing renewal (the local authority view), which we would emphasise, but instead the interlocking of preoccupations, fostering multiple and intertwined insecurities around different risks.

Acknowledgements

This chapter arises out of several pieces of research over several years by both of us in Teesside, on health patterns and air pollution, and more recently on perceptions of health, and the politics of epidemiology. We should like to thank David Sadler, John Vail and Jane Wheelock for helpful comments on an earlier draft of this chapter. We are also grateful to Mrs Maureen Taylor for her insights into the history of environmental issues in Teesside.

Notes

1 The central place accorded to pollution risks and insecurities in Beck's arguments may be linked to the larger ideological shift in Western societies from producers and production towards the perspective of the consumer and consumption. The language of 'distribution' (i.e. of 'bads'/dangers, favoured by Beck), or indeed of 'exposure' (as in orthodox assessments of pollution effects), can obscure the fact that many of our collective and cultural responses to pollution reflect our position as consumers of something unwelcome. The politics of environmentalism in capitalist societies is as much a child of our cultural preoccupations with consumption as it is a critique of those preoccupations.

2 Hudson (1989a: 336) quotes figures showing that in 1970 chemicals and steel accounted for about one-eighth of the entire Teesside land area. This was before much of the contraction of the late 1970s and 1980s, but equally was before the development of Seal Sands.

3 For example, total employment in steelmaking on Teesside fell from 23,000 in 1978 to 7,500 a mere six years later, in 1984 (Hudson, 1989a: 207).

4 Movement downriver was partly to take up available land, but was equally to ensure better access to deep water.

152 *Peter Phillimore and Suzanne Moffatt*

5 While the 'jobs at all costs' philosophy may have been increasingly difficult to sustain, it has not disappeared. The legacy of recession and lost jobs in the 1980s has been a strong 'retain what remains' ethos, and attempts to manage and control potential controversies about pollution and health need to be seen in the context of the overriding official objective of preserving existing jobs and at the same time attracting new sources of employment.

6 Wynne's discussion of 'the standardisation built into routine structures of scientific knowledge' (1996: 66) makes a similar point about neglect of local variations in environmental conditions, in the context of Cumbrian sheep farmers and the monitoring of radioactivity.

7 For example, the vicinity of chemical and steel operations (including coking) in South Bank and Grangetown, on the south side of the River Tees, has throughout this century been particularly severely affected. A report by Teesside County Borough on 'Prevailing Environmental Conditions in the District of Eston and Proposals of its Improvement' (1974) illustrates these contentions. With regard to smoke, it notes:

A marked decrease in smoke pollution is revealed over this period in Tees-side...the only location which showed no significant improvement in all Teesside was again in South Bank, at Albert House Clinic...the highest readings occurred naturally in the winter months.

For sulphur dioxide, it states:

Again a general trend to decrease in Teesside but two sites with a significant increase in pollution were Albert House Clinic, South Bank having the highest monthly average, and Normanby Clinic having the greatest increase. The largest readings were recorded in the months November to March.

And for ferric oxide:

There is no real evidence of a general improvement trend in Teesside in this pollutant and again the sites with the three highest monthly averages were in the Eston District in South Bank...Furthermore one of the sites in South Bank showed a significant increase in pollution. The highest monthly averages occurred in the spring months April to June again coinciding with the period of the local mists.

8 These quotations, and further quotations below, come from a survey conducted in 1992–3 on self-reported or perceived health in parts of Teesside and Sunderland, carried out for a wider epidemiological study examining the impact of industrial air pollution on health. That work was summarised in a report published in 1995 (TEES, 1995). Respondents were invited to add to the back of a postal questionnaire any further comments they wished to make, and these quotations are taken from the replies received.

9 Personal communication, Cleveland Emergency Planning.

10 The illustrations summarised in this section suggest that, alongside the two forms of insecurity faced by Teessiders, we should not overlook a different kind of insecurity on the part of the leading government and industrial institutions in Teesside, namely, an insecurity about the repercussions for Teesside of losing control over the discourse about risk and the environment.

11 As Beck has written, for example (1992: 45):

Protecting economic recovery and growth still enjoys unchallenged first priority. The threatened loss of jobs is played up, in order to keep the loopholes in prescribed emissions regulations wide and their enforcement lax....Those who point out risks are defamed as 'alarmists' and risk producers. Their presentation of the hazards is considered 'unproven'.

12 Enforced reliance upon 'expert' knowledge that you may in fact be sceptical about is a theme explored by Wynne (1996). We agree with his conclusion that (1996: 50): 'Lack of overt public dissent or opposition towards expert systems is taken too easily for public trust...the reality of social dependency on expert systems should not be equated with positive trust, when it could be better characterised as "virtual" trust, or "as-if" trust.'

10 Insecurities in contemporary country life

Rural communities and social change

Neil Ward and Philip Lowe

> Living and working in the country isn't easy and so much that makes rural life seem attractive to outsiders may cause despair. For some, despair may lead to suicide. In the farming community, the suicide rate is twice the national average. Farmers often live and work in isolation and may find it hard to share their problems. Never before has there been a period of such uncertainty and change in agriculture.
>
> Wherever you live and whatever you do, despair knows no boundaries. You can be isolated by your emotions, by your environment and even by those around you. Sometimes it seems life is too much to bear.
>
> *Life in the Country: Does Anybody Really Care?*, leaflet by the Samaritans (1996)

Introduction

Those wishing to draw attention to poverty or social exclusion in Britain's rural areas face a problem. Over the past two decades or so, the countryside has become increasingly equated in the public mind with middle-class affluence and security. The stereotype is one of Range Rovers and Barbour jackets, smart country cottages and picturesque villages. Of course, the ex-urban middle classes are not the only figures in this 'rural idyll'. There are the locals too, stereotypically cast in what John Short calls a 'pastoral myth'. 'The dominant image is of the happy swain, close to nature, connected to the rhythms of the earth and the seasons of the year' (Short, 1991: 30).

These images of tranquillity and contentment flourish despite evidence of the real, material hardship experienced by many people in rural areas. Detailed social research covering 3,000 households in twelve rural localities in England has recently highlighted the extent of poverty in the countryside. In nine of the twelve localities, at least 20 per cent of households were found to be at or below the poverty level (defined as an income level of less than 140 per cent of income support entitlement). Nationally, the proportion in this category was one in four (see Cloke *et al.*, 1994; Cloke, 1997). Such widespread poverty may appear paradoxical given the image of the countryside as a place of affluent contentment. Indeed, Rachel Woodward has written of 'deprivation' and popular representations of the 'rural idyll' as *contradictory discourses*. She suggests that the 'pastoral myth' serves to 'obscure lived experience in rural areas' (1996: 65). Yet recently, public concern about insecurity in rural areas has emerged in striking new forms with, for example, people marching through central London in hundreds of thousands to draw attention to the insecurities of contemporary 'country life'.

A cursory glance through the popular press in recent months yields a range of material about rural communities under threat. For example, Welsh farmers have blockaded ports to protest at Irish beef imports and the hardships and market uncertainties they have experienced through the 'beef crisis'. In a House of Commons debate on rural life, opposition MPs made and reiterated the claim that 'the countryside is under siege' (*Hansard*, 4 November 1997, cols. 176–220). Thirdly, the second Countryside March in London, organised by the pro-hunting Countryside Alliance, mobilised over 250,000 people to demonstrate on 1 March 1998 in protest at a host of social, economic and political issues impacting upon rural areas and rural communities. The proposed legislation to outlaw hunting wild mammals with dogs, catalytic in provoking this response, prompted pro-hunt campaigners to portray rural communities as marginalised and beleaguered, with their traditions and way of life under threat from an ignorant and sentimental urban majority.

This chapter takes the notion of insecurities in contemporary rural life as its starting point. But rather than lapsing into the simple dichotomy of 'town' and 'country', it instead critically examines the lived experience of insecurity among various rural communities and argues that contemporary processes of social and economic change are recasting the relationships between 'town' and 'country'. While the perceived tranquillity, changelessness and security offered by rural areas continue to attract migrants from towns and cities, new insecurities for some social groups are generated as a result. Often, insecurities emerge as part of a more general erosion of identities across society and a restructuring of social roles. The countryside has not been immune from these processes. The chapter begins by outlining the changing socio-economic composition of rural areas in Britain. It goes on to examine some of the prevailing representations of the countryside, and the relationship between these representations and notions of insecurity. It then presents two case studies of social conflict in the countryside which help to illustrate both commonalities and contrasts in the lived experience of insecurity between different social groups in rural areas. Finally, the chapter concludes with a discussion of the contribution that a sociological examination of insecurity in rural areas can make to wider debates about the insecurities of our age.

Rural restructuring and contemporary country life

The changing socioeconomic composition of Britain's rural areas over the past two decades is best understood in the context of two processes. The first of these processes concerns the diminishing role of agricultural production in rural employment, and in the local power structures shaping social change. The second concerns the urban-to-rural shift in population and employment, particularly since the 1960s. This process has turned the tide for many rural localities which are now, on aggregate, gaining people and jobs after decades of rural depopulation and urban concentration. These two processes, operating together, have profoundly altered the social composition of Britain's rural areas, and have set rural localities onto new development paths. These changes may be characterised as an overall shift in emphasis from production to consumption concerns in rural areas, with particular implications for relations between the 'urban' and the 'rural' and for lived experiences of insecurity in rural areas.

The decline of agricultural productivism

Following the Second World War, British farming experienced a technological revolution under what has been termed a national policy of 'agricultural productivism' (Lowe *et al.*, 1993). For more than four decades, a strong consensus surrounded the goals of agricultural policy. Through a system of subsidised commodity prices and public support for both agricultural research and development and business and technical advice, the agricultural sector was encouraged to increase productivity, expand output and modernise production.

Agricultural productivism was, in many respects, a successful policy. Domestic production of the main indigenous crops and productivity per acre rose dramatically. Moreover, productivism provided for the farming sector a secure economic and political environment in which to invest and expand. Marsden *et al.* (1993: 59–61) have spelled out five key dimensions to the security enjoyed by agriculture during the productivist period. The first was security of land rights; agricultural tenure legislation provided lifetime security for tenant farmers which, in turn, meant that for many *in situ* tenants freehold ownership soon became possible. Successive acts of parliament extended tenants' rights and provided statutory successional rights for three generations of tenants from within the same farming households. The second was security of land use; the 1947 Town and Country Planning Act accorded agriculture a pre-emptive claim over rural land and, by excluding other potential employers, helped ensure the supply of agricultural labour. The Act protected farmland from development pressures and established an institutional hierarchy around rural planning, with the Ministry of Agriculture, Fisheries and Food (MAFF) at the pinnacle and other rural planning bodies such as national park authorities and conservation bodies in a more constrained position *vis-à-vis* MAFF. The third dimension was financial security. The 1947 Agriculture Act and its system of guaranteed prices for agricultural products protected farmers from market fluctuations and cheap imports while encouraging them to produce more. Such financial security helped underpin accumulation within the sector, but also facilitated the concentration of production on larger and larger farm holdings and the rising value of agricultural land. Fourth was political security; in a classic example of corporatist political relations between the state and producer interests, the National Farmers' Union (NFU) enjoyed exclusive political access to the agricultural policy-making process and, in return, helped ensure the support of the farming community for agreed policies. Finally, the fifth dimension was ideological security. Agricultural productivism can be understood as a hegemonic discourse, supported not only by government and the NFU, but also by the agricultural research and advisory establishment and industrial input manufacturers such as agrochemical companies. As an ideology, productivism was linked to the national interest – by expanding production, farmers were feeding the nation and helping to address its balance of payments problems – and was cast as essentially protective of the rural environment and as a source of prosperity for rural areas.

Productivism helped give a clear sense of purpose to individuals and to various groups and organisations. Indeed, as the world became more complicated, productivism still served as the basis for a number of reliable nostrums. Its very straightforwardness was reassuring, and helped define the purpose of a number of different rural groups and functions. For example, the role of official agricultural policy was to increase output while containing costs. The remit of agricultural scientists was to boost yields. The remit of planners was to preserve, as far as possible, every acre of farmland. The remit of agricultural economists was to evaluate the efficiency of these developments in terms of their use of human and capital resources. This unity of purpose around productivism fed through into the processes of identity formation. Social roles and identities were clearly proscribed.

The different elements of security enjoyed by British agriculture under the productivist regime were largely maintained until the early 1980s. By then, however, a set of contradictions inherent in the system were becoming increasingly apparent as productivism became a victim of its own success. It was as if the security provided by agricultural productivism contained within it the seeds of its own demise which would, in turn, generate new types of insecurities for rural communities.

By the mid-1980s, the most pressing issues facing agricultural policy-makers had become how to curtail overproduction and bring down the costs of storing and disposing of surpluses, how to diversify the agricultural economy to protect farm household incomes – which, despite public subsidies, had been continually squeezed – and how to curb the damage being wrought on the rural landscape and natural resources by agricultural intensification.

The onset of the contradictions of productivism were such that food and agriculture 'increasingly became an arena of uncertainty' (Marsden *et al.*, 1993: 61), reflected in the sudden and unexpected imposition of milk quotas in 1984 to tackle over-production and broadening out into the 'farm crisis' of the late 1980s (Goodman and Redclift, 1989). In Britain, this crisis manifested itself in uncertainty within farm households about the future goals and direction of agricultural policy, rising farm bankruptcies and falling farm incomes, a search for new uses for 'surplus' agricultural land, wave upon wave of new regulations to improve food hygiene, animal welfare and rural environmental protection, and a loss of political legitimacy for the agricultural community both nationally and within rural localities.

Counter-urbanisation and social change

The second important process has been the net movement of people and jobs
from larger urban centres to more rural regions and localities. Taking population
change first, Britain has been in the vanguard internationally of counter-
urbanisation (Champion, 1994: 1504), with the first signs of the rural population
turnaround evident in the 1950s, and accelerating in the 1960s and 1970s.
Between 1951 and 1961, the population of metropolitan areas grew by 5.0 per
cent but this was matched by the growth in small towns and rural areas. Between
1961 and 1971, metropolitan population growth fell to 3.5 per cent, while what
Champion calls 'free-standing rural areas' experienced growth of 5.7 per cent.
But it was the 1970s that came to be labelled the 'counter-urbanisation decade'
by population geographers, with its evidence of a cascade of people from larger
towns and cities to smaller settlements. Although the population of metropolitan
Britain began to grow once more between 1981 and 1991, the free-standing
small towns and rural regions still saw their population grow by 6.0 per cent and
the rural areas in both metropolitan and free-standing geographical areas saw
population growth of 7.3 per cent and 7.9 per cent respectively (Champion,
1994). It would seem that the trend is far from exhausted. Recent opinion poll
surveys suggest that around 70 per cent of the English population would prefer
to live in the countryside than in urban areas (Murdoch, 1997). These patterns of
population change have transformed many parts of rural Britain, particularly
those more accessible parts of southern and central England and the rural
hinterlands of all the conurbations, into middle-class spaces. Indeed, several
commentators have questioned whether any truly *rural* localities remain. Thrift,
for example, refers to the Southeast as 'one vast created and manicured
urban/suburban space' (1987: 77).

Recent decades have also seen major changes in the nature of economic
activity and employment in rural areas. There has been a marked decline in
employment in primary industries, with large increases in the proportions
employed in financial and other services. In Britain, as in many other advanced
economies, the fastest growth in employment in recent decades has occurred in
the most rural areas (Townsend, 1993; Keeble and Tyler, 1995).

In addition to employment statistics, data on new firm formation rates show
rural areas in a favourable light in comparison with urban areas. Rural and semi-
rural counties have the highest propensities to generate new firms and, according
to Keeble *et al.* (1992), a fifth of new firm founders surveyed in remote rural areas
had actually moved to their new localities in order to set up their business, with
the perceived quality of rural life and quality of the residential environment
being important factors influencing their move. Keeble *et al.*'s study claims to
'unequivocally demonstrate a direct connection between recent environmentally
influenced population migration to England's rural areas and high rates of new
enterprise formation there' (1992: xi).

Together, these sets of changes have served to shift the dominant role and
functions of rural areas in Britain. For much of the postwar period, the
countryside was commonly conceived as a unitary national space whose primary

role was the increasingly efficient production of a growing proportion of the nation's food requirements. Such a conceptualisation was embodied in MAFF's concern with aggregate output of the main agricultural commodities and its statistical notion of the 'national farm' (Murdoch and Ward, 1997). More recently, agriculture's grip on rural space has weakened, not only as a result of the crisis of agricultural productivism, but also because of the movement into rural areas of middle-class migrants looking to find their 'place in the country'. The newcomers may, of course, have quite different ideas about how the countryside should be managed from other rural inhabitants; concerns for amenity, landscape protection and environmental quality tend to rank higher among their priorities (Murdoch and Marsden, 1994). Thus recent rural change can be understood in terms of a shift in emphasis from production to consumption concerns. The economic and political clout of primary production has been in decline at a time when more and more people want to 'consume' the countryside for its lifestyle opportunities and aesthetic delights.

These changes have also helped contribute to a shift in the relations between 'town' and 'country'. Not only are more and more people choosing to live in rural areas, but these areas also enjoy continuing popularity for leisure and recreation activities. The UK Day Visits Survey found that, in 1994, 1,300 million day visits from home were made to the British countryside. Some 62 per cent of people visited the countryside at least once a year (Countryside Recreation Network, 1996: 9), with walking or rambling the most common activity. Moreover, the diversity of types of recreational activities being pursued in the countryside seems to be growing. The Ramblers Association has around 100,000 members. Mountain biking has been claimed as Britain's fastest growing outdoor sport of the 1990s. War games and paintballing sites proliferate, as do Centre Parcs holiday villages and the construction of new golf courses (Clark *et al.*, 1994). In short, much of rural Britain at times appears set to become a vast 'play space' for the nation. These trends alter the relations between town and country, as a predominantly urban population feels it has a legitimate stake in what happens to the countryside, and articulates its views and concerns through the political system.

But this redefinition of the functions of rural areas is not welcome to all. The farming community and the residual rural working class are often cast as victims of the diffusion of urban values into rural areas, and are painted as beleaguered folk with their rural traditions and ways of life under threat from social change. 'If you're born a countryman you're harassed', complained a Cambridgeshire farmer on BBC Radio in 1995 (quoted in Cox and Winter, 1997: 75).

This notion of an 'embattled' rural community has been a common feature of a range of public and political controversies in recent years. These controversies include the foxhunting debate, the impact of the BSE crisis, concerns over farm animal welfare and the environmental problems of modern farming. Common ways of representing the countryside (or 'discourses of rurality') can be identified. One discourse usually associates the 'rural' with being somehow more 'natural', more enduring, more stable, but now under threat. In the next section, we examine some of the prevailing discourses of rurality – the common social representations of rural areas and rural life – and explore their relationships with notions of security and insecurity.

Country life and insecurity

Various researchers have examined the attractions of rural living for incomers (see Bell, 1994; Halfacree, 1994; Murdoch, 1997; Murdoch and Marsden, 1994). Halfacree (1994) suggests that two linked desires are central: the desire for a particular kind of physical environment (green, pretty, with open spaces, trees and traditional buildings) and a desire for a particular kind of social environment (safe, secure and with a sense of community). Halfacree's study of counter-urbanisers in six rural parishes in Devon and Lancashire helps highlight how a desire for security, stability and belonging underpinned the attractions of village life for incomers. He lists the following seven key social features his ex-urban in-migrants stressed as the attractions of their rural destinations: (1) the locality allowed them to escape from the 'rat race' and from society in general; (2) there was a slower pace of life, with more time for people, a feeling of being less pressurised, 'trapped' and crowded, and of feeling 'able to breathe'; (3) the area had a stronger sense of community and identity, and a sense of togetherness and less impersonality; (4) it was an area of less crime, fewer social problems and less vandalism, with a feeling of being safer at night; (5) the environment was better for bringing up children; (6) there were fewer 'non-white' people in the area; (7) the area was characterised by social quietude and propriety (Halfacree, 1994).

Such sentiments are of little surprise. They reflect an anti-urbanism which runs deep in British society (Lowe *et al.*, 1995; Robins, 1997). For example, former Prime Minister John Major defined the cultural roots of his political philosophy by invoking the imagery of 'long shadows on county grounds, warm beer, invincible green suburbs, dog lovers, old maids bicycling to holy communion through the morning mist' (Seldon, 1997: 370). In a recent interview in *Country Life* magazine his successor, Tony Blair, said 'I wouldn't live in a big city if I could help it....Bringing up children in the country is a million times better than in towns' (quoted in Robins, 1997: 72). Similar desires for security, stability and the timelessness of village life have provided a powerful attraction for rural living. But, crucially, it is a particular social class who are most able to 'buy in' to these attractions. Moreover, these sentiments also serve to cast the British countryside as a 'white' space, distinct from the multiculturalism of metropolitan areas (see Scutt and Bonnett, 1996; Agyeman and Spooner, 1997).

The class cleavages of village life were the focus of a detailed ethnographic study of a Hampshire village, dubbed 'Childerley', conducted by an American rural sociologist, Michael Mayerfield Bell. Bell examined how different social groups within the same rural community interact. The groups were differenti-ated, Bell argues, by class, with most Childerleyans coming from the 'moneyed' classes while around forty per cent were relatively poor (Bell, 1994). The two groups had distinct lifestyles and moved in relatively distinct 'sub-communities' with different cultures. The poorer villagers had a style that was 'informal, group-oriented, local, interactive and experiential', while the moneyed villagers, in contrast, had a lifestyle that was 'more formal, individualistic, far-flung, private and distanced' (1994: 52). However, these social distinctions between the different sub-communities were seen by both as being 'morally ambiguous' (1994: 78). Rather than dwell on the economic distinctions that structured their lives, Childerleyans preferred to cast themselves as 'country people'. This single identity, Bell argues, derives from pastoralism and the supposed proximity of rural life to nature. Nature, the Childerleyans would stress to Bell, is 'free from social interest' and 'something that stands apart from the selfishness, greed, power, and domination they see in social [that is, urban] life' (1994: 138). In clinging onto nature, both moneyed and poor villagers sought solace and a secure moral foundation for their lives.

But there is a risk here of overplaying a sense of harmony and cohesion. Other recent rural sociological studies have pointed to the ways newcomers to rural areas bring with them new ideas and values about how the countryside should be managed and maintained which can bring struggle and conflict. Newcomers tended to be more ready to protect their neighbourhoods against what they see as unwanted development or environmentally unacceptable practices (see Murdoch and Marsden, 1994; Ward *et al.*, 1995). But the politics of the newcomers, which would continue to preserve the countryside from new house building, industrial development or road building, also bring new social values to bear on a range of traditional rural activities. Paradoxically, in their search for stability, security and changelessness in the countryside, middle class in-migrants are themselves agents of change, bringing with them their own, often strongly held, views about the countryside and its purposes (Lowe *et al.*, 1997). Thus social change generates new pressures (and new insecurities) around certain environmental and cultural practices, prompting the claims that rural communities are 'under siege' from a 'new urban moralism' (Marr, 1996).

In the next section, two case studies are presented which document these processes and conflicts in more detail. The first concerns the increasing volume of environmental regulation of modern farming practices, and the second concerns the recent efforts to legislate to ban the hunting of wild mammals with hounds. Both issues are discussed as struggles between competing social and moral values which are frequently cast by commentators as a struggle between 'town' and 'country'. In the case studies, we pay particular attention to the prevailing social representations of the countryside invoked by the farming and hunting communities and the different lived experiences of insecurity and anxiety which they seek to articulate in their defence.

Case study: the environmental regulation of farming practices

While the mid to late 1980s may have been the high-water mark of the Thatcher governments' efforts at deregulation and liberalisation of economic life in

Britain, for the farming community the period saw the introduction of a plethora of environmental and public health regulations. The 1985 Food and Environment Protection Act legislated to tighten the environmental regulation of farming by introducing a statutory licensing system to approve new pesticide products for usage only after they had passed stringent environmental and health and safety tests. Several commonly used agricultural pesticides were withdrawn from use. Under the 1985 Act, the 1986 Control of Substances Hazardous to Health Regulations were issued, which strengthened health and safety laws governing the use of agrochemicals on farms and required that every farmer carry out a detailed risk assessment of health and environmental risks on the farm, a so-called 'COSHH assessment'.

Two years later, in 1988, there was heightened concern about the public health risks from salmonella in eggs, which became the first of several food safety scares to indict intensive farming practices. British poultry farmers saw the extermination of entire flocks of laying hens by the Ministry of Agriculture in an attempt to restore consumer confidence in eggs. Months later, Bovine Spongiform Encephalopathy (BSE, or 'Mad Cow Disease') hit the headlines and the price of beef fell by some 30 per cent. Diagnosed cases of BSE rose from 420 in 1987 to 37,755 in 1993 (Winter, 1996). Repeated media horror stories about the risks generated by modern farming helped recast the image of farmers in the public mind. Those who had once been guardians of the countryside and national heroes during the Second World War, expanding production and keeping the nation free from starvation, were being increasingly portrayed as the greedy consumers of taxpayers' money, used to subsidise the production of surplus food in ways that were both cruel to animals and polluted the environment. The sense of despair and alienation among the farming community was epitomised in the revelation that suicides amongst farmers were by the early 1990s at an all time high. Suicide became the second most common form of death among male farmers under the age of 45, and farming rose to fourth in the list of occupational suicides (Pugh, 1996: 32).

But it has not only been with the national media where the farming community has been on the defensive. Farmers also find themselves working in a changing rural world, surrounded by new neighbours with different values. In these conditions, environmental regulation can come to mean much more than merely an end to burning stubble and straw after harvest (following the 1990 Environmental Protection Act's efforts to curb air pollution) or having to wear more elaborate safety clothing when spraying crops with pesticide. Farmers feel themselves to be on the defensive in their own backyards as they increasingly encounter local criticism of their farming practices.

The ways these local social and regulatory pressures are fostering insecurity amongst farming households is well illustrated by the example of regulation to tackle water pollution from farming. The number of pollution incidents from livestock wastes more than doubled during the 1980s and dairy farming, in particular, came to be seen as a key contributory factor in declining river water quality in England and Wales. In response, the 1989 Water Act dramatically tightened the regulatory framework, empowering the new National Rivers Authority (NRA) to compel farmers to upgrade their farm waste storage equipment, and raising the maximum fine for causing water pollution from £2,000 to £20,000 (see Ward *et al.*, 1995; Lowe *et al.*, 1997; Seymour *et al.*, 1997).

The NRA talked tough, proclaiming itself to be 'Europe's strongest environmental regulator'. Its pollution inspectors not only found themselves armed with new powers but were also able to draw authority from an ascendant environmental morality which had transformed the dominant view of pollution from one of an unfortunate technical side-effect of efficient agricultural production to that of an environmental crime (Lowe *et al.*, 1997). Faced with the prospect of spending what sometimes amounted to tens of thousands of pounds of what they termed 'dead money' on installing new slurry stores, pits, pumps and settlement tanks or risk the public humiliation and expense of being taken to court and fined for pollution, many farmers came to see themselves as hapless victims of a capricious public mood, 'subject to shifts in the political and economic environment as erratic as the weather' (Lowe *et al.*, 1997: 132). Farmers felt they too were victims in the pollution saga. Often pollution occurred as a result of heavy rainfall and, in any case, specialised dairy farming – the main culprit when it came to water pollution – had been actively encouraged to modernise and intensify by successive governments. Such regulatory interference therefore challenged farmers' self-esteem as responsible countrymen as well as their farming strategies.

One strategy in the face of pollution regulation was to 'keep your head down' and hope that the problem would simply go away. This was the strategy of one farming couple we interviewed,[1] who were in their early forties with two teenage children. They had taken over the tenancy of the fifty-five-hectare dairy farm from his father in the early 1980s and had subsequently expanded the dairy herd from 40 to 50 milking cows, although pollution control facilities remained primitive. The cows were housed in concrete-floored cubicles but there were no storage facilities for the resultant liquid slurry which had to be spread on farmland daily, at great risk to local water quality, especially in wet weather. The farmer's wife mused 'I suppose we must be polluting, and our dirty water probably goes into the stream.' Most of the neighbouring farms had been visited by the NRA, but not yet theirs. The couple talked with evident dread of the possibility of an impending visit, commenting: 'Our days are numbered.' They were very worried about what scale of spending might be called for in harsh economic times: the farm's viability had tailed off sharply in the previous two years. They joked that their strategy would be to 'hide behind the sofa' when the NRA finally did call, although the wife did concede that it would be a relief to find out what expenditure might be required, to end the uncertainty and put their minds at rest.

Other farm families pointed to the ways that local social change brought new insecurities for their farming practices. 'New people' in the countryside were seen as the harbingers of the new environmental morality that saw farm waste pollution as an environmental crime. One farmer in his late fifties running a ninety-cow herd saw farming as 'under attack'. 'You get the city coming out to the countryside and telling us what to do', he said. This fear was most vividly encapsulated in the case of another farming couple in their mid-forties who were worried about social changes in their small hamlet in Devon. What was once a settlement comprising three working dairy farms had been transformed as the two neighbouring farmers had sold up, converting their farmhouses and barns into attractive residential properties. This couple were in the only remaining farm, but were now surrounded by eight private dwellings which housed newcomers. The farmer feared opposition to ordinary farming practices and wondered 'will they object to the noise and the smell?' The husband was fearful of objections, explaining, 'It's the new people in the countryside who will be imposing the regulations.' One of the biggest threats to the future of his farm was 'more town people in the countryside putting pressures on farmers....They don't like to see mud on the road and the like.' Asked to say what the biggest difficulty he faced was, he quickly replied, 'the uncertainty'.

Case study: hunting wild mammals with dogs

Our second case study concerns the efforts during 1997 and 1998 to introduce legislation – in the form of a Private Members' Bill in the House of Commons – to ban the hunting of wild mammals (such as foxes and deer) with hounds. In this debate, the protagonists quarrelled over what counts as right and proper conduct in the countryside and, again, notions of insecurity and beleaguerment were invoked by one set of interests, those who opposed a ban on hunting.

The struggle over the morality of hunting with hounds has been played out through several different discourses. Since the 1970s, those opposed to hunting with hounds have sought to occupy the moral high ground, pointing to the cruelty involved and portraying hunt followers as bloodthirsty and fanatical, driven by base instincts. Ever since Darwin's notion of human descent from the animal kingdom, animal welfarists have seen cruelty to other creatures as alarming evidence of the beast in man. They have assumed the mantle of a civilising force committed to rooting out bestial practices in striving for a higher humanity not wallowed in the evolutionary mire.

More recently, the counter-attack from the hunting lobby has drawn upon a similar vein of argument – of civilisation versus nature – but in which the moral polarity is reversed. Those opposed to hunting are thus portrayed as uncaring 'townies' who, out of ignorance, condemn an age-old rural custom. Hunting, it is argued, provides not only a vital pest control service and support for the rural economy and employment, but is also an integral tradition of rural life, part of the 'social glue' that binds rural communities together. Robin Hanbury-Tenison, former Chief Executive of the Countryside Alliance, recently spoke of how 'the countryside is a fragile entity held together through the skills of a small number of people. In some of the remoter parts of Britain the only cohesive force in the community is the hunt' (quoted in Daniel, 1997: 24). From this perspective, hunting – and thus by extension rural life – are poorly understood by a cocooned and naively sentimental metropolitan society that views country folk through a distant haze of rose-tinted hypocrisy. There are echoes here of a cultural pessimism with urban culture – seen as shallow and ephemeral but intolerant in its squeamishness – threatening to overwhelm a rural culture whose closeness to nature makes it more authentic, timeless and rooted.

These claims by the pro-hunting lobby have proved potent. They culminated in a 100,000-strong rally in Hyde Park in July 1997 under the banner of 'Listen to the Countryside', followed in 1998 by a second march involving more than twice as many people. Statistics were collected on the jobs that depend upon hunting as a measure of the threat a ban would pose to the rural economy, and testimonies were gathered from those who are normally taciturn and unheard, the farriers, the stable-lads, the kennelmen and so on – the humble countrymen in line to be victims. One elderly Cumbrian shepherd complained to a television crew: 'I think town folk should leave us alone up here. They want to look after their own.'[2] His local huntsman saw the proposed legislation as an attack on 'tradition' and explained, 'It's a proud thing for me to be the Huntsman of the Blencathra [Foxhounds]....Tradition is all important. Tradition and heritage are being lost all over the world, and now the sad reflection is that they're trying to kill it off in this country.' The same huntsman complained in the *Independent* of how he would lose everything: 'Number one, my job. Number two, my home. Number three, my vehicle' (quoted in Hart-Davis, 1997: 16).

It was estimated that the equivalent of around 900 full-time jobs were provided directly by hunts in Britain, and these would be the jobs most at risk from a ban on hunting with hounds (Cobham Resource Consultants, 1997: 57). One of these jobs belongs to Oliver Hill, Huntsman with the Hurworth Hunt in North Yorkshire, who lives with his wife in a tied cottage that comes with the job. He explained: 'It's all I've done all my life. People say you can retrain. But I'm a *countryman*. I don't want to go and work in the town. I've lived all my life in the country. I was brought up in the country. I don't want to go and work in the town. It would be totally alien to me, and there are few enough jobs in the countryside as it is.' His wife added her thoughts on what a ban on hunting with hounds would mean: 'It would be devastating. We would lose everything. We would lose our entire way of life....Ollie's job. We would lose our house.' Thus the insecurities faced by such folk are brought to the foreground by those who defend hunting with hounds. Legislation to ban hunting will, it is argued, damage their local rural economies, destroy their jobs and serve to unravel a whole rural way of life.

Insecurity and lived experience: lessons from the countryside

So where do these arguments about threats to rural society draw their strong moral appeal from? The answer lies in enduring beliefs in the sanctity and purity of the countryside. Such beliefs, in their modern form, emerged out of the Victorian and Edwardian reactions to industrialisation and its consequences for town and city life. In Britain, industrial society was constructed around a sharp, if ultimately elusive, distinction between nature and society (Latour, 1993). Whereas science and technology sought to subjugate nature, the industrial city separated people physically from the natural world. Rural areas, stripped of most of their population and their pre-industrial economic activities, became specialised spaces for producing food for the urban population. In this way the rural became equated with the agricultural. However, the rural also acquired strong associations during the period of industrialisation: it was seen as where most city dwellers had come from, and for many it also represented the last vestiges of their contacts with nature.

Rural values thus figured strongly in cultural reactions to the disruptions of urban industrialisation, and became a central feature in the definition and assertion of national identity against what was seen as the rootless and homogenising cosmopolitanism of the industrial age (Lowe *et al.*, 1995). The countryside was thus constructed as 'natural' and became a source of moral affirmation and condemnation. In contrast to the supposed innocence of rural life, the city was perceived as corrupting, not only of traditional morality and social hierarchies, but also of nature, through industrial pollution (Lowe *et al.*, 1997). This conception of the countryside served as an important unifying myth for industrialising society, cutting across the conflicting classes and strata of urban society and emphasising their common rural roots and dependencies.

But these rural myths often bear little relation to present-day realities. Late twentieth-century Britain is a highly mobile and thoroughly urbanised society, with complex, although often unrecognised, urban–rural interdependencies. It is one in which, for example, many of those who hunt have urban livings and most of those who live and work in the countryside are not involved in hunting in any way. A survey carried out by market researchers Produce Studies Group in 1997 found that only 9 per cent of those surveyed in rural areas ever participated in hunting (quoted in Daniel, 1997: 24), and a MORI public opinion poll in October 1997 found that 74 per cent of the 'rural population' would like to see an end to fox-hunting (RSPCA advertisement, *Guardian* 25 November 1997: 8).

Rural society is far from being an atavistic enclave. For example, it is more mobile than urban society, with higher levels of car ownership. Modern agriculture is also a high-tech, capital-intensive activity, often described as 'industrialised'. Indeed, many of the recent pollution and public health controversies – the contamination of beef, organophosphorus pesticides and sheep dip, the pollution of rivers, streams and drinking water supplies – have originated in the rural sphere. Conventional notions about town and country are thus being turned upside down, which is deeply unsettling for those who feel their lives anchored by such notions and the verities that cluster around them.

In the hunting debate, claims about insecurity were used by those in favour of hunting to draw attention to their plight and win sympathy for their cause. Likewise, when faced with environmental regulations to restrict farming practices, and with local social change bringing its new environmental morality, *some* farmers invoke the insecurities and uncertainties that now surround the struggle to make a living from agriculture in a changing rural world. For them, farmers and hunters are engaged in the timeless and vital task of husbanding nature. In stressing 'naturalness' and tradition, these groups are drawing on a rich vein of public sentiment about the role and function of the countryside. By invoking economic discourses about job losses in the rural economy, pro-hunting campaigners seek to cast the staff of hunts as hapless victims, whose current insecurities are generated by an alien urban moralism.

In this chapter, we have sought to examine how notions of insecurity and beleaguerment are invoked by certain actors when faced with the threatened imposition of new forms of social regulation in rural areas. Thus our concern has been to shed light on how some communities in rural areas – the farming community or the hunting community, for example – can draw on a particular discourse about country traditions which casts them as under threat from wider social change. Crucially, it is in response to these 'external' threats that these communities are being constructed.

For those invoking notions of insecurity and uncertainty, strong traditions exist which draw on narratives of continuity, of 'the present as a living embodiment of the past, an unquestioned absolute' (Cox and Winter, 1997: 82). Ironically, the 'siege mentality' that has recently been whipped up around the social regulation of some 'rural' activities can serve to powerfully cement the social cohesion of the group under threat. Thus it was widely remarked in press coverage of the second Countryside March in 1998 that the occasion mobilised an alliance of groups across class divides as large landowners and well-heeled country sports enthusiasts marched alongside humble farm and estate workers. Indeed, the march organisers were keen to stress this point, even though there was some evidence that rural workers or hunt members were compelled by their landlords, employers or hunts to attend the march (Beckett, 1998).

This chapter has illustrated how contemporary struggles over the rights and wrongs of country life can be understood in terms of the forging and mainte-nance of social identities or their defence in the face of social change. In this context, the chapter has shown how insecurities often emerge as part of the more general erosion of identities across society and a restructuring of social roles. The distinction between town and country continues to be one of the central defining dichotomies of modern society. It helps provide sites from which social identities are fixed or anchored. While the city becomes a site for the expression of a more open and multicultural society, the countryside has become a site where 'members of the middle class find a welcome retreat from the "confused" nature of urban life and, in so doing, find a sense of belonging which upholds the long-established, but constantly re-worked, forms of identity which are intrinsic to Anglo-centric culture' (Lowe *et al.*, 1995: 82). Such identities, with their connotations of stability and affluence, may of course serve to conceal the material hardships generated by poverty and social exclusion in rural areas. At the same time, the hardships and real insecurities faced by some groups in rural areas have been exploited politically by rural elites to protect their privileges and lifestyles.

Notes

1   See Lowe *et al.* (1997), Ward *et al.* (1995) and Seymour *et al.* (1997) for details of the conduct of our empirical research on farm pollution regulation among Devon dairy farmers and pollution regulators.
2   The quotations in this section, where not otherwise indicated, are drawn from a BBC North documentary, *Close Up North*, broadcast on 20 November 1997.

11 The road to nowhere

Youth, insecurity and marginal transitions

Robert MacDonald

> Young people already disadvantaged become more vulnerable to processes which disadvantage them further...for a growing minority of young people, the process of transition is destructive and debilitating. Policies directed at young people have increasingly worsened the opportunities and possibilities for this age group.
>
> (Williamson, 1993: 43)

This chapter concerns itself with some of the processes, problems and policies encountered by working-class young people as they carve out transitions from school towards adulthood in the context of high unemployment and a rapidly changing labour market. It focuses upon the experiences of young men and women who engage first-hand with the insecurities of youth transitions no longer underpinned by regular employment. It explores their involvement with more marginal, precarious and non-standard forms of working.

The chapter begins by describing how youth transitions in the UK have been restructured over the past thirty years, and illustrates this by examining the worsening of opportunities for young people in one area of particularly dramatic economic change (Teesside in the Northeast of England). This is followed by discussion of qualitative research undertaken with young Teessiders who, in the first instance, have attempted to join 'the enterprise culture' of self-employment and new firms and, in the second case, have engaged in 'fiddly jobs' (undeclared, cash-in-hand work while officially unemployed). The chapter concludes by contrasting these accounts of insecure livelihoods with those provided by underclass theorists, and by questioning the usefulness of government policies towards the 'welfare dependent' young unemployed.

The insecurity of youth transitions

Throughout the 1980s and 1990s, numerous writers have described how young people – differentiated by social class, gender, ethnicity, locality and education – follow different paths during the late teenage years as they leave school, enter the labour market and seek adult status and identity (for example, Banks *et al.*, 1992). These accounts all stress how these individual paths of transition have been transformed over the past twenty to thirty years by the virtual collapse of the youth labour market in the early part of the 1980s (Maguire and Maguire, 1997).

The sharp decline in the number of apprenticeships for skilled employment and in the number of entry-level jobs for young people has resulted in a series of policy interventions and other developments, most notable of which have been the introduction of widespread youth training provision and the expansion of further education to cater for those who might previously have entered jobs (see Roberts, 1995). As Craine (1997) points out, sociologists have deployed a series of adjectives – 'long', 'broken', 'extended', 'fractured', 'uneasy', 'protracted' – to try to capture the changes which have as a consequence been wrought in youth transitions.

Central to many of these accounts is the view that changes in the world of work, education and training have extended the youth phase. Coupled with welfare 'reforms', which have reduced entitlement to a range of state benefits (Dean, 1997), these changes have increased the dependency of young people on their families and delayed access to identities and activities which were previously regarded as signifying adult status (earning a wage, leaving the parental home, the establishment of long-term partnerships, parenthood). Family and housing transitions have thus been restructured for young people. Some progress has been made in unravelling the inter-relationships between these different aspects of youth transition (Griffin, 1985, 1993; Jones and Wallace, 1992; Coles, 1995) and the way that the profound restructuring of one of them (such as labour market transitions) impacts upon the others (such as the ability to form independent households, partnerships and families). Some have argued that youth transitions in the UK are beginning to emulate more closely transitions in continental Europe and the USA and that we here are now also seeing the emergence of a life phase described as 'post-adolescence' (see Jones and Wallace, 1992).

For some (see Chisholm *et al.*, 1990), this reformation of the youth phase is indicative of post-modernising trends in which the structuring hold of class (and the other social divisions associated with modernity) upon young people's identities, outlooks and activities has declined. They see new 'detraditionalised' and individualised routes to adulthood being pursued. Furlong and Cartmel (1997) provide a good review of these debates. Drawing upon a metaphor first developed by Roberts (1995), they compare the models of social reproduction and youth transitions which pertained to the postwar decades with railway journeys in which school-leavers, depending upon their class, gender and education, board different trains bound for predetermined destinations. Opportunities for personal decision making, to switch track and destination, were limited. However, 'we can best describe the changes occurring over the last twenty years as the wholesale closure of the railways' (Furlong and Cartmel, 1997: 6). The fragmented and allegedly individualised youth transitions of late modernity, through which young people move from class of origin to class of destination, are now compared to car journeys in which:

> The driver is able to select his or her route from a vast number of alterna-tives....The experience of driving one's own car rather than travelling as a

passenger on public transport leads to the *impression* that individual skills and decisions are crucial to the determination of outcomes…

(Furlong and Cartmel, 1997: 6–7, my emphasis)

That youth transitions have been radically restructured in the latter part of the twentieth century is not really in dispute.[1] My research on how working-class young people have experienced and responded to the dismantling of the structures which secured and framed youth transitions cast serious doubt upon these fashionable ideas of greater individualisation of transitions, as well as more sweeping postmodern claims. It is to the context of this research that I turn in the next section.

Insecure transitions: the case of Teesside

Teesside, in the northeast of England, exemplifies the transformations in youth transition in dramatic form. The speed and scope of the economic decline of a place which, as recently as the 1960s, was world famous for its industrial success provides for a particularly telling case study. It is difficult to think of another place in the UK where the change in economic fortunes has been so profound; and while there are aspects of Teesside's social composition (such as its quite small non-white, ethnic population) and economic heritage (for instance, the predominance of heavy manufacturing industry) which *might* limit its comparative value, it is likely that the processes and experiences described here will at least be familiar to similar old industrial regions in other parts of the UK and Europe (Hudson, 1989).

In 1965, the conurbation had an unemployment rate of 1.5 per cent. Full employment for men in relatively well-paid, long-term and skilled jobs in Teesside's chemical, steel and heavy engineering industries provided the economic security which underpinned social reproduction, cohesion and stability. As a result of fierce global competition, shifting policies towards nationalised industries and over-concentration in a narrow industrial base, restructuring and redundancy on a massive scale ensued (MacDonald and Coffield, 1991). Between 1975 and 1986, one-quarter of all jobs and one-half of all manufacturing jobs were lost (Cleveland County Council, 1986). In the 1980s Teesside became notorious for having some of the highest levels of unemployment in mainland Britain and joblessness persists at high levels in the 1990s, touching 40 per cent in some localities.

The impact on young people has been particularly severe. In 1974, when the 'lads' in Willis's famous study were 'learning to labour', the young men of Teesside were able to do the same (Willis, 1977). Then, 54 per cent of school-leavers moved into jobs or apprenticeships at the docks, steel foundries or chemical works.[2] By 1994, just twenty years later, only 4 per cent of school-leavers moved into work. Expanded youth training and further education provision now soaks up those left without 'proper jobs'. Around one-quarter enter youth training annually, and about one-half of sixteen-year-olds now continue in education: a figure which is still low by national standards, but which represents a substantial increase in an area with little widespread tradition of non-compulsory education. The remainder fall into Williamson's 'Status Zero' category (i.e. who are not in employment, training or education and, since the 1988 Social Security Act, are not usually entitled to unemployment benefits) (Williamson, 1997). This is a group which, again by rather sketchy official figures, seems to be increasing to around 16 per cent of the cohort.

Of course, these are only first destination statistics. The longer-term transitions of young Teessiders are even less clear. Despite the depressed nature of their local labour market, some will avoid social and economic insecurity in their early careers and make 'successful' transitions into mainstream employment in the long term. Many of these will be those from more socially advantaged, affluent families who are still able to trade on cultural capital and educational qualifications for relatively secure and rewarding employment. The widening of access to further and higher education may also have set in place new routes to more secure and rewarding futures for some working-class young women and men.

It is possible that the restructuring of the Teesside labour market over the past thirty years has brought with it a greater range of employment opportunities for young women as service sector employment replaces manufacturing industry. Yet we know that many of these sort of jobs are low-paid, low-status, low-skilled, part-time and temporary (Teesside TEC, 1995) and are unlikely to provide widespread, long-term, stable and regular employment careers for working-class young women (or men). Craine (1997) reports that one gendered response to this sort of restricted structure of opportunities is 'the mothering option', where young working-class women seek recourse to the traditionally accepted status and activities of motherhood. In one neighbourhood of Teesside (Hardwick) 27 per cent of 16–24-year-old women are lone parents (Teesside TEC, 1997).

Willis (1984) was one of the first to speculate about the impact of high and sustained rates of unemployment upon the identities and activities of young working-class adults. The wealth of studies on these subjects which have been undertaken since the early 1980s have, however, had little to say about the way that young people engage in more precarious and uncertain labour market transitions in which non-standard work outside employment work looms large. Formerly secure, safe and normal transitions for working-class young people from school at sixteen into working-class jobs have been replaced by transitions in which the movement to working-class adulthood is no longer framed by standard employment.[3]

One of my informants described Teesside as 'Schemeland', a place in which sisters, brothers, friends, relatives were all attempting to construct working lives through episodic involvement with a (to me) baffling array of government schemes. 'Government scheming' is, however, only one aspect of the cyclical transitions that interviewees described. 'Cyclical' is used here to denote the lack of any sense of progression or forward movement normally associated with notions of 'career' or 'transition'. The biographies that interviewees recounted certainly contained numerous and different labour market statuses patterned over time (and often within quite a short work history), but that these were somehow linked together, providing stepping stones upwards and onwards towards improved occupational locations, was not the case. Transitions were cyclical, and involvement with one or other of the various 'options' which presented themselves would often lead back to the same situation (typically poverty, unemployment and economic inactivity).

These marginal and insecure transitions usually incorporated permutations of training (on government schemes) and sometimes education (in further and occasionally higher education), together with more informal economic activity and non-standard employment, such as attempts to become self-employed, unpaid volunteering, undeclared paid work while in receipt of benefits and, of course, periods of completely inactive unemployment. Between 1988 and 1995, in separate research projects, I interviewed over 300 working-class men and women of different ages and ethnicities who had been engaged with these sorts of work.[4] About half of the interviews were with 16–25 year-olds. In the following sections, I draw upon these to illustrate some of the aspects of the lived experiences of young people who made insecure transitions.

Self-employed survival

My first studies of Teesside youth concerned the efforts of the young unemployed to establish themselves in self-employment through running small businesses and co-operatives. The book I published with Frank Coffield in 1991 was entitled *Risky Business?*, the title of which sums up much of the experience of the so-called 'young entrepreneurs' whom I interviewed.

The businesses these 'young entrepreneurs' established tended to be in the service sector, trading on skills developed as leisure interests in their teenage years. For instance, young women would become clothes designers and retailers or mobile hairdressers and beauticians. Young men typically became car mechanics and car valets, or computer games programmers. Virtually all the businesses were 'micro-firms' employing few if any employees, and virtually all had drawn upon support from the government's Enterprise Allowance Scheme (EAS) to start up.

The motivations of these young people to become self-employed were rooted in their personal experiences of a local labour market which had, up to that point, offered them little in the way of sustained and rewarding employment. Unemployment was for all a common and recurrent feature of their early careers. This pushed them into considering any alternative to continuing joblessness. Donna (aged nineteen, from Hartlepool) was typical in this respect. She had had a succession of part-time, temporary jobs and government schemes since leaving school, interspersed with periods of unemployment:

RM: What was it about self-employment that was attractive to you?
DONNA: It was a job. I wasn't – if someone had said here's a job, I would have took that. It was just that it was a way of working, that's all...//...I've

worked for lots of people. I'm quite happy working for employers...do you
see what I mean? It was just a job, you know.

Although motivations to start up were, in this sense, 'negative' and an example of what Storey and Strange (1992) call 'forced entrepreneurship', the
interviewees were able as well to identify positive features to self-employment, at
least in its early stages (feelings of autonomy and independence in their new
work, the promise of financial success, pride in self-achievement).

The experiences the interviewees reported of 'the enterprise culture' were
strikingly similar, and gender played surprisingly little role in differentiating the
accounts gathered. However, a proportion of the women who were young
mothers reported that self-employment offered them flexibility. Having their own
businesses – with flexible hours and a base at home – allowed them to maintain
household and family commitments at the same time as keeping a foot in the
external labour market (to which they hoped to return more completely in later
years). As noted above, the type of business started also reflected gender
stereotypes, while in their relationships with banks and other potential business
funders, young women felt doubly disadvantaged by their gender and by their
age.

Issues of ethnicity also played some role in the decision to start a business.
British Pakistani informants interpreted their labour market marginality in terms
of racial discrimination. Ranjeet, for instance, was a nineteen-year-old who was
running a small grocery on an estate in Middlesbrough. Prior to this, Ranjeet
had gained good 'A' level qualifications and had hoped to enter training for junior
management employment. Ranjeet showed me sheaves of rejection letters she
had received and talked graphically of how promising approaches to potential
employers (by telephone) terminated abruptly when her ethnicity became clear
to them. For young Asian people like her, issues of ethnicity and racism impacted
most directly upon self-employment in terms of the decision to start a business,
rather than upon the subsequent experience of self-employment.

Once trading commenced, the interviewees revealed themselves to be serious
in their intentions, committed to their businesses and prepared to go to
extraordinary lengths to keep them afloat. This is revealed in the bare equation
of hours worked for money earned. The young self-employed were working on
average around 60 hours per week, but even this never reaped substantial
reward. Pay typically never rose much above £1 per hour. It should be noted that
some of these young adults had families to support through these new firms.

Attention can also be drawn to the difficult social–psychological regimes
under which they were working. The strong attachment of the self-employed to
their businesses generated desperate feelings amongst the sample and was tied
directly to their perception that for them, self-employment was the last chance to
escape the poverty and monotony of long-term unemployment: to resist long-
term socio-economic exclusion and to gain greater economic security. Duncan
had been self-employed as a freelance cartoonist before closing his business and
gaining a job in a graphic design company. He said:

If this job hadn't come along I don't know what would have happened...it got dispiriting. You thought, well, there is no point in packing it in 'cos there's nothing there if you do. But you wonder whether it is worth carrying on with nothing coming in [when the £40 per week EAS grant ceased]. You were putting in a hell of a lot of hours and getting nothing back at all. Some days I was working from eight in the morning 'til eleven at night. Some weeks nothing at all. Nobody expects to pay for anything and everything's supposed to be done yesterday...It was just unfortunate. It seemed the only option at the time.

The following passage is from an interview with Fraser, who had been a self-employed joiner. He describes very well how 'becoming your own boss' does not resolve – but adds to – the general experiences of insecurity which motivated the move into self-employment and which, in turn, generated an arguably *over*committed approach to these new businesses:

Well, when it isn't going too good you're directly responsible. Security is one of the main things. I was never sure what would happen. I always hoped the next six months go as well as the last six months and you never quite know. You can see about ten feet in front of you but after that it's a bit hazy. That's one of the main disadvantages: the insecurity....It does get a bit depressing because you start to think to yourself what am I doing? Where am I going? It's a one-man band and nobody is looking after you...//...it's very easy to keep flogging a dead horse. You are very enthusiastic and you can go up the wrong road and keep putting in 100 per cent, plugging away and plugging away, when really you should be taking a step back and thinking about what you are doing.

Extensive involvement with various government training and 'make-work' schemes had not resulted in employment; creating your own job was all that was left. These perceptions led informants to expend enormous effort in their businesses. Self-employment became self-exploitation. Insecurity and fear of failure drove them to extreme lengths to maintain their businesses. Belinda, who had been involved in a small catering firm, captured these anxieties well:

I was putting everything I had into it and getting nothing back at all. I was leaving the house at 5.30 a.m. and not getting back in 'til 5.30 p.m. And all of that for £40 per week, which to me was peanuts. When we were doing outside work we would be working until the early hours of the morning as well. I would just come home and sleep. I thought as though we were just flogging our guts out for nothing at the end of the day...//...I didn't realise how much it can kill you. We were absolutely shattered. It was just a nightmare. I used to be seething that we were up to our eyeballs in debt...I used to cry all the time. I used to say 'I'm not going back – it's awful'. I used to be like that about twice a week. Worried about how much debt we were in and what we would do if we closed down – how we would survive.

This fear of failure led many to continue their trade beyond the point where it made commercial sense to continue. A number of those whose businesses collapsed commented that they should have decided to cease self-employment considerably earlier. Greg, the one person who had been running a manufacturing firm, was after four years in business employing over thirty staff and had won awards for 'Young Businessman of the Year', presented to him by Richard Branson. Shortly afterwards, two important clients failed to honour debts and his business joined the swelling list of new, small firms that went to the wall in Teesside in the early 1990s.

The collapse of businesses which were generally undercapitalised, run by people with little training and no experience in business management and which competed in a saturated and highly competitive marketplace, often brought with it devastating psychological and material consequences. Debts would often run into several thousand pounds, several were declared bankrupt, two informants lost family homes as a result and all those whose businesses had closed described a deep sense of failure and despair.

Trevor, for instance, was in his mid-twenties and had been running a car mechanics firm for a little over a year before it collapsed. The problems the business faced were numerous. To give a few examples: Trevor had had only one day's training in business management, had not 'served his time' as a mechanic (though he had picked up some basic know-how in his youth), was only able to invest a few hundred pounds, employed his 'friend' to work with him (who, it later transpired, had been stealing cash from the firm) and, despite the nature of his business, Trevor did not possess a driving licence.

These fundamental flaws did not prevent him from enrolling on the government's Enterprise Allowance Scheme, but soon after starting up he quickly faced further problems (clients refusing to pay for his work, competitors selling him faulty car parts, steeply rising rent bills for his garage, intense local competition). He worked exceedingly hard for very little financial return. Trevor, when asked to give examples of his working practices, described how he had bought one second-hand car for £300, spent a week repairing it and then sold it on for £375: close to sixty hours work for a 'profit' of £75 (from which he had to pay for the running costs of the firm as well as wages for himself and his employee).

In the main, interviewees explained their business failures in terms of their own personal shortcomings. Trevor's case is again illustrative of this. I met him again – in a youth enterprise agency – a week *after* he had ceased trading. He was now pawing over his original business plan in an attempt to discover what mistake he had included in it and, by rewriting the plan, to rectify this error on paper and to ease the sense of failure he felt. For these informants, experience of business closure was the latest in a series of perceived personal failures, ranging from their early 'failure' to achieve useful qualifications in school through to their 'failures' to find employment after participation in training schemes.

The experience that Trevor (and Belinda, Duncan, Fraser and many others) had of self-employment were not isolated ones, peculiar to the individuals who ran these failed firms. They were typical of an 'enterprise culture' which encouraged some of the least able and least qualified to attempt self-employment in the harshest of commercial environments. To paraphrase C. Wright Mills (1959), these were taken to be private troubles of their own making rather than the failures of public policy or their local labour market. As a consequence, many of these informants were, astonishingly, attempting to establish further new enterprises, convinced of the fact that if they worked a little harder, took a little less income, competed a little more aggressively (with similar businesses run by similar people in similar ways) then they too might eventually join the handful of young adults who had been able to establish long-term commercial ventures.

In 1995, the fortunes of those young adults who had stepped into self-employment at the end of the 1980s were surveyed (see MacDonald, 1996b). The results confirmed earlier fears. Of the seventy-one 'budding entrepreneurs' interviewed in 1989, only fourteen remained in business (around 20 per cent of the original sample) and only four of these could be categorised (by themselves or by myself) as being in any way successful. For these new recruits, the 'enterprise culture' promulgated by government ministers and business leaders during the 1980s meant nothing more than survival self-employment, which was motivated by, and which returned them to, the insecurities and unemployment of their local economy.

Fiddly jobs

The second example from this body of fieldwork concerns what are known locally as 'fiddly jobs'. These refer to casual work which is undertaken by people who are in receipt of unemployment benefits, payment for which goes undeclared to the benefit authorities. This sort of work represents one aspect of the growing informality of work relations which may be particularly relevant to localities in which economic restructuring has been widespread. The general findings of my study of the fiddly jobs undertaken by workers of all ages has been presented elsewhere (MacDonald, 1994). Here I will concentrate on the experience of teenagers and younger adults and comparison will be made with the insecure experiences of survival self-employment described above.

Self-employment and fiddly work clearly possess different normative and ideological status. The former is encouraged by state schemes; the young self-employed are applauded by government ministers and are presented with awards by national celebrities. The latter is the subject of screaming tabloid headlines, heavy policing by the Department of Social Security and young adults who engage in this sort of work are labelled 'dole cheats', 'scroungers' and 'benefit fraudsters'. Yet my research uncovered a great deal that was common to both of these non-standard ways of working. Furthermore, the accounts gathered about fiddly work and about self-employment should *not* be regarded as accounts of particularly different elements of the labour market or of the experiences of separate groups of young adults. Those who did fiddly work had in many cases been self-employed (and vice versa). Some of the self-employed had spent time running their businesses while unemployed (and receiving benefits) before making their trade more legitimate. Mary and Jane, before starting up officially, worked for a year in order to raise £1,000 to invest in their business. In this and the following passage we see the way that young adults perceived the morality of their endeavours and resisted the more usual labelling of these activities as wrong, deviant and fraudulent.

RM: A lot of people would say, though, that what you are doing is wrong, that it's benefit fraud.

MARY: It depends on what you're doing it for, if it's wrong or not. Like us, we're doing it for a reason – to raise the £1,000 to go on EAS. There's nothing wrong with that. It should be allowed. It's the people that are making £500 per week that annoy me. They're doing people who need the money out of it. So long as it's fairly small-scale there's no harm in it. The amount of dole money that people get – they can't afford to live on that.

Others, on closing their firms, continued trading irregularly 'on the fiddle'. Lynne, for instance, had become unemployed again following the collapse of her business. She now owed debts of around £10,000 which she was trying to pay off from the undeclared income derived from a fiddly job as a part-time secretary. She said:

If it's there [the chance of extra income], you can't really ignore it. I work two days a week and if I declared it they'd just knock it off my dole. It's just a way of keeping your head above water really.../... I'm just being enterprising, using my initiative.

Managers of Department of Employment and Department of Social Security fraud investigation branches concurred with the other informants to this study that fiddly work was inspired by 'need not greed'. The needs that motivated young people were diverse.

Firstly, and most obviously, there was material need. Similar to those in Jordan *et al.*'s study (1992), these people were struggling to maintain personal and/or household incomes in the absence of decent employment and under benefit regimes which only resourced basic subsistence. Muriel, who was in her early twenties, briefly worked full-time as a care assistant for elderly people. With her unemployment benefits, this gave a total of £70 per week income. Jane, who was twenty-five and been doing cleaning work on the fiddle, described it as 'a necessary evil – you've got to take every penny that you can'.

A group of young men who had been subcontracted to undertake physically demanding maintenance and cleaning work under hazardous conditions at a steel plant were paid £2 per hour and, again like the self-employed, were expected to work exceedingly long hours. One of them, Scott (aged eighteen), reported:

You're down underneath in like this sewer. You're not insured for the job because it's fiddly. You're not even meant to be there, you're signing on. Once I was standing there and this big lump of hot metal crashed through and landed five feet from me. I thought 'I have to get out of this'. A mate was working Christmas Eve and he got sacked cos he wouldn't work a triple shift through Christmas. I've known blokes be down there four days at a time, kipping in the shed. It was diabolical. They just used you because there was that many people desperate for work, to keep families going.

Scott was asked in more detail about why he had sought out such poorly remunerated, exploitative and dangerous work:

You've got to be on the dole to understand. I used to go on the fruit machines: addicted. Money after money was going in. And there were a lot of people worse off than me. But your attitude is when you're desperate you do anything. You're not bothered.

Secondly, informants described their need to demonstrate to others (to families, future employers and the world at large) that they were willing to work. They were unhappy to be perceived as idle, unproductive and unemployable. Fiddly work allowed them to show their work commitment to a society which deemed them to be literally useless. Like those in the sample who had undertaken voluntary work, it allowed them to demonstrate to themselves that they could still work, even if officially categorised as long-term unemployed. Thus, fiddly work preserved some remnants of self-respect and personal pride for a group of people whose experiences of unemployment had been detrimental to these aspects of their identity.

Thirdly, fiddly jobs served to maintain work disciplines and to limit the deleterious impact of long-term unemployment upon their potential as employees. Fiddly work demanded that they display the 'right' sort of attitudes to work (to be willing to graft for low pay, to be punctual, to be reliable, to take up work each and every time it was offered) and to the social relationships that underwrote this sort of work (to obey the rules of trust and non-disclosure upon which it was premised). Kenny talked about the importance of these informal social rules and expectations in getting fiddly work:

If you've got a contact you're working for and you're working well and you have got a good reputation – you get passed on. 'So and so needs a job doing.' It just gets around. The important thing is that initial contact, that initial break.

Fourthly, and related to the above, engagement in this casual work tied young people into the informal social networks through which both illicit and licit employment was distributed in their locality. Informants said that they needed to engage in this sort of casual work if they were ever to gain access to more legitimate employment. They reported that the same social networks and informal gatekeepers could provide entry into both 'proper jobs' and 'fiddly jobs'.

Ironically, the young people who engaged in fiddly work fitted the model of the entrepreneurial personality promoted through 'education for enterprise' texts (for example, Gibb, 1987) much better than did those who were occupied in survival self-employment. They had to 'network' with other similarly peripheral workers, to take greater risks, to be ever responsive to invitations to do fiddly jobs, to hunt out scraps of jobs wherever they could be found and to be able to market themselves (their skills, their experiences and their trustworthiness) to those who might be able to offer work.

In summary, this sort of work was typically insecure, even more so than that provided through self-employment, and was usually short-lived (lasting a few days or weeks), irregular, poorly remunerated, risky (in terms of the threat to benefits), often laborious and sometimes physically dangerous. It was very much perceived as second best to having a 'proper job' and was taken up by young women and men who had not succeeded in finding more long-term, regular, gainful employment.

Solving insecurity: from welfare to work?

The struggles of young people to become self-employed or to eke out a living through fiddly work are understandable as the survival strategies of working-class youth facing a labour market in which the structures which previously processed youth transitions have been dismantled. The apparent 'choices' and 'opportunities' presented by the changing culture of work are illusory. The similarities in the general experiences that the young people described in these pages had of self-employment, fiddly jobs and the other diverse, 'new', non-standard forms of work outweighed the differences between them. The overarching themes of their accounts were about the persistence of insecurity, the lack of opportunity, the limits to choice, the depressing acceptance of these precarious and short-lived alternatives to 'real work', and the pessimism with which they viewed their futures.

Earlier, we noted how Furlong and Cartmel (1997) compared youth transitions in the late 1990s to individualised car rather than collective rail journeys. In extending this analogy we might suggest that working-class youth still await the (re)construction of more secure and scenic routes along which to progress. The young people in these studies found themselves forever circulating roundabouts with a variety of exits to choose between, but which were all routes back to the insecurities and impoverishment of social and economic exclusion. The postmodern rhetoric of individual liberty which is gaining currency in the theorisation of youth transitions would seem, to borrow Robinson and Gregson's phrase, to be 'nothing more than a cruel joke' (1992: 46).

Indeed, interviewees shared a remarkably mainstream, 'old-fashioned' belief in the value of work and of providing for oneself and one's family; values which led them to engage in labour which was hard and poorly paid, insecure and risky. In places like Teesside, these cultural values no longer find obvious outlets in employment for many young working-class adults. The cultural values of the young working class, steeped in traditions, practices and memories of their parents' generation, have not kept pace with changing economic circumstances. This is quite contrary to accounts which regard the cultural identities of contemporary youth as being constructed chiefly in relation to consumption, and which see young people as the harbingers of new, postmodern values and outlooks (for example, Featherstone, 1991; Shields, 1992; Fornas, 1995; Polhemus, 1994).

Only a generation ago, in the 1960s, young working-class Teessiders followed what then seemed to be fixed, known, secure pathways into working-class jobs and adulthood. In the Fordist heyday of 'full employment', these work values found their place in jobs which were more regular, rewarding (at least financially), skilled and stable. Persistent, structural unemployment and widespread underemployment over the last three decades of the twentieth century has dismantled the economic base upon which this sort of cultural reproduction was built. Judging by this sample many working-class kids no longer get working-class jobs, or if they do, find them to be of a quite different sort to those encountered by Willis's 'lads' in the early 1970s (Willis, 1977). Yet young people growing up in the late 1980s and 1990s continue to prioritise working over non-working, labour market engagement over economic inactivity, self-reliance over dependency upon the state. Work remains of paramount importance.

It is especially important to re-emphasise these points given the contemporary influence of politics and policies which are premised upon a view of working-class youth as work-shy and preferring welfare dependency. Underclass theory, in particular, has picked out young people as prime candidates for membership of a new, anti-social, anti-work, welfare-dependent, dangerous class (MacDonald, 1997). Charles Murray (1990, 1994) – the champion of the conservative and most well known variant of the thesis – regards the young, poor and unemployed as largely responsible for their own predicament. For him, much youth unemployment is voluntary and a result of an infectious anti-work ethos fostered by over-generous welfare regimes. David Green of the Institute of Economic Affairs, which has done most to promote underclass explanations, talks of the 'behavioural poverty' of the underclass (1992).

Such theorists underestimate the way that the cultural and material values of work persist for young people. They also underestimate the creative and diverse ways in which young people *attempt* to resolve – albeit unsuccessfully – the problems of growing up in a time and place where economic security and social inclusion are no longer afforded through employment (see MacDonald, 1997). Unlike the informants to this study, Murray does *not* understand the desperate experience of unemployment. He fails to grasp the fact that, for young people attempting to make transitions from school, work continues to have a social, moral and cultural significance beyond the wage packet. Instead, he offers up moral castigation and partial descriptions which fail to connect with the lived experiences of the unemployed, and in so doing he perpetuates long-standing myths of the undeserving poor while peddling policy prescriptions which do little to resolve the real problems facing working-class youth and their communities.

The Labour government in Britain has perhaps gone even further than its Conservative predecessor in following this sort of right-wing thinking on unemployment, the underclass and welfare dependency. The flagship social and economic programme of the incoming Labour administration has been its 'Welfare to Work' strategy. The young unemployed in particular are targeted by even stricter policies to police and monitor their willingness and availability for work. Those claiming long-term benefits are offered places in subsidised employment, in education and training, in voluntary work or in an environmental taskforce. Failure to take up these opportunities results in heavy reduction in unemployment benefits (Convery, 1997). What the authors of these policies fail to understand is, first, that the young working class in areas of high unemployment do not need to be pressganged with the threat of benefit reduction. The second problem with the thinking behind the 'Welfare to Work' programme is the assumption that the problem of youth unemployment is in large part a problem of the young unemployed themselves: that they lack the skills and attitudes to work required by employers and this deficit needs to be remedied by participation in the government's programme.[5]

It is too early to say whether this set of interventions will be more successful than the long list of similar ones sponsored by the Conservative governments of the 1980s and 1990s. Some young people will, no doubt, proceed from welfare to work following participation. Currently, however, only one-third of Teesside youth trainees gain jobs after YTS (Teesside TEC, 1995). Where will further involvement with 'government scheming' lead? One of my informants, Malcolm, had left school at sixteen in the late 1970s and took part first of all in YOP (the Youth Opportunities Programme). By the age of twenty-nine he had worked his way through JIG (the Job Interview Guarantee Scheme), YWS (the Young Workers Scheme), CP (the Community Programme), ET (Employment Training) and various Job Clubs. When I interviewed him, he was setting up a small business through the Enterprise Allowance Scheme (EAS) to offer advice to others about how to cope with unemployment. He was not 'unemployable' (he had done much unpaid voluntary work for local welfare agencies), but he had never had a 'proper job'. In the absence of a more sustained and ambitious programme to provide long-term, secure employment *after* government training and 'make-work' schemes, it is difficult to see how the Welfare to Work Programme will do much other than reinforce the insecure cyclical transitions of economically marginal youth.

Notes

1   Roberts (1997) has usefully, however, added a word of caution and suggests that in reaching for evocative labels to describe these changes we should bear in mind the much more drastic disjunctures which have, for instance, so altered youth transitions in Eastern Europe.

2   The statistics in this paragraph were supplied by Teesside Training and Enterprise Council (1995).

3   The extent of the restructuring of the local economy was revealed most dramatically when interviews with older research participants were compared with the accounts given by young people. The opening interview question asked informants to recount what they had done since leaving school. Eric, who was sixty-one, used over one hour of audio-tape with his answer, in which he detailed a work biography commencing at fourteen when he started work at a local steel foundry. Over the next forty years he worked for the same firm, moving up the occupational ladder until he reached senior supervisor level. He had recently been made redundant and was attempting to become self-employed. The same question asked of those in their late teens and early twenties would typically receive a one-word answer: 'nowt'.

4   The results of these studies, and their methodology, are described in more detail elsewhere (MacDonald, 1994, 1996a, 1996b, 1997). The research was sponsored by the Economic and Social Research Council. I am indebted to them, to the editors and Colin Clark of the University of Newcastle who provided detailed and insightful critique of an earlier draft of this chapter and, most of all, to the people who took part in the studies. All names have been changed. The research was undertaken initially at the University of Durham with F. Coffield.

5   Although this chapter was written prior to commencement of the Welfare to Work Programme there have already been a number of telling criticisms made of the New Labour attempt to transpose a broadly American model of workfare to the British situation. Mead (1997) contains advocacy of workfare principles and policies, further elaboration of New Labour thinking from Frank Field and a range of responses from British social policy commentators who highlight some of the problems with this approach.

12 Boys will be boys

Social insecurity and crime

Beatrix Campbell

Boys will be boys...

When an apocalyptic debate about crime and community emerged in the early 1990s, it seemed to define the times. Its focus was the crisis in white ghettos, once the homelands of the respectable working class, now the locales of communities suffering the effects of economic insecurity created by the protracted withdrawal of public and private capital.

In the last two decades of the century, two distinct developments converged. Economic restructuring has been shadowed by the reform of relations between men and women, with the latter process propelled by women's permanent presence in the labour market, and by the women's movement. This convergence appeared in the political rhetoric of both Conservative and Labour leaders during the 1990s. Each showed a tendency to attribute community crisis to a synergy of unemployment and seismic shifts in relations between genders, in particular the loss of legitimacy attached to traditional patriarchal power. Indeed, this loss of legitimacy and traditional power entered conservative 'common sense' as the cause of crime and the collapse of civilisation as we know it. Poor neighbourhoods were no longer analysed as places that revealed the effects of national or trans-national redistributions of power and resources upon social classes and communities on the one hand, and the outcomes of local power struggles between genders and generations on the other. They became seen as places that reproduced poverty in their own local social relations.

While neo-liberals, communitarians and 'ethical socialists' varied in the weight they attached to the effects of economic restructuring, they were fatally attracted to each other's anxieties about gender, the new configurations of domestic relations between men and women, and the destabilisation of men's traditional dominance. Though palpable across all classes, loss of power and a privileged place in the social landscape were represented as having allegedly wrought havoc among poor people. In poor locales, lawless masculinity became perceived as both the effect and the cause of a crisis of community and public safety; thus a crisis of public peace in poor neighbourhoods became the symbolic courier of a regressive discourse about masculinity. Poor places, purportedly, were a warning: this is what happens to men when they lose their privileged place as breadwinners – they become mad or bad.

My argument here, however, is that the correlation between crime and masculinity is dramatic but historically predictable, and permanent. Far from representing a collapse of traditional masculinities, many of the characteristics of criminalised culture mirror the spatial strategies and cultural history of mainstream masculinities (Campbell, 1993: 202). With the decline of traditional manufacturing industries – and thus the demise of the male–breadwinner equation – many men found themselves suddenly having to share the same time and space as women. This upset the traditions which motivated the cultures of respectable, breadwinning masculinity. At the same time, poor communities witnessed struggles to conquer social space among criminalised coteries of young men. Community crime should be seen as a reassertion of mainstream, traditional masculinity imagined as difference and dominance, rather than as a crisis of traditional masculinity. What is often represented in 'common sense' as a crisis of men's privileged and separatist status is, rather, the reworking of masculine control over social space. The withdrawal of public and private capital from working-class neighbourhoods then leaves communities without the services and stewardship needed to mediate and protect public peace from a struggle for spatial control. This renders the community in general unprotected from the effects of a historic struggle by men for space and power, a struggle sponsored by crime.

...and girls will be women

The history of modernity is associated with the polarisation between 'public' and 'private' space and with the gendering of social space. The notion of 'full-time' waged work among men (which was one of the great goals of Western modernity) and the economic dependence of women confined to unwaged domestic employment has shaped the social landscape of modernity, the culture of respectability and the ideologies of masculinity and femininity. Men are breadwinners, women are mothers; men are public people, women are private; men's work is paid as well as public, women's work is private, personal and unpaid (Taylor, 1993: 262–3). Although these polarisations have always been contested and have only briefly defined the labour market (as argued in Chapter 5) they have been a potent influence on our imagined social space, on wages, social security and the gendering of rights and responsibilities. Throughout the industrial era, women have been in and out of the labour market, but since the Second World War, women have occupied both public and private spaces, engaged in a 'long march' into the institutions from which they had been exiled. Indeed, the modern woman's mobility and the multiplicity of functions associated with modern femininity disturb the very categories 'public' and 'private' and challenge the old mores of respectability.

This has not been a reciprocal movement. Men's relationship to women, children and domesticity has changed, but at a far slower rate, and masculinity is still defined *against* femininity, as a relation of difference and dominance. In the most traditional industrial communities, the dominance of men's work and play was palpable: in coal communities, for example, the local landscape was dominated by the pit, the miners' union lodge and the miners' welfare club, all institutions from which women and children were excluded. However, the creation of permanent and more or less mass 'unemployment' among men has changed many men's relationship to the domestic domain and to the 'local' community. In pauperised neighbourhoods with minimal access to a legal living, men find themselves marooned in the same time and space as women. This is an affront to the history of men's movements within Western industrial economies, which fought hard and long for the separation of men and women's spheres and for the exclusive equation between being a man and being a breadwinner.

This chapter analyses some of the debates in the 1990s about gender, crime and community. In particular, it takes the work of (among others) Norman Dennis as a classic case, showing that his early work on working-class men naturalises the social and political construction of gender, and takes for granted men's estrangement from the domestic world of women and children. His later work then accuses feminism of unmanning men, releasing them from the responsibilities of respectable fatherhood, leaving boys bereft of appropriate models of masculinity and thus fielding feral children in a life of crime. The chapter will argue that an anxiety about gender leaks across contemporary debates about economic insecurity, community and crime.

Crime and masculinity

Crime infuses a millennial debate about masculinity-in-crisis. In the 1990s, this crisis is assigned almost exclusively to the working class. My argument is that crime is a way of making masculinity. Crime therefore transcends class, and it does not reveal either an identity crisis, masculine dysfunction, or a tendency of masculinity bequeathed by biology. What I have to say offers a challenge to essentialist theories of masculinity, which is shared with a number of theorists of masculinity and crime in the 1990s. So, for example, Robert Connell argues that gender is a way of ordering social practices. Gender refers to bodies and what bodies do, but it is not reduced to the body. Indeed, 'gender exists precisely to the extent that biology does *not* determine the social' (Connell, 1995: 71). Commenting on crime and gender, Connell argues that masculinity 'is something that has to be made, and criminal behaviour is one of the ways of its making'. A great deal of crime 'only makes sense when it is seen as a resource for the making of gender, and in most cases that means it is a strategy for masculinity' (Connell, 1993: xi).

Crime is one of the ways men address the world as men. What is perceived as a breakdown of law and order is one of the effects of young men's display of masculinity as difference and dominance: in relation to the rest of their neighbourhood, in relation to other masculinities in the criminal justice system, schools and the statutory services, and in relation to women. It has its own lore of triumph and defeat, mastery and martyrdom enunciated in the criminal justice system. (This is one of the reasons why 'shaming' strategies designed to humiliate young men in public would prove pointless. The criminal justice system is merely one of the theatres in which modes of masculinity are displayed and their authority asserted against each other.)

Community crime among young men in dispossessed neighbourhoods is routinely explained in 'common sense' as an effect of their poverty. Poverty de-privileges these young men, and produces a pathology associated with their purported powerlessness in relation to women. Thus poor young men are represented as unmanned and pathological. In law and order debates, lawless masculinity is routinely believed to derive from the loss of economic power over women. Economic insecurity, so the argument goes, stripped men of their manhood. They are deemed unmanly in relation to women over whom they enjoy no economic power. They are deemed unmarriageable (Young and Halsey, 1995: 21). The resolution, therefore, lies in the restoration of young men's pride and privileged position as breadwinners.

However, these approaches erase the history of crime and gender. Crime sanctions modes of masculinity which, despite their lawless 'dangerousness', are bequeathed by the cultural history of patriarchal masculinities. The purported crisis of masculinity expressed in crime is something else: the reassertion of masculinity as difference and dominance at precisely the moment when patriarchal masculinity is losing its legitimacy. Pauperisation mediates men's place in what Robert Connell calls 'hegemonic masculinity' (Connell, 1995: 77–8). Poor men may lose out on the 'patriarchal dividend', a dividend all men gain 'from the overall subordination of women', because of their economic weakness, although they may still appropriate a working-class ethic of solidarity that is simultaneously misogynist (Connell, 1995: 116–19).

Thus crime is not so much a crisis of masculinity – a displaced, disordered identity struggling for meaning in a changing world – as a culture that moulds masculinity, forging an identity in the crucible of hierarchical, coercive, secretive and separatist coteries of men. This is not to say that criminalised masculinities are just like any other masculinity, that the characteristics of gender merely find their expression in any culture. Rather, it is to suggest that the cultural history of masculinity is reworked in new economic or political conditions. This is the sense in which crime – like waged work – is a context in which 'masculinity is made'. 'Criminal behaviour makes sense only when it is seen as a resource for the making of gender, and in most cases, that means it is a strategy of masculinity' (Connell, 1993: xi). Crime is unthinkable outside the imperatives of gender.

Crime is also a context and culture against which 'respectable' patriarchal masculinity defines itself (Campbell, 1993: 199). Often theorists are interested in what distinguishes lawless from lawful masculinities; as if criminality were always 'other'. There is a struggle in political discourse to disconnect dangerous from respectable masculinities. Respectable masculinity disconnects itself from the parallel culture of crime, but still defines itself against the challenges of women in the second wave of twentieth-century feminism. Indeed, the anti-feminism of these diverse discourses is evident in their more or less explicit attempts to mobilise the economic paragon of modern patriarchy – the breadwinner – in a critique which assigns the causes of crime to the loss of that privileged place in the community.

Back to basics?

In Britain, one of the most active proponents of the masculinity-in-crisis, bring-back-the-breadwinner thesis is Norman Dennis, a self-proclaimed 'ethical socialist' who found a political nest in the 1990s with the right-wing neo-liberal Institute of Economic Affairs. Dennis was emblematic of the realignment, around a misogynist matrix, of disparate political tendencies with a shared anxiety about gender, crime and community. This orientation has a long and formative history in British socialism. As early as the 1840s, the mass movement for democracy, Chartism, campaigned for 'separate spheres' for men and women, with men taking control of the labour market and public and political institutions, while women's freedom of movement was controlled and confined to the domestic domain. This patriarchal project was one of the founding moments in British Labourism, which produced it as a patriarchal project, as a men's movement. Representing the sound and fury of ebbing respectability – a culture which had been so influential in patriarchal working-class politics – Dennis is also splenetic about the intellectuals and left libertarianism of the 1960s, the sexual revolution and *fin de siècle* individualism.

In a manoeuvre indicative of the centrality of gender to traditional Labourism, Dennis lends his Fabian fury to the Institute of Economic Affairs, a redoubt of neo-liberal individualism, anti-statism and moral traditionalism. Though this seems like an odd alliance, given their polarised positions on economic individualism, what unites them in the 1990s is a shared repudiation of feminism's attempt to create a new historic settlement between men and women.

The scholarship generated by the women's liberation movement interrogated conventional histories of the working class, labourism and liberalism, and named the extent to which patriarchal priorities framed the politics of traditional Conservatism and Labourism alike. Barbara Taylor's history of socialism and feminism in the nineteenth century, for example, recovers the story of feminism's impact on socialist visionaries and utopians, and records the defeat of women's aspirations in the formative period in which labourism began to emerge (Taylor, 1983). That defeat of women in socialism and labourism produced a more modest, myopic form of class consciousness anchored in the men's movement, in misogyny. The narrowed political priorities of a socialist movement wrought in the image of the 'working man' were challenged on all fronts by late twentieth-century feminism. The collaboration between Norman Dennis and the IEA merely revealed the extreme edge of a more diffuse realignment within centre-left politics. This realignment was manifest in the priorities of New Labour in the 1990s around social authoritarianism as a response to two challenges: the challenge of feminism and the new social movements which emerged after the 1960s, and the impoverishment and insecurity of working-class communities.

Dennis joined the fray after the British riots of 1991, which erupted in mainly white, working-class council estates. Claiming to ground his case in a study of the riots, he proposed that crime was caused by dysfunctional, fatherless families. His texts scarcely refer to the riots themselves: indeed, he carried out no empirical research into the events. The riots and the communities in which they combusted were merely mobilised to support his hypothesis. His argument (shared with the American right-wing sociologist Charles Murray) is a protest against the growth of one-parent families, and an assertion that families without fathers contribute not only to crime and disorder but to a 'generational catastrophe' (Murray, 1990: 7). Dennis, like Murray, hailed the 1950s as the golden era of properly fathered families before the 1960s and the sexual revolution allegedly threw families out of control and into chaos.

Both contend that there were 'plentiful examples of good fathers' in the golden era (Murray, 1990: 11). However, Jonathan Gershuny's time-use studies of fathers and mothers since the 1960s paints a different portrait of parenting: the average father's dedicated daily time with children in 1961 was 11 minutes a day (Hewitt, 1993: 61). The lament ignores the great expansion in active fathering: in the 1990s, the average father spends four times as much dedicated time with his children than fathers during the golden era. What these writers might mean by 'good fathers' may be discerned from Dennis's own work on working-class communities in the 1950s, in *Coal Is Our Life*, an influential sociological text analysing an archetypal proletarian mining community. He describes – approvingly – a polarised landscape in which men and women inhabit entirely different locales, a social separation enforced by women's exclusion from waged work and containment within a domestic economy while men enjoy virtually exclusive access to waged work. Describing the extreme estrangement of this division of labour as 'a pure economic fact', Dennis eternalises and naturalises the male breadwinner. He erases the history of great campaigns waged by men within the trade union movement for their own wages to represent a 'family wage', and for women to be barred from wage labour. These initiatives were themselves constitutive of modern masculinity and the subordination of women.

Dennis's book thus rather disingenuously locates women's subordination in an innocent 'pure economic fact', rather than in the history of a sexual division of labour in which men sought to control women's freedom of movement, freedom of thought and access to a wage. Dennis does, however, signal the restlessness and reluctance associated with the 'pure economic facts' when he alludes to the heavy price paid by any woman who 'transgresses her confinement' (Dennis *et al.*, 1956: 211). He describes domesticity as a space in which women take care of men, a space in which a wife is 'ready to give him just what he wants'. It is her duty to 'see him off in a fit state' and to provide 'satisfactory conditions to which he can return' (1956: 174–5). Although Dennis claims that women accepted, even affirmed their domestic confinement, a sense of the fragility of this settlement is suggested in his comment that women's success or failure was 'very commonly under discussion' (1956: 181). His portrait of family life represents men as visitors to their homes: 'staying at home bores them'. Men typically returned home from work, were fed and watered before going out to play with other men, their mates. 'A man's centres of activity are outside the home' and as soon as he is 'rested' he 'seeks the company of his mates' (1956: 180–1). Indeed, men's social life is defined by their distance from women and children, and that distance in turn defines 'the exclusively male character of all spheres of popular culture' (1956: 211).

The family wage won by the male breadwinner was rarely offered to the family; men allocated their women a fixed sum and kept the rest. At least, ventures Dennis, this insulated family income from the insecurity of miners' incomes. The wage was the beginning and end of fathering. Fatherhood was legitimated, therefore, as absence and authority: 'The husband's duty to the family more or less ends at the handing over to his wife of her "wage" ' (1956: 196). Dennis admits that he found no evidence of any woman who enjoyed sufficient surplus income from the husband's wage to devote to herself and her children (1956: 200–2).

Coal Is Our Life, then, is a germinal text in the sociology of the working-class family. It maps the proletarian community as a polarised place in which men merely visited the homes they shared with women and children, in which men were the centre of women's attention while men's masculinity was fortified amidst their congress with other men, where men were providers rather than parents.

During the last three decades of the twentieth century, however, this quality of absence and authority has been challenged by both women and children. Increasingly empowered, they expected a culture of care and companionship rather than control. But for Dennis, like Murray, the tradition which had produced fathers as providers rather than parents is reinterpreted and reasserted as merely authority. Mobilising a Christian morality, they locate the purported crisis of community in the sexual revolution, in men's alleged estrangement and exile from the family and the community. This is not the exile of the golden era, when (according to *Coal Is Our Life*) men merely visit their homes. Rather, this exile assumes the loss of their responsibility towards women and children, and thus the loss of their authority, often at the insistence of women (Dennis and Erdos, 1992: xxi). Men's release from the shame associated with siring 'illegitimate' children generates men who no longer know how to be fathers, since the disciplining of masculinity depends on their dominance in the domestic domain. The social acceptance of illegitimacy and the decline of marriage have released men from responsibility. Stalked by original sin, it seems, men are doomed to dangerous bestiality.

For Murray and Dennis, contemporary crime rates could be explained exclusively by reference to illegitimacy and men's release from responsibility. Dennis wonders what motivates boys if not the holy grail of monogamous marriage and breadwinnership, if not the prospect of power in their family and community: 'It was because they had been deprived of the context of firm social expectations directing them to family responsibilities that British boys and youths became much more prone to deal with their frustrations by turning to crime'

(Dennis, 1997: 169). Moving on from his earlier commitment to the thesis proposed by Charles Murray in 1990, that families were being purged of fathers by the alchemy of Marxism or feminism or merely fecklessness (Dennis and Erdos, 1992: 70), Dennis now argues that it is not just absent fathers who create criminal tendencies in their sons.[1] It is the lack of personal and public constraints – primarily marriage and monogamy – that are the most important 'criminogenic effects' for young men. This was the product of men's emancipation from responsibility by the sexual reformation inaugurated in the 1960s (Dennis, 1997: 153). It certainly obliterated men's disgrace, their punishment for promiscuity.

For Dennis, therefore, marriage disciplined men; it saved them from themselves. Crucially, it announced their heterosexuality. Marriage, according to *Coal Is Our Life*, means above all the regulation not so much of men, but of the invisible other – femininity – by a masculinity that was shaped outside the home, beyond the world of women and children, down among the men in their privileged, separatist sphere. By the 1990s, Dennis's affectionate account of archetypal proletarian patriarchy had been bizarrely redeemed, though by now with an eye to the uncomfortable corollary: the oppression of women. The Labour Party's support for traditional family life, argues Dennis, 'had nothing whatsoever to do with support of women's subordination and restriction to the home' (Dennis, 1997: 2).

The journalist Melanie Phillips, who shares the critique promoted by Dennis and Halsey, invokes the spectre of marauding masculinity in a paranoid and victimised representation of family life deserted by fleeing fathers, whose flight has allegedly been encouraged by feminism and whose prospects are diminished by the women of their own class and community: 'Fatherlessness is likely to increase rather than decrease if young women flood the labour market, forcing out young men who become less marriageable as a result' (Phillips, 1991).

What is crucial here is a pessimistic and essentialist representation of masculinity that mobilises 'common sense' notions of original sin – men are beasts – to propose that young men will be naturally feckless unless disciplined by other respectable men and by their wives, suitably domesticated and dependent. In this version, which became almost hegemonic in the 1990s, the demise of respectability, in the wake of the sexual reformation, harvested itinerant, irresponsible and dangerous masculinities. The independence of women relieved young men of the disciplining responsibilities of patriarchy and threw them into crime and chaos. A correlation is assumed which claims that boys become bad in communities 'without fathers'.

The obsessive quest to connect crime with family circumstances – and particularly fatherlessness – is not supported, however, by Home Office researchers. Not that this deters Home Secretaries: researchers have long lamented the indifference of the politicians to empirical evidence. According to the Home Office Study *Young People and Crime*, published in 1995, gender remains 'an important variable': 'Among those males and females who are equally closely supervised at home and at school, who are equally attached to their school and their family and who have no delinquent peers, offending remains about twice as common among males as females' (Home Office, 1995: 48). Furthermore, 'there appears to be only a weak relation between starting to offend and both social class and the structure of the family'. Indeed, their significance 'disappeared'. However, a 'very strong correlate of offending' is gender, generation and friendship with other offenders (1995: 49).

Politically, the 'project of "reclaiming" the place of men in the family is equated with strategies of crime prevention, social responsibility and the father-right defence of the "normal" and "functional" family' (Collier, 1996: 23). Geoff Dench, of the Institute of Community Studies, exemplifies Collier's case. He proposes a candid version of essentialism and an unashamed defence of patriarchy in his argument that men are not naturally drawn to co-operation, collectivity or community, despite the evidence of masculine solidarities. Only through the breadwinner role are men domesticated 'and lifted out of egotism', a notion he shares with Dennis. Men's role as providers gives them a privileged place in the family and community. It was the 'patriarchal system that gave them the incentive to be active in the community'. If women strip men of their privileged place as providers 'they may unleash something worse'.[2] Men's status as providers gives the rationale for privilege: 'Giving men a place in society by making them responsible for women and children is to some extent bound to limit the freedom of women to develop and express themselves', he concedes (Dench, 1994: 217–18). But this, Dench believes, is a price worth paying: by 'inflating the importance of what they do – to pull them in – it legitimises them taking more than they give'. The privileges of patriarchy ensure men's co-operation with women and children: 'Promoting women's independence allows men's fecklessness full rein' (1994: 218).

The collapse of civilisation as we know it

A more covert misogyny can be discerned in interventions by Dench's director at the Institute of Community Studies, Michael Young, in a pamphlet written jointly with the Oxford sociologist A.H. Halsey (the proclaimed friend and mentor of Norman Dennis). Children are no longer well cared for, claim Young and Halsey (1995), who cite social services risk registers to support their claim that children's everyday life is getting worse. While it is true that children constitute one of the poorest constituencies in Britain, the rise in the numbers of children registered as being at risk of neglect, cruelty and abuse actually is an effect of greater vigilance among the child protection professions in the wake of a scandalous series of child deaths in the 1970s and 1980s. In the mid-1980s, the regulatory framework guiding child welfare professions insisted upon greater vigilance and robust intervention to support children at risk of harm by adults. Misreading the evidence, Young and Halsey conflate danger to children and dangerous children, predicting that Britain is on its way to 'becoming a moral wilderness filled with children seeking revenge' (Young and Halsey, 1995: 11).

Amplifying the 'collapse of civilisation as we know it' hypothesis, Young and Halsey subliminally echo politicians' response to the 1993 murder of two-year-old Jamie Bulger by two ten-year-old boys in Bootle. This event was a watershed moment in British politics, when Tony Blair inaugurated New Labour's social authoritarianism. Children (rather than the workers) appeared as the enemy within. Blair's mix of moralism and social authoritarianism was coined in an apocalyptic speech responding to the Bulger killing: 'We cannot exist in a moral vacuum. If we do not learn and then teach the value of what is right and what is wrong, then the result is simply moral chaos which engulfs us all' (Mandelson and Liddle, 1996: 47). Like Dench's reading of patriarchal masculinity and its furious reaction to its loss of privilege, Blair in his speech (and Young and Halsey) reinterpret children's traumatised aggression as revenge, rather than the more likely re-enactment and repetition of adult scenarios of domination and abuse.

There are common themes running throughout these texts, including the belief that masculinity is thrown into crisis when its access to exclusively masculinised cultures on the one hand, and a privileged and powerful relation to women and children on the other hand, are disrupted. It follows from this position that the rehabilitation of men can only be achieved by the restoration of their status as breadwinners. There is no alternative model for a boy than a man and the world of waged work. He enters this world with other men, with whom appropriate mores of masculinity are engendered. (There are further assumptions about the alien world of domesticity – the world of women – which he expects to enter as the centre of attention.) Crucially, all assume that disordered masculinity is an effect of an environment bereft of men, a world defined by women. The crucible of masculinity, then, is other men. These theorists draw attention to men's dangerousness not in order to understand it but to condemn it, and in so doing they ascribe it not to the cultural and political histories of masculinity, but to the morals of mothers. Despite their differences, not least in relation to both neo-liberalism and to feminism, they share a presumption that traditional fathers are an endangered species, that boys are being deprived of role models, and that the appropriate models are men, or rather, breadwinning men.

Communities and crime

My own work on crime and masculinity in impoverished, post-Fordist communities was ignited by the emergence of mass unemployment in the 1980s and the eruption of riots, public disorder and the prevalence of crime in the 1990s. Though the riots were represented in political discourse as the predictable outcome of poverty and/or bad parenting, neither poverty nor parenting offered an adequate explanation for the particular form of the riots, nor their connection to community crime and public disorder. This discourse did not explain the differential survival strategies adopted by different genders and generations. Nor did it explain the targets of the rioters, including variously community activists, Asian traders, and public facilities which serviced the community as a whole, such as the post office, community buildings and youth clubs. Young men and women may endure parity of poverty, but there is no expectation that young women – in contrast to young men – are somehow 'un-womanned' by their economic circumstances. Young men and old men may be equally isolated and insecure, yet old men do not become joyriders or burglars. Young men involved in TWOCCing (taking without the owner's consent) share more with young men in the police – the same passion for the chase, the same pleasure in cars – than with their mothers or sisters.

The assumption that criminalised masculinity is an effect of economic dispossession, stripping young men of their privileged place in the family or community, depends on a notion of masculinity fixed in a prior and predetermined destiny based on difference and dominance. This was not borne out by my experience in poor places, where proliferating modes of masculinity revealed the absence of any pre-given template of gender relations or ways of being male. Nor is it sustained by feminist criminology and politics, which – in contrast to social authoritarianism – contributes to an understanding of these phenomena as forms of masculine enunciation, ways in which young men address their world and assert their masculinity, which connect with the cultural history of mainstream masculinities. This approach challenges the representation of crime and public disorder as manifestations of disordered or dysfunctional masculinity. The correlation between crime, gender and generation is, of course, well established in crime statistics. But the study of crime as something men *do* has not been a subject of scholarship or politics until the 1990s. Moreover, problematic masculinity – in contrast to the masculinity problematic – has tended, in political discourse, to be stripped of the new gender politics and confined to the beleaguered strata of the poor.

Public order crises in impoverished neighbourhoods reveal an inescapably gendered profile: there is crime, organised by men, and community action, organised largely by women. These gendered responses to social crisis are mirrored in the statutory services, including the police, and the political system. Many of these neighbourhoods felt abandoned by the police, except for sporadic raids usually conducted without the co-operation of the community. Indeed, often the community felt left to manage dangerousness within, rather like a battered woman left to manage her man. A growing crisis of crime within poor communities also metamorphosed into a crisis of public peace and security. The experience of the mainly white, working-class suburbias that combusted in the early 1990s contrasted sharply with the experience of black communities subjected to obsessive attention by often racist white police officers (*The Broadwater Farm Inquiry*, 1985: 51).

Community crime, mainly associated with young men, contributed to the collapse of confidence in the maintenance of public safety. Crime is perceived by the community not so much as categories of offences but rather as a more or less organised and purposive culture of control. The characteristics which define these coteries of young men and boys are shared with the traditional template of respectable working-class masculinity described by Norman Dennis in the 1950s.

Crime provides a culture which celebrates men's control of social space. Criminalised coteries are sexually separatist, committed to the exclusive company of men unencumbered by the presence of the women with whom they live, or who belong to their kin, generation or neighbourhood. Indeed, their masculine ethos is established through the exclusion of women while relying on women, their mothers and other women, to make the homes in which they nest, to negotiate with schools, the local authority, the police and the courts. The authority of these young men is also asserted against other masculinities: against the authority of professional masculinities, particularly teachers and the police, and against the collective and co-operative discipline of their contemporaries, their generational community in school.

The estrangement of criminalised coteries of young men and boys from the school or the clubs associated with straight society is both a response to humiliation and failure, and a challenge to authoritative masculinity. It does not repudiate power and authority so much as challenge and claim it. In the absence of institutions in which to secure dominion, unstewarded public space and insecure private space are alternative arenas in which young men may assert audacity and authority. They are engaged in a struggle for mastery, a struggle that circulates between these young men and their neighbours, their contemporaries, their teachers, the police and other statutory services.

The struggle for spatial control is sponsored by crime. The street, or bus shelter, or shopping precinct becomes an arena in which to assert power. What is often represented as the behaviour of 'rogues' roaming around the edges of society is rather the exercise of spatial power. It can also be seen as one which mirrors the quest for sexual separatism and dominance which has characterised the great masculine assemblies associated with other classes or strata, from the craft trade union tradition, masonic cults, the professions and the political system. Criminalised coteries of young men are similarly disciplined by rules and rituals of authority which valorise dominance and obedience. Solidarity is also valorised, but on the basis of exclusion, secrecy and authority. To resist their dominion is to be designated a 'grass', a traitor to the secretive solidarities which exclude the rest of the community and yet demand collective complicity.

Like other criminalised cultures elsewhere, community crime requires the 'community' to be both audience and accomplice. Joyriding is a paradigm of this drama. Car crime is an almost exclusively masculinised form of crime, focused upon a commodity which occupies a unique place in popular culture. It is the commodity, historically, which men have given themselves permission to consume. It is also the commodity which conveys their mastery over space and movement, and their stewardship over the most grandiose commodity – other than shelter – possessed by most households. Joyriding throws a kind of chaos into the street by auto-acrobatics which disrupt the discipline of traffic, by imposing the joyriders' freedom of movement against the street's other users. It functions as a theatrical display of masculine virtuosity, playing with a commodity uniquely associated in popular culture with masculinity. Joyriding, like other community criminalities, demands an audience within the community whose space is requisitioned, and whose collective knowledge is controlled by the requirement that they keep the young men's secrets. In neighbourhoods where everything is knowable, the visibility of criminalised coteries is minimised by the imposition of sanctions against anyone deemed to be a 'grass'.

The displays also demand an audience among 'authority', that is, the police. Police attention is enlisted in a 'dangerous liaison' between young men united by the pleasure of the chase and the struggle for mastery. Their theatre is routinely monitored by a system of mutual surveillance. Joyriders' access to miniaturised scanners enable them to listen-in and monitor the movements of the police. Police helicopters trace stolen cars and guide police drivers to their routes, while joyriders' pleasure in their potency is rewarded by being watched from the heavens.

The passion and pleasure associated with cars has been, until the 1980s, almost exclusively associated with men as both buyers and users, and infuses the culture of respectable mainstream masculinities no less than criminal masculinities. The degree to which the umbilical cord between cars, masculinity and car crime is accepted is revealed in criminal justice strategies. These assume that the 'cure' for addictive car crime among joyriders is to give them cars. Implicitly accepting that their gender identity is somehow tied up with cars, there is an assumption that their redemption can be achieved through having cars, messing about with them and driving them in fields and other empty spaces, rather than stealing them and showing off in them. The need for the car, therefore, is not open to question, since that, presumably, would expose the generic relationship between masculinity and cars to interrogation.

The difficulty of both the police or career politicians (mostly men) in confronting the culture that sustains car crime (and thus confronting themselves) is palpable in the resistance to attaching gender to crime prevention programmes. A senior police officer in Oxford, who assiduously trailed round the city's schools as part of a car crime-prevention exercise, was asked whether the police inscribed gender awareness in the programme. The senior officer hesitated, looked bewildered and then ventured: 'that's a matter for the parents'. In 1998, a senior civil servant attached to the reform of juvenile justice took part in a discussion about poverty and young offenders. Challenged about the government's apparent determination to excise gender from its strategies, he replied that it was difficult to know what to do about masculinity; as if gender was an act of god, rather than a creation of culture.

Sexual separatism and secretive solidarities derive from the tradition of exclusive collectivities which produce masculine authority, through competition with other strata of masculine authority, and their distance from the universe of women and children. In the context of a mass experience of poverty and isolation from the institutions associated with waged work, crime provides dispossessed young men with a cultural legacy that valorises conquest and domination.

The 'work' of criminals associated with petty property crime is often represented as if it were performed for the benefit of all, a notion embedded in the

Robin Hood myth and the heroism of banditry. I recall a discussion among a group of young men in a northern prison about the meaning of riots – in which some of them had been participants – which had been a massive confrontation between organised crime and the police. They saw their creation of a public order crisis in their community as a gesture of defiance towards the statutory agencies which had been rewarded by massive state investment in the refurbishment of the built environment. Women involved in this discussion, including a community activist who was friendly with some of their mothers, were horrified: rioters' activity had threatened the public safety of the streets these men shared with their mothers.

But what the mothers experienced as routine menace and terror tactics, as a coercive culture by which the community's space and values were controlled by men, was perceived by the young men as behaviour that was in the collective interest. In other words, their specific interests were universalised, in much the way that the restrictive practices and exclusive rites of men in trade unions, professional associations and the military services have historically been represented as natural, and as cascading benefits to the rest of their community. Criminalised young men have been represented as the feral outcasts of respectable society, rather like the bad 'black' lion in *The Lion King*, as malevolent as he is indolent, loitering with giggling hyenas, scavenging on the edges of a cowering community of lions bereft of masculine leadership.

This representation of poor, criminalised young men as bestial and beyond human culture was palpable in the Home Office campaign against car crime which dominated public hoardings in the early 1990s. Car thieves were represented as hyenas, rapacious, slithering into pristine, shimmering cars, as though their visible and confident repudiation of the law or their exclusion from the institutions disconnected them entirely from popular culture and collectivities. However, their passion for cars implied not their exile from popular masculine culture, but their connection to it. Their patterns of consumption established not their estrangement, but their embeddedness in a masculine community of interest. Young men committed to cultures associated with crime readily testify to their belief and pleasure in force and coercion as a way of exercising control over social space, while simultaneously asserting their identities as men.

Notes

1   Charles Murray, who strongly influenced Ronald Reagan's social welfare strategies and who was fielded as an important commentator in Britain by the *Sunday Times* and the IEA in the early 1990s, argues that the purported flight of fathers was the effect of a purge. The impact of both Marxism and feminism among the poorest people – presumably unbeknown to themselves – produced communities bereft of men (Murray, 1990: 11).
2   This conservative 'common sense' is as prevalent as it is pessimistic. Francis Fukuyama, professor of public policy and former adviser to the US State Department, for example, locates the problem in biology and the solution in patriarchy: crime has not only environmental causes, 'but also has a biological dimension: crimes

are overwhelmingly committed by young males. In virtually all societies around the globe...this is the result of their underlying psychological make up rather than culture'. Men's 'promiscuity needs to be controlled by the institution of marriage, male aggression needs to be controlled by paternal authority' (Fukuyama, 1997: 35).

13 Democratic vistas

Imagining a twenty-first-century security

John Vail

The democratic imagination and security

> Did you…suppose democracy was only for elections, for politics, and for a party name? I say democracy is only of use there that it may pass on and come to its flower and fruits in manners, in the highest forms of interaction between man, and their beliefs – in religion, literature, colleges, and schools – democracy in all public and private life…
>
> Walt Whitman, *Democratic Vistas*

Whitman spoke of the 'region of the imagination' as the proper vocation for poets, politicians and the public alike. He believed the imaginative faculty was one of the most important aspects of a democratic society: the power to envisage innovative solutions to deeply felt problems, to promote harmonious resolutions to entrenched conflicts, to harness the energies of the entire population in the search for the common good. This imaginary realm is not simply an issue of individual self-awareness but of collective deliberation, an arena not of wishful thinking but of social learning. By subjecting the terrain of political, economic and social power to a critical scrutiny, democratic vistas expand the capacity of a society to imagine a credible view of what form of social change is both essential and feasible. Indeed, Whitman was contemptuous of those who 'try to cut the fabric of democracy to the sorry measure of their own tiny imaginations'.

One of the most profound effects of our insecure times is the way in which insecurity has acted as a constraint on our collective imagination. Indeed, the prevailing imaginary horizons at the end of the century are neither expansive nor democratic. For all the exhortations of 'Third Way' politicians to 'think the unthinkable', their political rhetoric is essentially a means of ratifying (by 'modernising') the neo-liberal hegemony of the past two decades. Truly radical projects that seek to reconfigure political, economic and social life around democratic principles are dismissed by these self-proclaimed 'pragmatists' as irrelevant, out of date and utopian. Those who suffer most from our present insecurity have learned to adapt to their circumstances and often come to believe that it is right that things should be this way, that their afflictions represent a deeply rooted personal failure rather than entrenched social dilemmas. The paradox of insecure times is that just at the moment when the introduction of a new form of security is urgently required, our abiding paralysis of the imagination seems to foreclose this very option.

This chapter is conceived first and foremost as an act of democratic imagination. It is an argument that security and democracy are inextricably linked. Only democratic norms and practices can ensure that individuals are treated with equal regard and respect; that resources are distributed fairly and equitably; that individuals are given a direct say in how political and social life are organised; that individuals are empowered to resist, both individually and collectively, those forms of insecurity which they experience as oppressive, arbitrary or exploitative. It insists that our political economy must be designed to enhance our social and institutional capacity for innovation and experimentation. This is critical, because any fulfilment of security will require radical institutional and social change and a transformation of economic, social and political relations and institutions.

I envisage a twenty-first-century security that is predicated on the extension and deepening of democracy in the economy, civil society and the state (Amin, 1996; Held, 1995). This political economy envisages a democratic internationalism, rather than a neo-liberal globalisation where the coercive aspects of market discipline are counterposed to the enhancement of the democratic coercion of civil society and the state. It imagines a politics of production that incorporates the need for sustainable development and ecological responsibility. It envisages a vital civic community that resists the unjust redistribution of insecurity and at the same time reorient gender relations and the practices of social reproduction. It envisages a democratic polity that maximises participation of the excluded and strengthens the capability for collective discussion and solution of collective problems. In short, it envisages a democracy that flourishes in political life, in our communities, in our households and in our economy.

I recognise that the current environment may strike many readers as an inauspicious moment for such a democratic initiative. Democracy has never been more widely esteemed as a system of political organisation than at present, yet as a political force capable of restructuring society, it has lost all its momentum. 'Democracy is indeed more widespread than ever', wrote Perry Anderson. 'But it is also thinner – as if the more universally available it becomes, the less active meaning it retains' (Anderson, 1992: 356). Politics has been transformed into a realm of virtual simulation: a land where pollsters, focus groups, advertising consultants and spin doctors reign supreme, where electoral politics has metamorphosed into a marketing campaign designed to package political principles as if they were brands of cereal. This debased democracy has produced a deeply cynical, dispirited and de-politicised population. At the same time, the market has become a truly universal system for the first time in history: its disciplinary logic has penetrated just about every aspect of human life and nature itself (Wood, 1997). All around us we see the wreckage of an untrammelled capitalism, highlighted by Jane Wheelock in Chapter 2: declining incomes, families struggling to make ends meet, devastating inequality, a ravaged environment, individuals deprived of their capacity for full human development.

Indeed, our insecure times bear an eerie resemblance to the circumstances depicted by a nineteenth-century social theorist who wrote that the 'atmosphere in which we live weighs upon everyone with a 20,000 pound force' (Marx, 1856, in Tucker, 1972: 427). An abiding fear of change in a fragmented world where there are few sources of certainty combined with a collapse of trust in political institutions hardly seem the best circumstances in which the democratic imagination can flourish.

Yet, potential opportunities are often obscured in periods that ostensibly seem unfavourable. The devastating consequences unleashed by the East Asian financial crisis of 1997–8 – countries thrown into massive depressions, millions left unemployed and in abject poverty, the danger that the crisis would spiral out of control into a global conflagration and threaten even the strongest economies with ruin – has actually made the case for democratic control of the market appear more necessary and feasible than ever before (Wade and Veneroso, 1998). Mass discontent with political life has sparked a genuine hunger for a meaningful alternative. The seemingly unstoppable spread of insecurity across greater sections of the population means that all are now forced to imagine what our lives would be like if they were suddenly placed in the same circumstances as those of the less fortunate. They are more likely to consider collective solutions than ever before. In short, the time may be ripe for an egalitarian security.

The essential values of a twenty-first-century security – equality, autonomy, solidarity, fairness, responsibility – are basically the values that have animated the progressive left throughout the past century. The debate on the left today consists precisely in whether these objectives can be met in what is assumed to be a qualitatively different strategic environment that places distinct limits on the realisation of those values (Giddens, 1994b). Security is assumed to be a moving target: something better understood as a process rather than an end state. It must be guaranteed and ensured not as a once and for all condition but rather as an ongoing relationship that is continually reaffirmed through democratic practice and contestation.

There are no clear blueprints for success in establishing an alternative basis for security. 'If the twentieth century holds one political lesson', writes John Dryzek, 'it is that we should beware of anyone peddling such blueprints, be they socialist paradises, fascist Reichs to last a thousand years, or free-market utopias popularised in the Anglo-American world in the 1980s and exported in the form of "shock therapy" to several East European countries after 1989' (Dryzek, 1997: 192). Instead of the politics of end states, we need to endorse what Anthony Giddens calls a 'generative politics', which seeks to apply a constant set of democratic norms to rapidly changing circumstances (Giddens, 1994b). Claus Offe argues in a similar vein that security should now be concerned with 'avoidance criteria', of 'guaranteeing minimums rather than realising maximums' (Offe, 1996: 36). The object of policy making should be to ensure that no single person or social group is deprived of either the means necessary to live a dignified life, or their fundamental human rights. Within this framework of basic rights, there may be considerable latitude for an active experimentation with what form of society best fulfils these goals.

In the next section, I offer an account of the institutional arrangements (in the economy, civil society and the state) that would underpin an egalitarian political economy. The final section examines the redistribution of work as a policy which illustrates how these institutional arrangements could be realised in practice.

An egalitarian political economy of security

The discussion that follows investigates the relationship between democracy and security in three interrelated domains: the economy, civil society and the state. It proposes a series of democratic initiatives to underpin an egalitarian basis for security: democratic oversight of the market and the gradual weakening of market relations over social life, the democratisation of civil society to create the potential for broader political participation in decision making and governance. This section is premised on the democratic imagination, but is also grounded in a measured sense of the outer limits of what is politically feasible in the contemporary political context.

Democratising the market

The case against markets has been raised throughout this volume and is obviously central to a rethinking of security. Markets are inherently unstable, inefficient and inequitable. They subordinate all issues to the myopic criteria of the 'cash nexus' and reduce individuals to little more than factors of production, treating them instrumentally rather than as ends in themselves. Markets on their own are incapable of providing the security goods that every democratic society requires: clean air, public health, good quality jobs, free education and social safety nets. The global restructuring of capitalism has dramatically intensified these problems. It has generated tremendous inequality between and within national economies, increased rates of poverty, malnutrition and disease, and devastated the natural environment. It has reoriented the balance of power in our societies, enhancing the power of capital at the expense of workers, citizens and democratic states. It has exercised a stranglehold over the democratic imagination, serving as the conventional wisdom for countless politicians who proclaim that there are no longer any meaningful choices to make in the political economy.

The task for an egalitarian political economy is to begin to find ways of reversing these trends. It requires us to discover the basis for an economy that sustains innovative activity, provides for a socially efficient allocation of resources, guarantees fairness and equity, is ecologically sustainable, and is supportive of our families and communities. I envisage this strategic dilemma as a twofold problem involving the capacity to exit and to exercise voice in the economy (Hirschman, 1970; Pollin, 1995). The internationalisation of economic activity represents an unparalleled expansion of capital's exit options: the freedom to move around the globe as it sees fit, the freedom to avoid the implementation of environmental, labour or human rights safeguards, the freedom to escape from its collective obligations to civil society and governments. Globalisation contributes as well to a grievous reduction in the effectiveness of voice. It undermines the capacity of national governments to promote policy objectives (such as full employment and sustainable growth) that challenge market imperatives, and weakens the bargaining power of workers who had scant leverage against the threat of flight by capital. A political economy of security therefore needs to first place distinct limits on this ability to exit, by limiting the financial speculation that creates massive instability and prevents long-term calculations, and by foreclosing the growth option of downsizing, low wages and high job insecurity that has taken such a tremendous toll on people's lives. At the same time, we need to provide a more effective foundation for the democratic exercise of voice that creates an alternative democratic capacity to influence economic strategies, binds market actors to collective obligations, and engenders a higher level of private commitment to wider democratic objectives and concerns.

There have been a number of innovative proposals for circumscribing the options of capital. Foremost of these is the proposal by the Nobel Prize-winning economist James Tobin to impose a small tax on all international transactions that are aimed at profiting from small changes in currency exchanges and stock markets (Haq *et al.*, 1996). A 'Tobin tax' would undoubtedly reduce the levels of speculative trading and the revenue garnered could underwrite a 'Global Reconstruction Fund' to lower Third World debts, improve social conditions in the South and provide funding for the development of stronger formal links between transnational civil society organisations (see below). There have been similar proposals to promote an alternative trade strategy. This would build institutional mechanisms into the world economy to level wages up rather than down, strengthen standards for environmental protection, labour regulation and human rights in agreements such as NAFTA and GATT standards, and make decision-making processes more democratic and transparent (Ekins, 1992). In the domestic economy, 'living wage' campaigns in the United States have pressed for a substantial rise in the minimum wage to make the low wage route less feasible for corporations (Pollin and Luce, 1998). An expansion of employment in the social economy would likewise give low-skilled workers added leverage to refuse or walk away from the most insecure jobs in the labour market (see next section).

One of the most effective methods of empowering democratic voice in the domestic economy would be to reinstate full employment as a central objective of economic policy. Full employment is an essential means of fighting inequality and social polarisation, reducing poverty and improving the bargaining power of workers, each of which has the potential to augment the influence of workers in economic decision making. A similar policy in the international arena would be the cancellation of the crippling debt (at last count over $2.5 trillion) owed by governments in the South to financial institutions and governments in the advanced economies (Strange, 1998). This would free up substantial resources for basic needs (housing, health, education, infrastructure) that are desperately lacking in these societies and which act as a permanent obstacle to participation. There have been numerous proposals for improving democratic voice in corporations and financial systems (Kelly *et al.*, 1997; Pollin, 1995). These include mandating greater representation on company boards of directors for workers, consumers and communities, promulgating new regulations for widening shareholding rights, changing the nature of pension funds to allow for worker representation, and greater investment in socially useful projects. Greater funding for public broadcasting (in television and radio), wider access to the Internet and other advanced communication technologies and increased start-up capital for new public media ventures would help create a democratic sphere of communication that could act as a counterweight to the hegemony of the corporate-dominated media.

Ultimately, the role of democratic voice is to spark forces that can resist the insecurities of the market and lobby for democratic mechanisms for its containment. These forces must initially concentrate their energies on the terrain of the nation-state, but eventually they will be forced to expand their horizons across state borders. An embryonic transnational civil society is beginning to form at present, composed of international groups such as Greenpeace and Amnesty International, the non-governmental organisations represented at the environmental, women's and development summits, and in the tentative alliances made across borders by national trade unions (Ekins, 1992). This empowerment of civil society represents an important attempt at re-imagining the bases not only of economic power and security, but of the very nature of community itself.

Regenerating civil society

Security is linked to democratic participation in all walks of social and political life. To place participation on a permanent institutional and social footing requires the deliberate fostering of the broadest possible capacity for self-organisation and group formation (what some call 'social capital') in civil society. It has been well recognised in recent years that societies with a rich supply of social capital enjoy considerable advantages in economic efficiency, public health, social cohesion and effective governance; I wish also to highlight the distinct contributions it makes to an egalitarian security (Putnam, 1995; Wilkinson, 1996). Group formation in civil society tends to replicate existing social inequalities, with some groups (the rich) overrepresented while others (the poor) are underrepresented. Associational networks contribute to security first by helping to remedy initial imbalances of power. Individuals with limited resources, by pooling their limited advantages together through organisation, improve their collective potential to resist dominant cultures of exploitation and oppression. Collective organisation is also a necessary (although not sufficient) condition to prevent an illegitimate redistribution of insecurity landing on the backs of the disadvantaged.

Participation in civil society enables individuals to broaden their understanding of how the world works, and to become aware of the relations of domination that shape their everyday lives. Activism engenders a politicised reflexivity that illuminates the wider context of local struggles, reveals the structural dimensions of what had hitherto been perceived as personal troubles, and permits an awareness of commonalities of interest beyond one's own particularistic concerns. This critical analysis sometimes requires individuals to undergo an often painful reassessment of their world views, but it also serves as a foundation for a profound commitment to social justice which encourages us to construct alliances across diverse constituencies and rebuild fragile communities. Participation also allows disadvantaged individuals to broaden the political and social understanding of insecurity and thereby formulate a more inclusive definition of security. Environmental justice activists in the United States demonstrated an inextricable link between inequality and environmental risk when they revealed that the siting of toxic waste dumps and noxious incinerators, long associated with a myriad of health problems such as cancer, birth defects and blood disorders, was frequently concentrated near working-class and racial minority neighbourhoods (Bullard, 1994). The women's movement similarly challenged the criminal justice system to treat domestic violence as a legitimate offence and lobbied for changes in police practice and greater resources to support groups.

Activists in these associations are rewarded with significant interpersonal benefits as a result of participation. Finding the courage to speak in front of an audience for the first time, learning to chair a meeting, confronting a person in authority about a grievous injustice: all of these provide an invaluable boost to an individual's self-esteem and self-confidence. They also represent an important reservoir of civic skills and citizenship training as well: associational members develop an appreciation of the public virtues of dialogue and negotiation, and learn the habits of inclusion and mutual regard upon which a cohesive society depends.

Although the density of social capital in society is deeply conditioned by political culture, historical legacies and socioeconomic structures, it is also a product of political crafting (Cohen and Rogers, 1995). Governments can stimulate collective organisation and collective action by ensuring equality of access to important resources such as skills, education and information; by entrenching the right of representation at all decisive stages of decision making; by mandating publicly funded day care and public services; and by requiring public recognition of trade unions and regulation of unfair labour practices. The state has an equally important role in influencing the political character of the groups themselves. Civil society is not simply an ideal realm of co-operation, trust and equality as is often assumed, but rather should be recognised as an arena of coercion, exploitation and domination as well. Associations in civil society that promote self-respect and co-operation among their members may at the same time be exclusionary in their membership practices, support particularistic conceptions of the common good and work to constrain the democratic rights of other citizens. In circumstances where groups fail to treat other citizens with equal regard and respect, or are intolerant and repressive of aspects of difference (sexual preference or race), or seek to deny the democratic rights of citizens (such as the reproductive rights of women), governments should act to ensure they become more inclusive in their relations with the wider society.

Of course, the problem remains that only a state that has deep roots in civil society and fosters widespread political participation would have the necessary legitimacy to enact such measures. However, this itself would require an active democracy movement in society to bring about such political changes. Michael Walzer perfectly captures the paradox: 'only a democratic state can create a democratic civil society; only a democratic civil society can sustain a democratic state' (Walzer, 1995: 24).

Deliberation and democratic governance

A democratic state involves more than just sustaining popular participation; it concerns establishing institutional spaces and procedures that require democratic norms to be satisfied in policy making and political practice. Deliberative arenas are necessary to provide opportunities for competing interests to articulate their concerns, to find some common understanding about the nature of competing claims and demands, and to widen the scope of available solutions to pressing problems. They are indispensable to facilitating broader relations of tolerance and mutual respect across divergent communities. In the past decade, there has been a remarkable experimentation in numerous countries and across various issue areas with various deliberative forums such as citizen juries, study circles and focus groups. Benjamin Barber offers the imaginative proposal of a government-funded and independently administered 'national civic forum' which would allow, via satellite link-up, various town hall meetings throughout the United States to discuss in common a particular public problem. Barber sees this innovation as a way of countering the influence of demagogic talk shows and sensationalist news reporting that has so poisoned deliberative discussion in America in the past decade (Barber, 1998). Cities in Great Britain, Sweden and Brazil have engaged in participatory planning and budgeting exercises to involve citizens in the identification of critical needs and priorities and the disbursement of municipal revenues for capital improvements (Sousa Santos, 1998). These initiatives should be encouraged and promoted as an integral feature of a security project.

The state should be transformed from a form of power over people, an external authority that is distant, bureaucratic and feared, to a network of institutions that are experienced by people as a site of genuine consensus building and reciprocity. It requires the state to engage in self-limiting behaviour of its own by widely dispersing the bases of political power throughout society. The state would thereby shift 'from first problem solver to first organizer of social capacities for their solution' (Cohen and Rogers, 1995: 236).[1] This means devolving responsibilities for policy making and governance from the state to organisations in civil society. For instance, in the provision of welfare services, civil society organisations enjoy a distinct competitive advantage over state bureaucracies by virtue of their unique ethos and institutional architecture. Associations are premised on high levels of altruism and trust, and there is an intuitive understanding that social services that rely on those values are best delivered by organisations that are committed to them. Associations place a premium on flexibility and creativity in their efforts at problem solving, a distinct advantage in a context of rapidly changing demands and needs. Associations are predicated on a belief that the well-being of their members and service recipients is inseparable from their creative empowerment and self-confidence, an ethic that is at odds with the passive recipient culture of the traditional welfare state. There should be few limits to the diversity of services that associations could undertake: literacy training, crèches and other child care facilities, drug treatment centres, sports clubs for youngsters, housing regeneration, community enterprises and hospices for the infirm and dying.[2]

Joshua Cohen and Joel Rogers also argue for providing a more direct and formal governance role for associations as an essential feature of an associative democracy (Cohen and Rogers, 1995; see also Hirst, 1994). In the matter of the regulatory arena, they sketch out a series of conditions in which the state's competence to monitor compliance of regulations, or to enforce standards, or even to set the appropriate ends of regulatory policy, is severely compromised. The ability of associations to gather local information, to promote co-operation between various actors and to monitor compliance therefore makes them indispensable to a more efficacious regulatory regime. As an example, governments have a difficult time enforcing occupational health and safety because the large number of workplaces, and the corresponding small number of state monitors, mitigates against any serious efforts at mandating compliance. In these circumstances, the ideal solution is to enlist those groups (trade unions, works councils, employers) who have both a direct interest in effective regulation and the capacity to monitor changing conditions, and give them direct involvement in regulation (typically through worker–management safety committees at the workplace).

Associational participation here promises a number of distinct advantages. It provides an important measure of personal security to workers and improves their representation in government policy making. It enhances state capacity and efficacy through better programme implementation and regulatory compliance. It makes an important contribution to a societal capacity for social learning by increasing the range of solutions to social problems that are taken seriously, promoting a heightened awareness of the interdependence of social problems, and encouraging norms of trust and co-operation in place of adversarial relations. Similar arrangements for environmental regulation (such as reduction of source emissions) could involve ongoing negotiations and co-operation between employers, workers, local community groups and environmental activist organisations.

More far-reaching is the contribution associative democracy can make to social integration and cohesion. Participation in the deliberative arenas of the associative democratic framework would foster relations of mutual respect among citizens and encourage inclusive forms of solidarity premised on common purposes and discussion. These would constitute a 'solidarity of citizenship' counterposed to the organic (and often particularistic) solidarities of class, community and family, a solidarity that is 'based on people with common concerns treating one another as equal partners in the resolution of shared concerns' (Cohen and Rogers, 1995: 251). By fostering the acceptance of collective obligations among diverse and competing interests, these deliberative arrangements could lay the foundation for what Wolfgang Streeck calls the 'political reconstruction of community' (Streeck, 1995: 184), a development which our insecure times surely demand.

However, it must also be the case that as the state opens itself up to alternative sites of power, and changes the relative power status of various social groups, the potential for a multiplication of conflict among groups will be heightened. The issue which I fear will be most destabilising is that there may be profound objections from key social actors about the need to participate in these associative forums. As an example, it does not strain the imagination too much to envisage that capital has very little interest in accepting a diminution of its unilateral decision making in arenas such as workplace health and safety or environmental policies. The success of associative democracy therefore relies on the efficacy of democratic coercion: on the ability, that is, of both the state (and popular movements) in making recalcitrant employers an offer they cannot afford to refuse.

Security policies: redistribution of work

Work is so central to the attainment of security, whether material, personal, political or even spiritual, that it is only natural that employment policy should be a critical focus of an egalitarian security. In this final section, drawing on arguments developed in greater detail elsewhere by myself and Jane Wheelock (Vail, 1998; Wheelock and Vail, 1998), I show how a policy to redistribute paid and unpaid work can promote a more even sharing of the burdens of insecurity and the benefits of security. Redistribution of work underpins an egalitarian political economy of security through its potential to democratise the market, regenerate civil society and broaden deliberation and democratic governance. How do we want to distribute our time between employment, other forms of work including caring for the young, the old and the sick, and the time to do what we please; and what makes a fair distribution? Putting the redistribution of employment on the policy agenda enables debate on how to ensure a more equitable and fulfilling relationship between the ways we gain our livelihoods and the lives we lead. We thereby open up Walt Whitman's 'region of imagination'; we can use our imaginative faculties to expand a democratic vista of how to relate our public and private lives. But redistributing employment is also a 'feasible capitalist' solution to insecurity, and it is here that I start.

The true test of an employment–work policy that leads to egalitarian security is whether or not it is able to successfully fulfil a number of interrelated tasks. Employment policy needs to restore full employment and thus substantially reduce poverty, inequality and insecurity for those without work. It should contribute to overall economic growth and productivity without damaging the environment, and at the same time provide the foundation for a sustainable economy that encourages the development of social wealth and productivity. It should lessen the persistent job insecurity of workers, and ensure the satisfaction and more humane treatment of those in employment, including fair levels of pay. It should reorient the structure of caring responsibilities that leave women in a state of permanent disadvantage in the labour market, and thereby abolish the artificial divisions between paid work and unpaid work and between market production and social reproduction.

A redistribution of work policy begins from the premise that the current pace of current technological change makes full employment impossible without a massive co-ordinated increase in world demand, but that this is ecologically unsustainable and politically unfeasible. This only leaves a deliberate effort to redistribute working opportunities. A redistribution of work relies on three mutually reinforcing policy means: the reduction of working time, the creation of jobs in the 'third sector' or social economy, and the provision of a basic income (for a detailed discussion of each alternative see Wheelock and Vail, 1998). Proposals for a rethinking of working time include a number of different approaches: reducing overtime hours worked, longer holidays, early or gradual retirement, parental or caring leaves, job sharing or job rotation, and reductions in the standard week to thirty-five hours, as has been proposed by the Jospin government in France. The social economy alternative entails state-financed but locally organised job creation (and hence service provision of socially useful activities) by the voluntary sector, co-operatives, community enterprises and Local Exchange Trading Schemes (LETS). A basic income would provide an unconditional grant to every citizen on an individual basis, without any means test or requirement for past or current work performance.

A redistribution of work meets all the criteria for an egalitarian employment policy, and redistributes security to those in most severe insecurity.[3] Stuart Holland, in a study for the Socialist group of the European Parliament, estimated that between 9.5 and 11 million jobs could be achieved through work-time reductions, and another 4.5 million from third-sector employment. When added to an additional 4.5 million created by the direct investment stimulus of a revitalised European Investment Fund, he calculated that 20 million new jobs could be created in Europe, more than enough to end mass unemployment (Holland, 1997). Third-sector employment could be targeted to the sectors of the population (youth, racial minorities, disabled, elderly) who are systematically excluded from the labour market and would provide meaningful employment opportunities in areas of high social depression and poverty where private sector job growth is virtually non-existent. A basic income would provide economic security to the most disadvantaged in society, and attenuate the various poverty traps that plague so many social benefit systems.

A redistribution of work would also make a positive contribution to employers' need to sustained innovation and productivity in the global economy. Workers who had the benefit of a basic grant, or the knowledge that there was a substantial pool of quality jobs outside their own workplace, would be far more receptive to the 'flexibility' which employers need to ensure their competitiveness (Standing, 1992). Workers would be less resistant to changes in workplace organisation or the introduction of new technology, and more inclined to contribute to productivity improvements, when their legitimate fears of losing their jobs could be reasonably allayed. This would represent a 'democratic flexibility', premised not on compulsory insecurity imposed by employers but rather on the ability of workers to enhance personal autonomy. Critics of a basic income have charged that it would erode incentives to work, but in fact it would offer people the freedom to engage in part-time work, or to invest in self-employment.[4] The added security of a basic income would give workers more bargaining power to walk away from the most exploitative and alienating dead-end jobs, a freedom that over time could lead to the elimination of the most insecure arenas of the labour market by giving employers the incentive to create better quality employment.

Work redistribution would contribute to a wider notion of social productivity and sustainability as well. Third-sector employment would provide services that meet a variety of critical social needs (in education, health, community care and environmental protection) that are undersupplied when left to the vagaries of the market. Non-market employment of this kind furthermore provides a sustainable, ecologically sensitive alternative to the productivist orientation of market-led accumulation. Likewise, although any transformation to a sustainable system would undoubtedly involve a series of short-term costs that would have to be borne by the working population, these sacrifices may be more easily contemplated when workers are assured of an independent income and have access to wider employment opportunities in the social economy (Offe, 1995). Finally, a redistribution of work is likely to make a significant contribution to gender equity (Bruegel et al., 1998). A basic income would give women greater power within unequal relationships. Changes in working time could help reduce the double burden women face and help underpin a new relation of domestic democracy by encouraging male participation in caring responsibilities and domestic work. Caring work could also be provided by civil society associations or organised by local labour exchanges where individuals provided child care or caring in return for a reciprocal service provision (Offe and Heinze, 1993).

A redistribution of work also enables us to expand our democratic deliberation about wider issues involving employment. For example, what constitutes a 'socially useful activity'? How can workers be given a sense of dignity and control at their workplace? How can we ensure that relations between employers and workers are not predicated on domination and subordination? How should we distribute our time between paid employment and other forms of work? At the same time, work redistribution promises a substantial expansion in the possibilities for personal autonomy. By freeing up time and offering a modicum of material security, it would give people the ability to choose between a much richer range of life chances and opportunities. It would enable individuals to develop their talents to the fullest and thereby provide an egalitarian basis for social mobility.

The contribution to a vital civic community and democratic spirit would also be profound. The withdrawal of many citizens from active political and civic life is undoubtedly affected by the time paradox of modern employment highlighted by Jane Wheelock in Chapter 5: that time-poor/income-rich individuals are chained to the world of work with little time to participate in social affairs, while those who are time-burdened/income-poor have plenty of involuntary free time on their hands but are beaten down by the grinding weight of poverty. Reducing work hours could be an important step in revitalising public life and opening the way for a democratic renewal. Third-sector organisations are incubators of an active and informed citizenry, help inculcate and strengthen an ethic of service and responsibility, and represent the 'social capital' that enriches the fabric of the community and polity (Putnam, 1995). An independent income would give idealistic young people the opportunity to embark on challenging projects of social activism that could never realistically hope to offer a decent wage.

Lastly, a redistribution of work has the potential to start constructing a new framework of material relations of power that substitutes a democratic logic for an all too pervasive market logic. Working-time reductions implicitly embrace the principle of establishing democratic control over the workplace that could be extended to wider areas of the economy. Basic income has the potential to weaken the coercive force of market commodification by partially uncoupling income from the labour market. Third-sector employment posits a social logic of development that can be counterposed to the private logic of the market. In short, the most important and far-reaching aspect of a redistribution of work may be its ability to establish the material foundations of society along non-capitalist criteria, even while it is satisfying the very criteria for a successful capitalist economy (Van Parijs, 1995).

Let us heed Whitman's warning not to 'try to cut the fabric of democracy to the sorry measure of [our] own tiny imaginations'. In our insecure times, where the worldwide spread of market relations ravages the very society it rests upon, a policy which promises protection against the market by reducing the reach of capitalism itself has the potential to attract support across much of the population. An egalitarian security, with its foundation in the democratisation of the economy, civil society and the state, may very well constitute the general interest of the next generation.

Notes

1   I want to make it clear that by advocating this conception of the state as a guarantor rather than provider, I in no way construe this as an endorsement for an enhanced role for the market. Private provision of state services has dire consequences in this

regard, reducing altruistic, public-spirited behaviour within the state, exacerbating inequality, limiting the supply of necessary public goods and destroying the capacity of the political realm to act as a site of alternative visions of the public good. In other words, I do not think security can be provided if we remain agnostic (or to use the moderniser's rhetoric 'pragmatic') about the means: what is best is not simply what works (either the state or market or civil society), but what ensures security for the greatest number which rules out the role of the market by definition. For the contrary view, see LeGrand and Bartlett, 1993.

2   There is no question that civil society associations would be transformed by their compact with the state. Being held accountable to state authorities can impose immense burdens on organisations with shoestring budgets and little managerial expertise. Contractual obligations with the government can begin to squeeze the life-force out of an organisation, changing the looser, friendlier modes of operation to more professional styles of conduct, weakening or even abandoning the original animating ethos of the association, and becoming an instrument of social control of the state rather than an advocate for the locality (Taylor, 1996).

3   A redistribution of work would face a number of important constraints (institutional, ideological and political) that could jeopardise the feasibility of such a policy, but there is also good reason to believe that these obstacles could be overcome success-fully. For a discussion, see Vail (1998).

4   Critics of a basic income have long claimed that individuals who receive a grant will have an incentive to withdraw from labour market participation altogether and thereby 'free ride' on the hard work of the rest of the population. It is curious that they are so animated about this form of potential shirking, yet tend to ignore the most widespread form of free riding in society, namely men's free riding on women's domestic work and caring responsibilities.